# John Louis

*A Life in Speedway*

First published in November 2015 by
**Retro Speedway**
**Tel: 01708 734 502**
**www.retro-speedway.com**

Designed by Jan Watts
Printed by Henry Ling Ltd
Distributed by Retro Speedway
103 Douglas Road, Hornchurch, Essex, RM11 1AW, England
Distribution email: subs@retro-speedway.com

ISBN 978-0-9559340-9-4

I WOULD like to dedicate this book to my late parents, Vera and Jack Louis.
Dad for his incredible self-taught engine expertise which underpinned all my early successes in
scrambling and speedway.
Mum for her devotion in collecting and compiling all the endless press cuttings from my very
early days until the late 90s. Without her scrapbooks the level of detail we have achieved in this
book would simply not have been possible.

# Acknowledgements

As well as my parents, I would like to thank Elvin King for getting this project started with his interviews and for drafting all the chapters which provided the framework on which the book was based.

I must also say a big 'thank you' to Sue Stevens for her tireless dedication in going through all my mum's scrapbooks to gather a detailed account of my career. This played a huge part in bringing back so many memories of things I had done throughout my life (my ability to recall events in the past can be lacking at times – I put it down to too many knocks on the head . . . who said Jeremy Doncaster can take credit for some of that!). Sue's patience in helping me combine all of this with the work already done by Elvin has ensured that I have produced the book that I imagined when Retro Speedway's Tony McDonald first asked me about writing my life story.

I hope you all enjoy reading the book – I have certainly enjoyed reliving everything.
*John 'Tiger' Louis*

Retro Speedway would also like to add our thanks, in particular, to Elvin King and Sue Stevens. Andrew Skeels, deputy editor of Speedway Star, has also been a big help, while Mike Bacon (EADT/ Evening News), Peter Thorpe, *Speedway Star* editor Richard Clark, Nigel Pearson and those Halifax devotees, Martin Jackson and Jason Ward, have been very helpful in spreading the word.

Many of the photographs used came from John's personal collection and although we have done our best to credit all photographers where they are known, we apologise if anyone's name has been omitted in error.

Special thanks for use of pictures must go to Dave Kindred, who not only covered JL's speedway career from the start in 1969, but also snapped him in scrambling events. It was, of course, Dave who captured the front cover image of JL at Foxhall wearing his iconic 'Tiger' leathers.

Other photographic credits: *East Anglian Daily Times, Ipswich Evening Star,* the late Alf Weedon, Wright Wood, Mike Patrick and Trevor Meeks (whose vast volume of work now form part of the John Somerville Collection), Ken Carpenter, Christchurch Press Co. Ltd (New Zealand), Karlof Karlof (Poland), Gianni Tomba (Italy), *Speedway Star,* Steve Waller, Phil Hilton, Geoff Cable, Jeff Higgott, John Booth, Carl Squirrell, David Ebbs and David Walsh.

Last, but not least, thanks to Dave Feakes, Kevin Hammond and Roger Payne for statistics.

# Contents

In the pits with Bob Radford, such a good positive influence in my early speedway days, in 1971.

# Foreword

## By Bob Radford

**I WAS very honoured when John asked me to contribute to this book – and I can't wait to read it all. After 47 years of writing for** *Speedway Star***, I am now retired but can look back on my long and varied time in speedway and say that John was, and still is, my personal favourite British rider of the entire era.**

That is not to decry the fabulous talents of Peter Collins, the late Peter Craven and so many others. We all knew John was a late starter but what an impact he made. To my mind he was the rock on which the great Ipswich Witches teams of 1975 and 1976 were built.

As a local family man who was no mean moto-cross rider, he was a walking publicity magnet for the shale sport in and around Ipswich. Little did either of us know that our paths would soon cross in his debut season, 1970.

I was then announcer and press officer for Newport Speedway, then in the British League first division, but for the Wasps' away matches the team manager could be any one of five people. So when asked if I'd cover the away match at Leicester, I initially declined because of one guest the promoters planned to book.

John Louis, enjoying his first season with second division Ipswich Witches, was the man I wanted as our guest and I was pleased when he eventually turned out for us that night. John and I walked the old Blackbird Road circuit together and just after we had passed the starting gate I told him that this was where the other three riders would be rolling off the throttle in his first race, Heat 2.

Having never ridden myself, I doubt that he believed me, but he roared through the field to win his first-ever senior league race in any case. Thereafter, the Newport promotion agreed with me that we should book John whenever possible. He finished second in the Wasps' final averages that season behind Sandor Levai, who would later ride for the early Ipswich Division One teams.

In his first book, *Confessions of a Speedway Promoter,* the late John Berry noted that I, almost alone, shared his belief that John was going to be world class. I believe the following winter he had to fend of offers to move John up into Division One – and with typical spite the BSPA banned him from senior league guest appearances

The bonus for Berry and Ipswich was that John had proved he was not overawed in senior racing, paving the way for the Witches to move up in 1972. Clearly, John Louis was much more than a big fish in a little pond.

We share a personal favourite moment. Newport were at Wolverhampton and John got off to a winning start. I then confided to him that he would record his first-ever maximum – despite Great Dane Ole Olsen spearheading the Wolves side, they never opposed each other.

I knew the changes I would make to the programme, and they were to keep the Wasps in the match. Later, over a Chinese meal, John was still amazed that I had predicted a maximum and that he had achieved it. Also, we had only lost 40-38, which was then considered a good away result for the Wasps.

Often en route to my much-loved Scandinavia I stayed over with the Louis family in Ipswich before catching the ferry from either Harwich or Felixstowe bound for Gothenburg. Although we gradually lost touch, the bond of friendship remained and I was pleased to see him on the World Final rostrum at Wembley in 1975 and, by then, well established as an England regular. By 1973 I had managed Reading to the league title, and two years later John captained the Witches to their first championship and was placed third in the world.

In my time with John Berry, who I liked and respected enormously, he stressed how much effort he and Ron Bagley (his most effective assistant over the years) had put into the making of 'Tiger' Louis the superstar.

After long discussions with JB while visiting him on my two holidays in Perth, he finally agreed he had been wrong to move John on from Ipswich in 1981. Did JB say that to boost sales of his own wonderful *Confessions* book? My answer is an emphatic 'no' – he had simply reflected further on the successes that John Louis had led the Ipswich Witches to achieve.

A wonderful rider, modest and approachable but with an inner-drive and self-confidence . . . those are my words to describe John Louis.

Today he is still involved with the club and it is high time people with local influence submitted his name for the honours list.

*Bob Radford*
*August, 2015*

# Introduction

## By John Louis

**T**HEY say that you need to be slightly mad to be a speedway rider and race at 70mph-plus around a confined shale track, against three other riders, on a 500cc methanol-powered motorcycle that has no brakes or gears.

That's partly true but you also need ability, commitment and the desire to always be the first one past that chequered flag. I'm proud that all the hard work, combined with a natural ability on a bike, led me to winning world titles and reach the top of the tree in my chosen sport.

I'm especially proud of my long association with my hometown club, the Ipswich Witches, as a rider, team manager and promoter, winning league titles and trophies along the way. It's now 46 years since I completed my first (very cautious) lap at Foxhall Stadium.

It was in 1969 that I first ventured onto a speedway bike, aged 28, and I've been one of those fortunate people able to make a living doing something he loves.

My life has been very full and I have experienced many things. Some of them were scary or even mad, some of them brought great pleasure and pride and there were some sad times as well. I have met so many people along the way, some of them real characters, and some are still my friends today. I hope you will enjoy hearing about them all as my story unfolds before your eyes.

When it comes to gaining success on the track, it's all been down to skill and focus, and making sure that I was always well prepared and performed to the best of my ability. I look at it as being similar to a surgeon, who has the skill to repeatedly perform the most delicate of operations, deal with the unexpected and sew a patient back up time and time again.

I had the ability to analyse every race, during all four full-throttle laps, and reach the chequered flag in front of my opponents, regardless of what challenges I had to overcome. And like a top medical man, it didn't come straight away. I've had to train hard, work hard and be 100 per cent committed to achieve everything that I did.

There can also be no fear. If you are worried that you might hurt yourself, then it's probably best you don't even sit on a speedway bike. You have got to believe you can do it and never falter in that belief. I've given my heart and soul to speedway and I would not change a thing about my life.

Yes, like most successful people, I've been lucky – lucky with injuries, as I thankfully never suffered a serious one, and lucky that an enterprising John Berry joined forces with Joe Thurley to bring speedway back to Foxhall Stadium, Ipswich in 1969.

I was doing well as a scrambler but was persuaded – rather reluctantly at first – to try my hand at speedway. Almost overnight (or so it seemed) everything slotted into gear and my life opened up so that I became a celebrity in my home town and travelled around the globe doing what I did best.

These days, I am co-promoter of the Ipswich Witches with my son Chris but now happy to take a back seat and give advice when needed. Chris does everything else.

John Berry proved himself to be the best promoter around and made a lot of money from running Ipswich Speedway when it attracted average crowds of around 6,000 a week.

A number of local scramblers followed my path into speedway and the Witches enjoyed halcyon days in the mid-70s with a side made up of Suffolk talent, plus Australian 'Adopted Son of Suffolk', the late Billy Sanders.

But after a decade of riding my heart out for the club and still almost averaging nine points a meeting, JB discarded me in a most callous way. Yes, I'd made good money, but nowhere near as much as I'd helped JB make.

It was the saddest day in my involvement with Ipswich when I was told to go in 1981. The ups far outweigh the downs, although it still grates today the way I was sent packing – thankfully only briefly - from the club that I love.

I went on to ride for two more clubs, Halifax and King's Lynn, before finally calling it a day at the end of 1984. Needless to say, it wasn't long before I got involved in the other side of the sport, as team manager and assistant track curator before becoming a promoter myself.

Because I had set myself very high standards as a rider, I have always felt comfortable questioning riders representing my teams if I think they fail to make the most of the talent they have and opportunities they are offered. I can be a hard taskmaster when it comes to anyone failing to fulfil their potential but that's because I want them to enjoy that feeling when you achieve success, whether it be as an individual or as part of a team. There's nothing quite like it!

*John Louis*
*October, 2015*

Chapter 1

# Childhood

**"JOHNNIE, slow down and stop doing that this minute – you will fall off and get yourself killed!" These were the words being screamed at me by my mum as I yet again came hurtling down our road on my three-wheeled children's bike, flat out and loving it. I was around three to four-years-old at the time but already showing the first signs of being a daredevil on two wheels!**

I was born on June 14, 1941 in Ipswich, Suffolk to parents Jack and Vera Louis. The arrival of my brother Tony in 1943 and sister Pat in 1946 completed our family.

My dad was very keen on motorbikes and I'm sure my attraction to bikes came from him. He used to ride a Norton back then; apparently he would lean over so low when cornering that Mum used to wear her shoes out after only a few rides! I think he would have liked to ride in grass-track meetings but he never had the money to be able to do anything like that.

I was always on the go as a young child and when Mum couldn't find me in the garden, she had a pretty good idea where I was.

We used to live in Suffolk Road, which was a side road off a bigger one called Hervey Street. This is on quite a steep hill and I used to pull my little bike to the top before turning it around and hurtling down. My feet were soon off the pedals as, by this time, they were spinning round at a rate of knots. When I got to Suffolk Road, I remember naturally leaning as I took the left turn – obviously a skill that would be of help in a later career.

 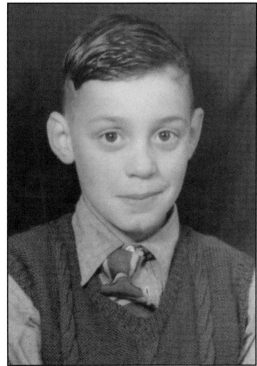

The earliest photos I have from my school days in Ipswich. I was more interested in riding my bike.

As I approached our house, Mum would be standing in the middle of the road, arms in the air, screaming and shouting at me to stop. I would then get marched back to our house, have a few smacks and be told (again) not to go out into the road. I would do as I was told for a bit but the thrill of that ride was too hard to resist and sooner or later I would slip out of the front gate again ready for another high-speed descent. Looking back, I realise how lucky I was that there were so few cars on the roads in those days.

A few years later, when I was seven, Dad got into greyhound racing. He owned a dog (whose name escapes me) that ran regularly at the now-defunct Ipswich Stadium that was located near the town centre.

He used to sit me on the dog and get me to walk the animal around the garden, as apparently it would strengthen the dog's legs. We regularly walked to Christchurch Park in the centre of Ipswich as part of the dog's training.

My job was to hold the dog back while Dad walked 100 yards or so away from us. Dad was a great whistler and as soon as he stopped and whistled, I was able to let go of the dog, which would charge off to catch him at full speed. We would then reverse the run and by the end of the 'training session', my hands were red raw from restraining the dog between his runs.

Dad was working as a lorry driver then and one day he called at the house to take me out for a ride with him. At the time, the United States was still operating at two big airbases on the other side of Woodbridge (about 10 miles from Ipswich). They were strategic centres in the Cold War with nuclear weapons rumoured to be stored underground.

When we arrived, he parked the lorry at what I found out later was the very end of the runway while he went to complete his paperwork before unloading. Suddenly, I heard this roar that gradually got louder and louder, getting closer and closer. I had no idea what was happening and thought the world was coming to an end.

The noise got so loud that it felt like my ears were bleeding and I was terrified as this huge plane went over my head within touching distance. Dad got back in the lorry shortly afterwards and I told him that the noise had frightened the life out of me but he just shrugged his shoulders and said it was only a plane landing and wouldn't hurt me.

Little did I know that this experience would help me many years later to cope with the noise generated by 90,000 fans at Wembley Stadium or by the more partisan crowds in Poland!

When I was about 12, I took up something completely different by joining the Sea Cadets. I think my parents thought it would help in the discipline department. Seven creases in the trousers was the order of the day for the bell-bottoms we used to wear as part of our uniform. We did the obvious things like learning to tie knots and learned all about sailing, plus we had a few trips in a Motor Torpedo boat that was kept in Ipswich docks.

My two main memories from the cadets both involved standing still for a very long time, which was extremely difficult for someone who prefers to be always on the go! The first one was marching to, and then standing along the top of, Lloyds Avenue in Ipswich town centre with my whole section outside the Odeon Cinema to mark the release of a film called The Cruel Sea.

It was quite an ordeal standing to attention for so long (it seemed like hours but was probably only about 30 minutes) and in front of so many people. Finally, the inevitable happened as one of the cadets in front of me slumped to the ground after fainting. I remember he was picked up and carried away but the rest of us didn't move as we had been trained to do (but I was laughing inside…).

The second memory was travelling to Trafalgar Square for what I think must have been to mark Trafalgar Day. We joined up with Sea Cadets from all over the country and had to stand to attention in lines while the ceremony took place. Afterwards there was an inspection by the Duke of Edinburgh and I was lucky enough to be singled out for a handshake. It was a big experience for a

**School awards for swimming and athletics.**

**Dressed up for the Sea Cadets.**

boy who had barely been out of Suffolk.

Something else that I enjoyed in my middle teens was hiring a horse for half-a-day and going for a ride on the roads around the edge of Ipswich. I'm not saying that I had any ambition to be a jockey despite being the right build, but at that time horses were just as interesting to me as machines.

I would usually ride from the stables back towards my house, to show off the horse, and then go over Rushmere Heath near Foxhall Stadium. It was great fun and I really looked forward to my days in the saddle.

One day, it all went wrong and, ironically enough, I was close to the main cemetery in the town when I thought my number was up. With no warning, we were galloping down the street and, as hard as I pulled on the reins, the beast just kept charging along. My legs were straight out in the stirrups as I tried to gain some sort of control. It was ducking its head down almost to the ground to show its displeasure at being asked to slow down!

We went over one road where, thank goodness, there were no cars and I must have then pulled harder on the nearside rein as we veered towards some houses and I grazed my leg as we brushed a brick wall. My hands were red, my face was red and, to be honest, I was terrified. A main roundabout on the Ipswich by-pass was approaching with the horse frothing at the mouth.

Thankfully, or I might not be here now to tell the tale, it decided to slow down and for the last mile it behaved itself. I have since been told that horses know when they are heading home and that this type of behaviour can happen, especially when they are hungry.

From that day on, I decided I much preferred to have my legs astride a machine I could control rather than an animal I couldn't – my days in the saddle were over.

But an interest in horses has continued through my daughter Joanne, who began riding from around the age of 10 on a horse called Quinn. She not only rode him but also happily cleaned out his stable and groomed him as well. In fact, she has a natural close affinity with horses and still rides to this day.

My first paid 'job' was delivering newspapers and I volunteered to do a round that the other lads were frightened of. This was because there was a number of long drives that, in the winter, you had to negotiate in the dark.

Another perk was that there was an orchard in one of the houses, where I used to go scrumping mid-round and take apples back to my mum. I told her they had been given to me but I'm not sure she believed me.

The newsagent, Borehams in Woodbridge Road, paid me an extra shilling (10p) a week for my trouble and they also gave me a trade bike.

Being able to take my trade bike to school had its ups and downs. I went to Copleston School from 11 years old and some days I spiced up the ride home when I got together with five of my pals.

I put one on the handlebars, two in the front basket, one on the crossbar and one standing at the back holding my shoulders. The hard tyres on the bike were nearly bone flat and we needed a push off by some other lads to get us going.

On one occasion, the headmaster, Mr. Scott, spotted us and drove his car alongside. "Louis, in my office, tomorrow morning!" he barked as my friends all froze in terror. I knew what was coming so I put on three pairs of underpants and, true enough, I had the cane, the big one, while bent over his desk.

Another time when I was a bit cheeky to a lady outside of school, several of us were asked to line up for her to find the culprit. I tried my best to distort my face and was pulling all sorts of grimaces but the lady had no hesitation in picking me out. This time, I was given the cane that had four strips on it and there was no chance to put on extra pants!

In total, Mr. Scott had three different canes depending on the seriousness of the offence and I probably felt all of them during my time there. Looking back, I can see that, in my case, it wasn't a bad thing as it ensured I left school knowing that if I did wrong, I would get punished.

Like many boys in my year, I preferred sport to sitting down doing lessons. I played football for the school team and enjoyed athletics – the long jump was my best event, which I know is hard to believe given the length of my legs!

However, just in time, I realised I needed to get my head down, as I would need much better exam results to get a job when I left school. To my surprise, and probably my teachers' too, my English, Maths, etc. improved by a huge amount in that last year and I finally got a good report.

My dad also believed in punishment if any of us misbehaved. On one occasion, I was told that I mustn't go out and that at the age of 14, I had to stay in and keep an eye on my younger siblings.

The lure of cycle speedway got the better of me and I went out to a track in the recreation ground, which was just round the corner from where we lived. My mates were all there and I wanted to have a laugh and ride with them.

**I spent every spare moment I could riding my pushbike.**　　　　　　　**Possibly my final year school photo.**

Unfortunately, I didn't get back before my parents and Dad was waiting for me when I got home. I knew I had done wrong and took my punishment. Mum didn't like to see this but she knew that I had to be taught a lesson. She always told people that I had been mischievous from the day I was born and that I would always fight against being held back from doing what I wanted.

Dad was very strict when I was growing up but later on he was a huge help to me throughout my scrambling and speedway careers and I'm pretty certain I would not have achieved what I did without him. He worked tirelessly on my engines, despite having no formal training. In fact, he proved a genius at working on my machinery until he died in 1978, aged only 58.

He had a tiny shed in the garden and he used to sit in there for hours on end thinking about what to do next to make his son go faster. All my early success came on equipment that Dad had done and he often drew plans as he sought ways of improving speed, with Mum regularly having to go down to the shed to bring him in for dinner.

I remember we were one of the few families to have a car in our road and Dad decided to completely dismantle the engine one weekend. Tony and I were asked to do some of the fiddly jobs before Dad got a winch affair to lift the engine out. He stripped it down completely and put it all back together again. The end product was virtually a whole new engine and, for someone who had never worked in a garage, he was a fantastic mechanic.

He also motivated me in another way when I started my speedway career that I didn't realise until after his death. Mum told me the reason he always timed my first few speedway races was that he wanted me to be the fastest but didn't want to appear to be pushing me. The fact that I knew he was timing me always spurred me on to try and beat the track record so it had the desired effect.

Dad even adapted my cycle speedway bike so that it would go faster around the bends by straightening the front forks. This meant I caught my toes to begin with, but not for the last time I learnt how to adapt my riding style and to ride on the balls of my feet. I loved the sport but never reached the standard reached by my brother Tony. The only track I ever rode on was at the local recreation ground against a few of my mates.

**May 8, 1945 and families unite to celebrate VE Day in Cemetery Road, Ipswich, which adjoins where I lived in Suffolk Road. Somewhere in this photo is my mum holding me, a month short of my fourth birthday.**

Tony was very good at cycle speedway, becoming Suffolk Champion in both 1959 and 1960. He rode for a local team called the Kesgrave Panthers at the same time as the late Dave Hunting. Dave continued in the sport to become a top national cycle speedway official.

Many years later, Dave's company, Hunting Hire, were to become the first team sponsor when I started promoting the Witches. Someone else who rode for the Panthers at that time also went on to become a big part of Ipswich Speedway when I rode. His name was John Earrey . . . 'So Long As We Know!'

Tony was also a good footballer in his younger days. Again, far better than I was as I used to get out of breath too easily. He had a trial with Ipswich Town and played for the Orwell Works team in the Ipswich leagues.

Tony later moved to Derby to work as a fitter in a power station. He used to visit local speedway tracks to watch me whenever he could. Our sister Pat also moved away after she got married but came to watch me when I was riding near her new home in Manchester. Unfortunately, Tony's choice of career was to lead to his premature death at the age of 60 due to asbestosis.

As I've already indicated, I could not have wished for better parents or a better upbringing and it was sad that Dad did not live to see my whole career. Mum died in 2010, aged 84, and was able to follow me right through to my promoting days at Foxhall Stadium, always giving her support and encouragement.

As you have probably spotted by now, I was a bit of a lad in my youth and always up for a giggle.

I also liked a dance. Later on, you will see that dancing is now playing a big part in my life. Around the time I left school, I was often out on the town whenever I could, as I was rock 'n' roll crazy.

Along with some mates, I went to see a Bill Haley film at The Gaumont cinema and the music got the better of us. Before we knew it, we were out in the aisles dancing away. The film included songs that we loved to dance to and before long half the audience was bopping away.

There were bouncers lined up along the back wall but they were happy to let the place swing. Eventually, a gang of us jumped onto the stage and began dancing away in front of the film. It was fantastic, and something I will never forget.

When the film ended, we danced our way out of the cinema, down the steps at the front and carried on right along Carr Street, a road that ran right through the middle of the town!

As I think I was to prove later in life, I was never one to go into anything with half measures, and I went to lessons at the Tom and Pat Lait Dancing School. It was a bit too traditional for me so I then tried the Victor Sylvester small ballroom that was situated inside The Gaumont, but again it was too formal.

There was another ballroom in Museum Street called The Arlington. This was right up my street and I could do all the rock 'n' rolling I wanted. I loved it and, at one time, dancing looked as though it would dominate my teens.

Mum used to come and watch me whenever she could and was so pleased to see me having so much fun. I think Dad thought I was a bit of an idiot!

Bikes were still a big interest though and, in the end, they won. I used to ride my cycle outside the house and could wheelie 200 yards or so up Renfrew Road where I lived from the age of seven.

The neighbours used to come out and watch; the Welchs, with sons Brian and Michael, the Hammonds and the Clarkes. Several of them went on to follow my speedway career and are still Ipswich supporters today. Some days, I would set myself a target of doing a wheelie all the way to school, which was probably a mile away. I don't think I ever managed it, but I gave it a good try a few times.

My love affair with bikes had been with me since those early days riding that trike for all it was worth down Hervey Street, and that affection was going to intensify.

**Scrambling gave me such a great adrenaline buzz.**

Chapter 2

# Scrambling

IT was some 13 years after I left school that I rode my first speedway race, so there were a lot of other experiences to be had first. My first job was as an apprentice fitter at Ransomes and Rapier Ltd. in Ipswich. It was a huge engineering works with a worldwide reputation for quality. They produced sluice gates, railway turntables and large cranes, including massive walking draglines used in open cast mining.

R & R provided work for a large part of the local working blue-collar male population, along with other companies such as Ransomes, Sims and Jefferies, Crane Ltd. and Cocksedges. Sadly, they have all closed down now apart from Ransomes, Sims and Jefferies (now just Ransomes), who are still world leaders in lawnmowers.

Initially, all apprentices spent time in a training department where we were tested for aptitude in a variety of skills. After that, we were allocated to different departments. I went into fitting where I worked on sluice gates. I enjoyed myself immensely during this time as I went through all the training and learned a lot of new skills. I also went to the local Civic College one day a week and managed to get my Certificate of Engineering.

I was earning the princely sum of one pound 18 shillings (£1.90) a week and Mum took £1 for housekeeping, leaving me with 18 shillings for 'spending money'. As you can imagine, I had precious little spare to finance any leisure activities.

Setting off from home at Renfrew Road, Ipswich for my first scrambles meeting, at Claydon in 1959.

**Before I went racing full-time I studied at college to gain my mechanical engineering qualifications.**

However, I did get one opportunity to earn slightly more when it was announced that Ransomes was to be used as a film set for *The Angry Silence* starring the late Richard Attenborough. They wanted to film the mass exodus of workers pouring out of the front gates at clocking off time. Volunteers were asked for and I thought I would give it a go, as it's not every day you get to appear on the big screen even if it is only as an extra. I was paid £40 for my 'starring role' – the easiest money I have ever made!

I had been taken by my dad to various scramble meetings at places like Shrubland Park and really enjoyed them. Plus, I had a work mate called Tim Robinson whose dad and uncle used to take part and I spent quite a bit of time at the garage where they worked on their bikes.

It wasn't long before I had set my sights on joining the scrambling scene but I needed some extra money to get me started – and to be able to buy a bike.

Dad was also keen for me to go into scrambling. Perhaps he could see that I had talent or he wanted to make up for being unable to take up grass-track himself. Unfortunately, his desire to see me riding did not go as far as providing any financial support simply because he did not have the cash to spare.

However, he was by then a tanker driver for Thomas Allen and helped to get me some evening work there to raise some extra funds. After working all day at Ransomes, I would go to the outskirts of Ipswich docks and, armed with a hose and long-handled brush, would clean the tankers for three or four hours in the evenings.

During one of my evening shifts, I had a bit of a hairy experience. I hadn't passed my test or even driven seriously but they trusted me to drive the tankers around the yard. One day, it was bit icy and I ended up going into a broadside.

The brand new DOT bike that I bought for £200 in Manchester in 1962.

Dad (right) pictured beside the tanker he drove for Thomas Allen. I once had a scary experience at the wheel of one of them.

**With my bike loaded and ready to go, a quick pose with the banjo. Not exactly the next Beatle!**

The hairs on the back of my neck stood up and I thought, 'here we go, we're heading for disaster'. But I found myself automatically steering into the slide and I soon had it back under control. For the first time, I realised I had a natural flair for driving 'on the edge'.

Dad also started helping me with a few riding techniques while taking me to work on the back of his bike. He had a Velocette by now and we wore no crash helmets in those days as we swerved in and out of the early morning traffic across town. It was my first time learning how a motorbike sways and how to react, with Dad telling me to 'lean when I lean'. This I did and it proved great advice.

Two of my mates had motorbikes; one a James and the other a Francis Barnett. With my new-found skill learned riding with Dad, I would sometimes play up when riding pillion behind them. Instead of leaning into the corner to help, I would hang off the opposite side of the bike and force them to go straight.

We used to frequent the cafe/coffee bars in the area and carrying on my rather madcap approach to life, I was the instigator of a crazy trip we used to do from the Classic café in Woodbridge Road East in Ipswich along four miles or so, down a country lane through the village of Bealings, to the Flamingo café at Martlesham.

It was full throttle all the way with me at the helm 90 per cent of the time. Luckily, the roads were a lot quieter then; if we had met with any traffic, it could have been curtains for us all. What made it so wild was that there used to be four of us on board. We had one on the tank of the bike, two on the seat and one sitting on the mudguard at the back. Brian Greenslade was one but unfortunately my memory lets me down on the others.

Having survived that episode, and I think my parents finding out, it was time to get serious about testing my motorcycling skills against others off the public roads. I had managed to scrape enough money together to buy an old AJS road bike on my 16th birthday but that had to go so that I could buy a second-hand DOT ('Devoid of Trouble') for £40. This meant having to go everywhere by bus for a couple of years but if you want something, sacrifices have to be made.

# Louis triumphs in a 'two-horse' Lydden

**W**ITH one or two exceptions, most of the riders at the Eythorne Club's scramble at Lydden Hill, Kent, on Sunday might just as well have stayed at home! For the main events developed into long, hard fights between just two men, John Louis (360 CZ) and Jim Connor (360 Greeves). At the end, Louis was the undisputed top man, three races to one.

In the first leg of the moto-cross he led from start to finish, but in the second he slipped on the chalk of the last bend and Connor, always on his tail, shot through to notch his lone win.

Senior Moto-Cross. Overall: 1 J. Louis (360 CZ); 2 J. Connor (360 Greeves); 3 M. Ballard (360 Husqvarna); 4 L. Neve (256 Husqvarna).

One of the countless newspaper cuttings Mum kept throughout my racing career.

I was about 18 at the time and I used the DOT both for trials and scrambling in those early days. It enabled me to gain experience on all terrains but it soon became clear I would need better equipment if I wanted to progress in scrambling.

I also frightened myself at speed because I just couldn't hold the bike straight, simply because I wasn't strong enough. Thankfully, one of my mates, John Mann, who lived just behind our house, and a couple of his mates were into bodybuilding at the local YMCA in Ipswich.

They put me through a stringent course of action and had me pushing up weights to such an extent that I just could not push anymore. And they did the same for my legs. This part was essential as

Eyes on the job . . . tackling the slopes ahead of John Ford at West Stow, Suffolk in 1961.

With my proud parents, Jack and Vera, and fellow riders and officials at the Triangle Motorcycle Club awards dinner-dance held at the Regal Restaurant, Felixstowe in 1962.

around 90 per cent of the time you are racing a scrambling bike, you are standing up. To be at your best, you also need to be strong in the chest and back and I saw a survey somewhere that said moto-cross was a more strenuous sport than football.

The added strength I built up was vital and before long I was enjoying a bit of success on the scrambling circuits in the region. Through working two jobs, I was able to save some money, which enabled me to take a trip to Manchester with my future brother-in-law Dave Wilkins to take possession of a brand new DOT for the princely sum of £200.

Dad also helped out as he customised a trailer he put on the back of his car so that I could travel to meetings at places like Washbrook, Bentley, Sudbury and Chelmsford. My first meeting on the new DOT was at Woodham Ferrers where I was satisfied to come 10th out of 30.

As I progressed from junior to senior racing, I was able to purchase a Morris pick-up to get us about and, after I found my feet, I used to regularly finish in the top four competing with the likes of Norman Messenger, Peter Smith, John Pease and John Ford.

During this time, I switched jobs after finishing my apprenticeship. I moved to the nuclear power station at Sizewell that was being built at the time on the Suffolk coast near Leiston.

I was asked at the interview my reasons for wanting the job and why I wanted to travel 25-plus miles each day to work. As far as I was concerned, it was simple. "To earn more money," I replied, as I knew the wage structure at Sizewell was much better than anything of a similar nature in the area.

Being frank, I have to say that I was amazed to get the job. I was only just out of my indentures, yet I was given the responsibility of setting up guide tubes that would house the uranium rods. There was so much security around the place – and still is, I'm sure – and it was very new in those days to be working with radiation.

Well aware of the importance of the job, I got my head down and made sure that the guide tubes were dead level so there would be no problems when the rods were inserted.

We worked behind 15-foot concrete walls and four-inch thick metal and had to wear special clothing to maintain a clean working environment. When we got behind with the schedule, we used to be asked to work what we called a 'Ghoster', which meant up to three days of work, non-stop.

I'm unsure whether the powers-that-be realised what was happening but I have to admit – for the first time in public – that we used to sleep through much of the evening. There were strips of quite thick foam lying around and they made good beds. It was asking a great deal to expect us to work virtually non-stop for up to 48 hours.

Although I enjoyed my new job, I didn't let it get in the way of my motorcycling fun. If there was a good meeting on a Sunday and I was down to work, I used to ask a workmate to stand in for me.

He would go in and clock on himself, and then go round the back and come in again – perhaps wearing a different hat or something – and clock in for me. For this, I was happy to pay him half my day's wages. I was picking up some prize money from scrambling by now as I began to establish myself in the sport.

Another couple of memories from this time . . .

Firstly, the journey to work on a double-decker bus provided by the company. Our driver liked to drive 'flat out' and several of us would sit on the top deck above him and stamp our feet to encourage him to go even faster. One day, he misjudged a corner and veered off the road, with the bus ending up in a ditch. Luckily, none of us was hurt and he was back on the gas the very next day.

Secondly, despite being 21, I was still unable to buy a beer in pubs because they wouldn't believe I was over 18, so I always had to get my mates to buy my drinks.

Looking back, it was a good time money-wise for me and I stayed at Sizewell for two happy years before I moved to a job more closely linked with motorcycle sports.

I was offered a job as stores manager at Dave Bickers' Motorcycles in Woodbridge Road, Ipswich

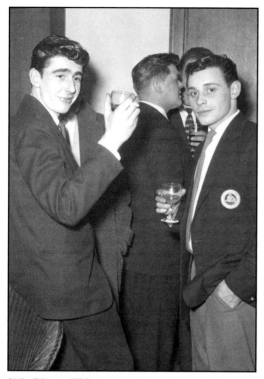

At the Triangle MC Club dinner-dance with Brian Osborne, who went on to have a brief career in speedway as a rider and promoter at Scunthorpe.

Me and my friend and fellow scrambler Jim Aim, one of my main competitors, show off our nifty footwork.

Showing the ladies how to jive. I still love dancing today and attend two-to-three modern jive sessions per week.

With my work-mate from Ransomes, Tim Robinson, who shared my passion for scrambling.

– just a stone's throw from where I had lived in my early years. Okay, riding was still a hobby I did at weekends but I was involved in the 'industry' and my life was starting to point in the direction it was going to take.

The success I was gaining at scrambling was the reason I was offered the new job as I had built up a close relationship with Fred Cotton, who was a top official at the Triangle Motorcycle Club. Fred went on to become one of the unsung heroes in speedway – a behind-the-scenes man who acted as machine examiner at Foxhall Stadium for many years.

He worked for Dave Bickers and was instrumental in my appointment as stores manager, although I don't know where the 'manager' bit came from as I was the only person in the 'department'! We offered a service whereby we guaranteed every order by 'phone or letter was despatched the same day.

Fred was an exponent of a little known sport but one that he helped to make popular at the time – moto-ball. This was like polo but with a big ball and on motorbikes, rather than horses. It was great fun and shows how many different 'angles' and how much fun you can get out of riding a bike.

Dave Bickers lived just outside Ipswich in a village called Coddenham and our paths were to become linked for several years. He was a far better scrambler than I was and went on to win many international events before getting into films in a big way by providing mechanical props and preparing stunt sequences for James Bond films and the like.

He was a natural rider and I made it my business to watch him and find out how it should be done. The first hour of meetings is taken up with practice and I would always watch how Dave went about the course. I learned a huge amount from him and took on board how to take corners and make jumps the right way.

There was a difficult jump on the course at Tuddenham and I'd watched Dave Bickers clear it with

Trevor Rumsey (a sidecar racer) and me in 1963, admiring the Triumph engine fitted in the frame built by Trevor.

Competing at Icklingham, near Newmarket, in October 1962.

Airborne: Briefly suspended in mid-air during another Eastern Counties event where I learnt my trade as a scrambler.

Looks like I'm about to leap over a couple of spectators' heads in 1963.

Blazing through the Essex countryside at Halstead, near Colchester, in 1960.

Unlike speedway, you had to tackle right-hand bends on the scrambling circuit but the humps and bumps stood me in very good stead when I later encountered rough shale tracks.
Below: With my early mentor Dave Bickers, who sponsored me in scrambling and later gave me a job as his stores manager. In this picture we're taking a close look at the impressive new Greeves Challenger, which I rode with Dave's backing from the spring of 1964.

Scrambling was not always as easy as it looks in the photo above. As you can see (below), the wet and mucky conditions often created some hairy moments.

ease without taking the easier, but slower option. It took some while for me to decide whether to follow suit and eventually I had to make a decision – and I was able to follow in the successful tyre tracks of Dave and gain ground on my rivals.

One of my friends, Ian Towns, also decided to try this difficult jump. Unfortunately, he got it wrong and went tumbling over and over. It shook him up but he was soon back on his feet, thank goodness, and none the worse for wear.

That experience gave me extra confidence in my ability, and I took this on to a meeting at Cockfield. I made a poor start and was at the back of a 40-strong field. At one point in the track, there was a drop where you had two options. Everybody else took the safe option and I probably would have done the same myself if I had not been left adrift. I'd been studying that section of the course during practice and convinced myself that I could handle the dangers as the race panned out and after I had passed a few other riders.

While others in front of me slowed down to take the easier drop, I wound up the throttle in fifth gear and went for it. Thankfully, I got it right and, going flat out, I landed okay before speeding off on the rest of the course.

I ended up going from last to first and I'll never forget fellow racer Terry Folley saying to me afterwards: "John, do you know you jumped right over my head?"

By now, I was riding a BSA Victor 420cc but I only kept it for a season as I just didn't get on with it. Dave Bickers then part-sponsored me to ride a Greeves for a couple of seasons. He later took up a CZ franchise which he rode himself with great success, both locally and internationally.

**Trying out the Greeves at Debenham, Suffolk in 1963.**

At about the same time, I also had a bike with a Triumph engine and a frame built for me by Trevor Rumsey, a well-known local sidecar racer. I only kept this for a season as I had problems with a weak headstock.

After the Greeves, Dave part-sponsored me for a couple of CZ bikes, one was a 250cc and the other a 360cc. These were the best bikes I rode by far and gave me enough ammunition to stay at the forefront of the regional scrambling scene. I went on to ride a 380CZ the following season.

Using these bikes, I won the 250cc Eastern Centre Championship and was runner-up in the 500cc championship in 1969.

I never made it big like Dave, who was one of the very best riders the sport has produced. He could mix it with the big boys and his proud record of international victories proves how accomplished he was.

As far as I was concerned, there was no one like Dave on the track and, as I indicated earlier, I watched his every move whenever I could. The tips and tricks of the trade I picked up went a long way to getting my speedway career off the ground in the quickest possible time.

He taught me indirectly how to handle a bike. It has to be your friend, there is no point battling with it as I did in my youth with that pesky horse. You have to be a partnership and work as one. I never forgot what I learned from the 'master'.

I became good enough to ride in some international meetings, although it was on the local tracks riding mainly in Suffolk, Essex, Cambridgeshire and Norfolk where I collected an array of trophies. I went on to win numerous trophies in my racing career, from expensive, thick glass mementoes to the less impressive, and perhaps almost plastic-like, shields at lesser events.

But I valued them all. If someone has gone to the trouble of putting up a prize – from a world title downwards – and you had to beat others to win it, then you have to take pride in what you take home and what you have achieved.

When Dave was at the height of his powers, there used to be a weekly television Sunday lunchtime spot for scramble racing. This helped to make Dave's name and a host of other British, and foreign, riders. I didn't reach those heights, although I did feature in a few of the TV meetings with the publicity helping to swell attendances.

There was a superb track at Shrubland Park just outside Ipswich and this used to attract top riders and hold some of Europe's most prestigious meetings. A large Georgian mansion is situated in the grounds and at that time it was being used as a health spa, attracting many well-known celebrities – and even, it is believed, royalty. But the celebrities I was interested in were those on the track, and one I remember watching with most interest was a talented Swede called Stig Rickardsson who rode a works Husqvarna.

He was one of the best riders in Europe, although not a regular winner. But I liked his style and used to be glued to his progress around the course. I loved the way he rode. He used to stand up for most of the race without touching the seat and I thought, 'this is the way' – the way to get the balance right and to get the best from both man and machine.

I adopted some of Stig's methods during my scrambling career and gradually increased the amount of time spent standing up, especially on long, undulating stretches of a course. Little did I know that our paths would cross many years later when his son Tony first started in speedway.

There was another type of off-road activity at Shrubland Park that fewer people knew about. In fact, it was only the five of us who took part. We used to meet up occasionally at midnight in our vans and with Dave (Bickers) leading, we would roar through the main entrance, down the driveway and off on to the grass driving up an extremely steep hill. This was on a curve, which we had to take at very high speed before dropping back down on to the driveway and returning to the main road. Completely mad, but great fun!

Sadly, Dave Bickers died in 2014, having enjoyed a long, successful life, doing what he loved best and creating memories for many that will live forever. I attended an event at his house where numerous marquees were set up to exhibit all the bikes he had collected over the years. Many of them had been raced but some were just collectors' items. It was a hugely impressive display. Although a sad occasion, I met up with many people I had raced against in those early years and it was great to reminisce about those times.

Mum used to keep a scrapbook of my scrambling exploits from the *East Anglian Daily Times* and *Ipswich Evening Star* that used to give excellent coverage. She continued this right through my speedway career.

It was during this time that I met my first wife Pat, who is the mother of my son Chris and my eldest daughter Joanne. She came from Great Bentley, Essex, and I met her at a Dave Bickers fan club social evening at Chelmsford.

Despite all my success in scrambling, it was always just a hobby and one that I expected to continue to enjoy until age took a hold.

But things were to change when the Berry/Thurley duo moved in at Foxhall Stadium to create a new speedway track inside the old one after the sport's absence in the 60s had seen the original circuit concreted over for stock car use.

Ipswich Witches were about to take off in a big way – and I was going to be at the heart of it all.

British motorcycle sport lost one of its all-time greats when Dave Bickers passed away after suffering a stroke on July 6, 2014, aged 76. Less than a couple of months later, on August 31, a number of us local former scramblers attended a memorial reunion in Dave's honour organised by Woodbridge and DMCC at Blaxhall, Suffolk, while a moto-cross meeting staged that day also marked the club's 50th anniversary celebrations. In this picture, I'm fifth from the left in the dark top with my arms folded. Many Witches speedway fans will probably also recognise Tony Davey kneeling (front left).

Aboard my new Jawa-ESO two-valve speedway bike in 1969, with (left to right) Dave Bickers, Fred Cotton, John Booth, Joe Thurley (Witches co-promoter) and Mike Horne (press officer) for company.

Chapter 3

# Unleashing The Tiger

**IT has been documented many times that I took a great deal of persuading to take the plunge into speedway. If I had known that I would take to it basically like a duck to water, and that it would bring me so much and make me into a bit of a celebrity, I would have taken it up with no questions asked.**

But I had my doubts, and my fears. The first time I got to the pit gate to take my first ride on a speedway track, I backed away. The thought of taking those bends at speed with a heaving 500cc of engine power between my legs was too much.

My dad had first taken my brother Tony and me to Foxhall Stadium when I was about 11, soon after it had became a purpose-built speedway venue. Like numerous others in the area, I can reel off the names of the riders who graced the blue and white Witches colours in the early days, when up to 20,000 fans used to regularly cram into the stadium.

I remember my particular heroes were Junior Bainbridge, Bert Edwards, Syd Clarke, Charlie Frenzl and Tich Read but I had no expectation whatsoever that I might one day follow in their tyre tracks. Dad and I even visited Charlie in hospital after the injury to his arm that ended his career.

I cannot leave that era without mentioning the impact that Bert Edwards made on me when he attended the club's 50th anniversary celebrations in 2011. He was invited back to Foxhall, along with many other ex-riders including Norfolk-based Tich Read, whose real name was George Snailham (he had to change it, didn't he!).

Bob Jennings, a former rider and a very loyal servant to the club, brought along a JAP bike he had maintained. No sooner had Bert took the throttle and warmed the engine up, tears started to stream down his face. The memories had come flooding back. Sadly, he passed away a few years later.

Now back to Foxhall in the 60s. Unfortunately, the stadium was closed for several years but as I was busy working and establishing my scrambling career, this perhaps had less impact on me than other fans.

John Berry and Joe Thurley, former school pals from north London, brought speedway back to Ipswich in 1969. They were both very enthusiastic about its potential and Joe had even briefly dabbled in the sport as a rider. John was the owner of a fish 'n' chip shop in east London at that time. They were granted a licence to compete in British League Division Two but they were required to appoint someone with proven experience as an advisor. An obvious choice was Howdy Byford, who had previous connections with the club and was a renowned character.

Ipswich was a hotbed for speedway back then and the crowds soon started to flock in again, although not to the levels they were a decade or so earlier. But every promoter in the country these days would be smiling all the way to the bank if they matched the 6,000 or so fans who regularly watched the Witches in the early 70s.

John Berry had many talents and one that was to serve him well was his desire to track a side of local riders. He understood that if the public knew the riders, or a friend of a friend did, then they were much more likely to build a connection with Foxhall.

Local press reports of the scrambling scene were very good and I know that John used to read every word to see what potential there was. I was winning at 250cc level most weeks and also doing well on 360cc CZ in the 500 class. JB often used to come to Dave Bickers Motorcycles where I worked and lean on the counter, chatting about me having a try at speedway. I always had an excuse

This time I'm on my original speedway JAP, surrounded by (left to right) Stan Pepper, Bob Jennings, Joe Thurley, Brian Osborne and Howdy Byford.

In my first set of 'Tiger' leathers with the club mascot.

Hugging the inside line in practice at Foxhall.

– 'I don't have a bike' – but John would come back with something like, 'I can get one sorted out for you', so then I had to think of another excuse to keep him at arm's length.

Along with some mates, I was regularly watching the action from the back straight and, because of my scrambling experience, I used to boast that I could do better. Words are easier than deeds, as it turned out, but I have to admit there was a small part of me that wanted to test my ability on the shale surface.

As the 1969 campaign moved on, I became more and more interested and this is where 'Chunky' played a big part in transforming my life. This was the name Rex Garrod, who was a very good scrambles rider, had christened a JAP bike that Dave Bickers had previously owned.

Rex, who I believe later got into films, found out that the runway at the former military aerodrome at Mendlesham, on the Ipswich-to-Norwich Road, was okay for practising on.

At one end, there was a huge pile of sugar beet and when lorries came to load up to take this to the factory near Ipswich, they used to leave plenty of dirt (a mixture of mud and earth) at the end of the runway. This provided a good surface for broadsiding on and that's where I learned the basics that were to stand me in good stead later on.

I don't think Rex was too serious about taking up speedway. He just loved to mess about on bikes and two other scramblers, Adrian Yallop and John Gibbons, joined in as we took it in turns to ride 'Chunky' on the airfield.

With John Berry and Joe Thurley still pestering me, I agreed to go back to Foxhall and one afternoon we took 'Chunky' to the track. The blessed thing refused to start – perhaps because it didn't want to lose any of us to the sport where we would end up with our own machines.

Anyway, we had to get it going so I sat on-board while we got roped up to a Ford Anglia so that it could give us a pull. We got up to a fast enough speed for the bike to start but the outcome was not what I wanted as the car stopped once its job had been done…and I went full pelt into the back of it.

It was a hard lesson to learn – that speedway bikes do not have any brakes!

Now we had got the bike started, we didn't want to risk it stopping again so we kept it running between each of us having a spin by parking it on the footrest and just topping up the fuel and oil. Rex went round first and looked good as he swung into the corners, with Adrian following and then John.

During those first laps, I found that I was broadsiding okay, helped by my spins around the sugar beet mess on the airfield. In scrambling, the bends were easier to negotiate because of the banking or burm on most corners.

I was quickly realising that speedway was certainly a different skill and you have to have perfect control of the throttle to get the best results.

After I had completed a few laps, I decided I would have an 'official' try-out. The next time John Berry came to see me, I agreed to do a few laps after a meeting on a Thursday night. I did ask him to put out all the floodlights first, so fans would leave the stadium thinking there was nothing else to watch. Word must have got out though because when the lights went back on, there were still people on the terraces.

Ron Bagley, who was to become one of my Ipswich team-mates and an early mentor, allowed me the use of one of his bikes. I had no speedway gear, of course, so I turned out in scrambles trousers, boots and an ordinary brown leather jacket that looked, from a distance, to fit the bill. They pushed me off and off I went – my life was changing.

I got a bit carried away, did several laps and then realised I was being waved down. Scramble races are over 10 to 12 laps and I had forgotten I was now on a speedway track where only four are required.

I'll be the first to admit that I was not very fast but I felt comfortable enough, despite a searing pain in my left foot. Nobody had told me anything about wearing a steel shoe and I wore a hole right through my boot so that I could see my sock!

Soon after this – I think it may even have been the following week – I was offered a chance to ride in the second-half when a rider called Mike Coomber became unavailable.

I was again able to use Ron's bike and everybody kept telling me that speedway racing was no big deal. Still relatively nervous about it all, I asked to go off the outside gate so that I could stay out of the way.

The tapes went up and we were away, with me several yards behind the other lads. I locked up going round the first two bends and when I came out of the second corner, they were halfway down the back straight. But I took great satisfaction from finishing the four laps no further adrift than where I was after the first half-a-lap.

I had completed my first 'real' race and from then on, I knew in my heart that I could make an impact in this sport, although winning world titles was the last thing on my mind at the time.

What I also took on-board was that I had to get my starting right. From that very first competitive race, I had learned that, without a fast starting technique, I was not going to have a successful speedway career.

I can remember going to former Norwich rider Ken Last after the meeting for advice on how to get the bike from the tapes in the quickest possible time. He kindly gave me some initial advice that held me in good stead and, until the day I retired, I continued to work on getting the best out of myself to the first corner. As an aside, his daughter Julie became the advertising manager for Ipswich Speedway when I started promoting in 1989 and she is still there today.

If you have ever started off in your car in third or fourth gear, you will have some idea of what getting off the start entails for a speedway rider. I found it was best to give it about a half of throttle and feather the clutch to get me away in the fastest manner.

Once you had that sorted, it became automatic and I used to fly away from the tapes. The other important technique that many riders take a long time to master (and some never do) is how to hold the throttle in such a way that your hand and arm are positioned correctly when you are starting and also when you enter the corners.

You want to have your hand over the throttle so that when you have wound it up to the maximum, your arm is straight. It's the same with the left hand; arrange your starting position so that when all the clutch work is done, both arms are straight to improve your balance and your control.

When I looked at other riders and saw their clutch lever was angled up from the handlebars, I used to smile to myself – they were not going to have their arms in the right position to achieve a good start.

All the techniques I used during my career – and I have to say successfully – were developed by me through trial and error. I soon picked up the best technique for Foxhall but, of course, it took longer on other circuits because I did not ride them so often.

During away meetings, I made sure I always studied, at close quarters, how the top two riders in the home team made their starts and the lines they rode on the track. If they were scoring double figures, they were clearly doing something right, and I wanted some of that.

Towards the end of August (about three weeks after my first race) I was put down as a reserve for the Dave Bickers Best Pairs meeting at Foxhall. Graham Miles missed out because of a collar-bone break so I stood in still using one of Ron's machines. I'd like to think that I did okay without pulling up too many trees and scored seven points, with my partner Barry Thomas suffering engine problems after a couple of races.

When I arrived for the meeting, I checked the programme to see if my name was in there and was surprised to see a 'Tiger' Louis listed in the line-up. I went into the office and asked, 'who is this

'Tiger' Louis?' They told me that Joe Thurley had thought of it based on the yellow jersey and black and yellow trousers I frequently wore for scrambles.

A few weeks later, I was drafted into the Ipswich team as they were short of riders against an All Star Select side. The match preview in the local paper had this to say about my inclusion: "The Witches will be hard-pressed by an extremely strong All Star side, but they have taken the opportunity to blood one of their second-half juniors. With Bernie Aldridge and Neville Slee suffering from acute motor troubles, John Louis is brought into the side at No. 7. Louis is a well-known scrambles rider and only took up speedway midway through this season. He did well as a reserve in the Dave Bickers Trophy meeting and his keen style of riding has already earned him the nickname 'Tiger'."

I rode in four races, but failed to score. However, it was more about the racing experience then and getting more laps in against other riders.

Then, in early October, Ipswich faced Berwick in a challenge meeting at Foxhall and I passed another milestone by winning my first-ever race in Heat 2. I came third in my next race and managed to get past their skipper Mark Hall to take a second in my third heat, finishing on six points overall.

When all is said and done, I had ridden enough by this stage to want to give speedway a go and the

Another picture of me practicing at Ipswich. I didn't find the transition from scrambling to speedway too difficult.

way I had been brought up meant that I was not going to go into it half measures.

Apparently, Howdy Byford also thought I had the potential to go far, often making outrageous predictions in the Ipswich programme about how an Ipswich team, full of local lads led by me, would win the Division Two title and then go on to take the Division One title as well. That was certainly a lot to live up to but who knows what the future might bring?

I approached John Berry and asked him if he could guarantee me a reserve place for the next season and I, in turn, would get a new bike, leathers, etc. and have a real go at it. I received a typical JB response, which was: "We don't make rash promises to other riders and I'm not about to start with you."

Despite that, I decided I would get myself prepared anyway…

There were winter training schools taking place and I wanted to have some of that – I wanted to be much more professional and competitive by the time the tapes went up for the first time on the 1970 campaign.

There was a two or three-day course at Long Eaton run by the Swede, Olle Nygren, who later became an Ipswich rider but was, at that time, captain of the West Ham team. He split us into three groups and I was put into the slowest lot. As you can imagine, this did not go down too well, but it was probably a fair enough assessment of my first day or two at Long Eaton.

Olle put us into mini races and I managed to work my way up through the middle group to the 'elite' gang. I was really buzzing and I beat Alan Bellham, who was at the time a fully-fledged rider with King's Lynn. He later joined the Witches when they moved into Division One but only did one meeting before moving back to Division Two with Scunthorpe. After he finished riding, he ran a parts van at Foxhall for many years.

There was a school at Boston that I also went to and because I wanted to keep the costs down, I used to sleep in the car between sessions. I learned a good deal from Olle and the other tutors but, at the end of the day, it is how much you want it yourself.

So much of my craft, I figured out for myself. I used to draw diagrams and pictures with a line going through my body to determine the best posture and positioning to get the most from the bike. It was all quite technical but I loved doing it, and was perhaps a throwback to my dad who would spend hours in his shed puzzling out similar scenarios on my engines.

The tweaks I had put into my game during that winter worked well for me and I got a call from Dave Lanning to see if I would like a ride at West Ham. Off I went down the A12 and somehow the fact that I was going to ride in London found its way back to JB.

As we were approaching Romford, a car pulled in front of us and began frantically waving us down. It didn't look like the police but we thought we'd better stop, so we pulled onto the verge. Out jumped JB and I have to say that the air turned somewhat blue. He was not a happy man, and was ranting and raving as to why I should want to ride at West Ham.

To be fair to Dave, who had been advised by Olle to sign me up, he had only asked me down to have a spin and there was no attempt on his part to get me to sign. But what it did make me realise was how much JB thought of me, and how keen he was to see me in his 1970 side.

JB, who mellowed somewhat as our relationship grew, had no doubts about plonking me into the team but, before we started racing in earnest, I upset the boss once again. He called me a cheat and some of those other names that had lit up the Romford air a few days earlier.

I was invited to Foxhall for their practice day and JB asked me to sign for Ipswich before the session started but I refused! He then told me that I had to pay for my own insurance if I wasn't an official team member but I still wouldn't sign.

During the session, JB pitted me in with established riders John Harrhy and Pete Bailey. To save having to set up the regular starting gates, JB used some thick elastic that he stretched across the track and then let go.

John and Pete were the best that Ipswich had at the time, but I beat them away from the start every time. Using all the knowledge that I had learned so far, I was out like a rocket, reaching the first bend in the lead.

"You're a cheat, you are," stormed JB. "You must be."

I wasn't, it was just that I was quicker on the draw and benefited over John and Pete in that I was more used to elastic starts as they were regularly used in scrambling.

If I was on the inside and the elastic zinged past me first I'd be off, not waiting for it to clear the whole width of the track. To me, it was just basics, but JB would have none of it. He argued with me a lot of the time and I'm still unsure today whether it was just his rather aggressive nature or whether he was trying to toughen me up to become a better competitor. Whichever it was, it worked and his perseverance paid off – not only for me, but for him as well.

Anyway, I signed that form after the practice session and the rest, as they say, is history.

End-of-season social at Ipswich in 1969. Howdy Byford, Brian Osborne and John Harrhy are standing behind me, with Pete Bailey and Ron Bagley sitting to my right.

Showing more body movement in the saddle at the 1970
pre-season practice. The new Jawa looks bright and shiny.

Chapter 4

# 'Speedway's Most Wanted Man'

**I**T was not something I had planned to do but, as things turned out, I've certainly no regrets at taking up the opportunity offered to me when speedway returned to my hometown of Ipswich in 1969.

In preparation for the start of my first full season, I sold most of my scrambling bikes and purchased a brand new Jawa from Czechoslovakia. It was even put on display for a while at Dave Bickers' shop, where I was still working as stores manager.

I kept my 360 CZ scrambles bike to help maintain my fitness levels. Whenever I had a chance, I went over to Chippenham, which was a very challenging scrambles track, and did about three sessions of about 10-12 laps. This stretched me to my limit but I believe it improved my overall strength and stamina for speedway.

The Witches began their season at Romford and due to the growing popularity of speedway in Suffolk, the A12 was awash with cars and coaches as hordes of Witches fans made their way to watch our first meeting of the 1970 season.

My memories of that night are of the low concrete wall that went round the outside of the now-defunct Essex circuit and that I managed seven points from a reserve berth. I had to be happy with that.

I took the chequered flag in my first race, beating team-mate Neville Slee, Kevin Holden and Ian Gills. That 5-1 helped the Witches pull off a 41-36 victory against a Bombers team tipped to do well in the second division that year. According to the local press report afterwards, I had 'joined a relatively small group of riders that have won their first-ever league speedway race'.

This guaranteed a bumper attendance figure for the Good Friday afternoon return fixture with Romford and the atmosphere was terrific as we repeated the 41-36 win. I won the reserves' race and scored seven points again, this time from four rides, as opposed to the five I had ridden the previous evening.

Although it was early days, I was already feeling confident that, with more racing combined with a natural ability, this was the sport for me.

I took a while to find my feet, although I was still scoring nicely and quite happy with how it was all going. In fact, after only six meetings, I moved to the No. 5 berth in the line-up. Each away track I visited provided a different challenge but I took each one as it came and tried to record set-ups used, etc. for future reference. This was something I continued to do for the rest of my career.

Towards the end of April, Ipswich staged a double header at Foxhall. In the first, a league meeting against Peterborough, I won my first three heats but was then beaten by Pete Seaton, spoiling the hopes I had of completing a full house.

I went into the next meeting, a Knockout Cup tie against Crayford, with something to prove. And it worked out perfectly as I put together four straight wins for my first 12-point maximum.

A few weeks later in early June, I won my first piece of speedway silverware, partnering Ron Bagley in the Dave Bickers Anglian Best Pairs at Foxhall. We needed a 4-2 in the last heat to win the event and we were up against arch-rivals from King's Lynn, Ian 'Tiddler' Turner and Russell Osborne. I managed to gate first with Tiddler hot on my tail and Ron behind him in third.

Apparently, it was a very exciting race to watch before Turner overdid it on the third lap and got disqualified for stopping the race. Ron and I made no mistake in the re-run, scoring a 5-1 to lift the trophy for Ipswich. Scores: Ron: 6, JL: 17. The local press report said: "Three of the smallest men in speedway – Dave Jessup, Ian Turner and John Louis – made this a night to remember."

I was getting quicker all the time and at the next home meeting against Berwick, I broke the Ipswich track record for the first time, lowering it by 0.2 seconds. Two weeks later, when Eastbourne were the visitors, I scored my first 15-point maximum and lowered the track record again, this time by 0.6 seconds.

Dad was still maintaining my engines on his own and also encouraging me in all areas of my racing. As I mentioned in the first chapter, he always timed my first few races as he wanted me to go as fast as possible. I knew that he was doing this and subconsciously I think it spurred me on to always try and improve my times at Foxhall. He never verbally mentioned why he did it or put any pressure on me but his technique obviously inspired me, because the track record got lower and lower!

At this point, I started to get second-half bookings at Division One tracks, such as Hackney, Leicester and West Ham. After I beat Hackney No. 8 Barry Thomas on his own track, Hawks' promoter Len Silver apparently rang JB wanting to buy me, regardless of the price. The response was very short and to the point: "He is staying here until the end of the season, at least."

My scores were obviously attracting a lot of interest but I wasn't expecting to hear that the Young England selectors had picked me for all five Tests against a Young Sweden team. After one of the meetings, a journalist asked me how old I was and I replied: "How old do you think?"

He said: "I would say about 18." I agreed with him and he went away happy, while I laughed my boots off that I could still pass for a teenager. I scored 51 points in those meetings, which I was happy with as we won the series, winning four matches and drawing one.

A month later, in August, I was selected for another series – this time against Czechoslovakia. It gave me a very busy racing period where I did seven meetings in 10 days! I scored 14 points at King's Lynn, 17 at Ipswich and 12 at Rayleigh but the young Czechs proved a bit too strong for us, winning the series 4-3.

A fortnight later, more recognition of my improving results came when I made my First Division debut. Newport manager Bob Radford booked me as a guest for an away fixture at Leicester. I won the second heat in a time equal to the winner of the first and top scored on eight points but unfortunately we lost 52-26. Bob was convinced I had the talent to go far and was very supportive, giving me more guest bookings whenever he could. I am indebted to him for giving me the chance to ride against the top boys, that experience was invaluable.

I also had chances to ride for West Ham, Oxford and Wembley as a guest but I don't really remember much about those meetings. It's the Newport ones and Bob Radford's support that stand out.

Back to Foxhall and our Knockout Cup semi-final against Rochdale, which turned out to be an unforgettable night but not necessarily for the racing. It was an incredibly close meeting with Rochdale needing a 5-1 to force a draw in the final heat. I was up against their No. 1 Eric Broadbelt and knew I had to beat him out of the gate.

Few of my races stick in my memory but I can recall this one clearly. When the tapes went up, we both made good starts. He was not in the mood to be second best and he took me right out, so that I clattered the fence on my way round the opening two turns.

Being left adrift of the field, I was not in the best of moods and did not take long to pass the other two riders in the race. I was breathing fire and, by the time we reached the back straight on the last circuit, we were level. In my mind, I was going 100mph, I was so wound up and I went under Eric who then slid off. Did I touch him? I can't remember! But the referee was happy, which is the most important thing, and I took the three points.

Looking relaxed in the Romford dressing room just moments before Witches' first meeting of 1970, my first full season in speedway.

I expected to be congratulated by supporters as I did my lap of honour but the appreciation was more intense than it normally was. The shouting from the terraces found its way through my helmet and I was smiling to think that my race win meant so much to the fans.

Little did I realise that Eric had by this time picked himself up and, not wasting time to dust himself down, had grabbed a rake that was lying on the centregreen. He was making his way towards me as fast as his legs would take him. Supporters had been warning me of the impending danger. Although I was oblivious to the anger Eric possessed, JB could see what was going on.

Apparently, he leapt over the fence and it became a race between him and Eric as to who would get to me first. It must be the only running race staged at Foxhall and, thankfully for my well-being, it was JB who came out on top – literally!

Before Eric could strike a blow, JB flew into the air and rugby tackled him – holding him down until the red mist had evaporated. The fun and games certainly amused the crowd and I bet from JB's point of view, he would have given much to have similar dramas every week to pull the punters in.

I had the last laugh as I then went on to win my first Silver Helmet challenge against Eric, but without any added drama this time.

I never spoke to Eric after the meeting. It was probably best that we were kept apart, particularly as he was given a two-week ban, but I did see him much later at a meeting at Belle Vue.

He came up to me and gave me a nudge with a bit of a friendly smirk on his face: "Remember the rake?"

Ipswich Witches 1970. Standing, left to right: Pete Bailey, Dave Whittaker, myself, John Harrhy. Kneeling: Ted Spittles, Bernie Aldridge. Skipper Ron Bagley is astride the chrome JAP.

Feeling tall alongside King's Lynn II's Ian 'Tiddler' Turner, eith Canterbury's Barry Thomas in the background. Those two, plus Canterbury's Graeme Smith (tussling with me below) were three of my biggest rivals in 1970.

It was always a great honour to represent my country and my first opportunity to do was when Young England faced Young Sweden in July 1970. Above: Our line-up, including three Witches, before the fourth Test at Reading. Standing, left to right: Richard May, Dick Bailey (team manager), Dave Jessup, Pete Bailey, Reg Fearman (promoter), Barry Crowson. Kneeling: Myself, Mike Vernam, John Harrhy.

Below:  A month after smashing the Swedes 4-0, we met a stronger Czechoslovakia side and this time lost the series 4-3. In this shot from the second Test at Canterbury, my race partner Richard May seems to have overcooked it.

I replied: "Yes I do and that I won the race and the Silver Helmet!"

Like the majority of sporting flare-ups caused in the heat of moment during tense battle, we have laughed about it several times since.

Probably my best meeting that first season was when I guested for Newport again, this time against Wolves at Monmore Green. Given that I had never ridden the track before, I went out and scored a 15-point maximum. I was riding as a reserve and Bob Radford managed to prevent me from meeting Wolves No. 1 Ole Olsen for the whole meeting.

He also stayed with me in the pits all night and encouraged me all the way. As Newport's top scorer, I should have been able to challenge Ole for his Golden Helmet but guest riders were not eligible to compete. It would have felt pretty good to hold both the Gold and Silver helmets at the same time!

Ipswich still had the Knockout Cup Final against Berwick to complete and we won the first leg 47-31. Ex-scrambler Tony 'Shrimp' Davey, who was 19, made his debut in that meeting. The second leg followed two days later when we travelled to Berwick and lost 43-35 but we had won the cup on aggregate by eight points.

There would be no league title but that just meant we had more to aim for in the next season.

It has to be one of the biggest thrills you can get to represent your hometown sporting team. It certainly felt very special to me. Not only was I with a club run by a man who went on to become one of the best promoters this country has produced, but I was in a position where my family and my mates could follow me at close quarters. It was a real bonus as far as I was concerned and, on top of that, I could see what was going on with JB looking to bring in other local riders to fit in the side around me.

JB was extremely influential in my career and he was also very clever. He could see that the more fans could associate with the team, the more likely they were to come through the turnstiles. And

My first silverware, presented by Dave Bickers after Ron Bagley and I won the Best Pairs at Foxhall.

Getting my hands on the Silver Helmet after beating Eric Broadbelt in August 1970.

Where it all started in terms of Ipswich winning major team honours following their 1969 revival. I'm holding the British League Second Division Knockout Cup after Witches defeated Berwick on aggregate in the 1970 final. My team -mates (left to right): John Harrhy, Pete Bailey, Tony Davey, Ron Bagley, Ted Spittles, Stan Pepper.

With dad, Jack, who was a constant companion in the pits and took very good care of my engines. I will never underestimate the key role he played in helping me to achieve what I did in speedway.

it worked with 7,000 to 8,000 fans regularly coming to those early 70s meetings as speedway re-caught the imagination of the Ipswich public.

We rivalled Ipswich Town for the affections of local supporters and this was at a time when Bobby Robson was beginning to make the 'Tractor Boys' (as they were to become) a dominant force in the European game.

I got to know Bobby and he used to come to some of the sporting social events that were organised in and around the town. He had time for people, made you feel important and was the down-to-earth type that I admired. In the few dealings I had with him, you could see how he became so successful with so many top football clubs, and England as well. He earned respect.

Mike Horne was the local speedway correspondent at the time and, after a spell away reporting on Blackburn Rovers, he returned to Suffolk and began working full-time at Foxhall Stadium as JB's speedway manager.

The relationship with Mike was excellent, as were the ones with top photographers Dave Kindred and Owen Hines who used to snap away at most of our home meetings. Their photos were some of the best that ever appeared and the press coverage we received was first class. I remembered Dave from my scrambling days when he used to literally lay in ditches hoping to catch riders mid-air as they jumped over him. Some of the resulting photos were spectacular to say the least.

As you will have appreciated by now, John Berry was to have a big bearing on the way my life was going to pan out. I had some issues with him later in my career when I was 'dumped' due to Dennis Sigalos and John Cook moving in (more of that later) but I can say fair and square that I would not have achieved as much as I did on a speedway bike without him.

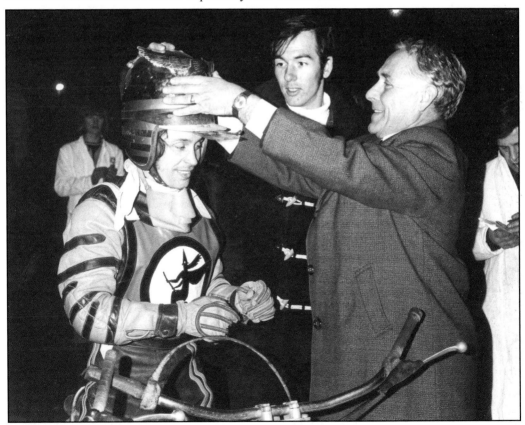

Another successful defence of the Silver Helmet in 1971. This time Bradford promoter Les Whaley presents me with the headgear, watched by John Berry, after I beat Dave Baugh at Odsal.

The Eastern Counties Championship individual event at Rayleigh in 1971 turned out to be a good night for the Witches. Pete Bailey and Tony 'Shrimp' Davey complete the top three.

It is well documented that JB was not always the easiest person to get on with; his desire to succeed and be the best often caused him to ruffle feathers. However, we generally had a good working relationship and the desire to succeed rubbed off on me so that after I had decided the shale sport was definitely for me, I knuckled down to make the very most of the opportunity – and the skill – I had.

Joe Thurley played a big part in my early days but he moved on after a couple of years at the club and it was left to JB and Ron Bagley to become my 'father figures'.

Ron went from captaining the team to becoming team manager by the time the Witches hit the real heights. He was a very calming influence and contrasted nicely with JB, who was never afraid to speak his mind, regardless of who might be upset.

When Ron spoke to you, he always did it in a calm way and was constructive in what he said, which was just what I needed. Having willingly let me borrow his machinery for my first tentative laps at Foxhall, he carried on helping me when I was paired with him in the team. He taught me the importance of teamwork and that going all out for the win was not necessarily good for the team.

All-in-all, it worked in my favour and I have to thank both JB and Ron for their help in my early years. I still see Ron occasionally at various Ipswich reunions and we often reminisce about our time spent together.

John Harrhy and Pete Bailey were the top men for the Witches in 1970, as befits the experienced Coventry loanees, but I'd like to think that I helped to create extra interest in the club with attendance figures having improved dramatically.

Pulling a locker during the third Test between Young England and Young Sweden at Eastbourne in 1971.

Ready to take on the bouncing Czechs at Romford in 1971. Left to right: Richard May, myself, Geoff Maloney, Malcolm Shakespeare, Brian Foote, Barry Crowson, Dave Jessup. On bike: Phil Woodcock and team manager Maurice Morley.

My first full season was over, and what a season it had been. I had achieved an average of 8.74, was holder of the Silver Helmet (since August), reached many 'first' milestones and thoroughly enjoyed every bit of it. But there was plenty more to come…

I found some records recently that show I spent just over £1,000 on equipment that year. I had to buy a second bike when the first one failed mid-season, plus there were the usual fuel and maintenance costs. In the Second Division, a rider who won all four races and the second-half could make a whole £16 per meeting. In the top division, this increased to £45, which was quite a difference.

I was 'Speedway's Most Wanted Man', or so some of the headlines in the speedway press would have had me believe in the close season of 1970. I know that Newport, West Ham, King's Lynn, Hackney and Leicester had all asked about me moving up to the First Division after the scores I got during guest bookings I had taken (I think I averaged about eight points at that level).

There were so many things to consider and just when I thought I had made up my mind, something else would make me think again.

For example, if I signed for Newport, I would be faced with a very long journey just for home meetings. Was I ready for that yet? If my scoring dipped and my income was reduced, what impact would it have on the family finances? I wasn't a youngster with no responsibilities, I had a young family to support.

Also, in my own mind, I felt I hadn't done enough to be certain that I was ready to move up a level. I had only started to go really well halfway through the season and perhaps I had just been racing against second strings in the First Division. I had also been lucky that, on some occasions, poor track conditions suited me better as an ex-scrambler.

My way of thinking was that if I found I was stretching myself too far, too early, it would affect

**Romford's Brian Foote tries to force his way past me on the inside, with my team-mate Clive Noy behind.**

After a successful first defence of the Silver Helmet match-race title against Romford's Colin Sanders at Brooklands at the start of 1971.

We enjoyed good rivalry with Rayleigh. Here I'm competing at The Weir with Rockets' Allan Emmett.

Wheel to wheel and no-one's giving an inch, me and Eastbourne's Gordon Kennett go for it.

It's only practice at Foxhall but Ron Bagley, myself, Tony Davey and back marker Pete Bailey are not easing off.

Some fresh air at last as I go for the win during a home league match in 1971, our last in the second tier.

my confidence and end up reducing my ability to make as big an impact in the sport that my professionalism demanded.

By staying where I was, I could build on what I had already achieved and, at the same time, increase my confidence with what I hoped would be a succession of high scores. All in all, I thought it would be best to leave it a further year and earmark 1972 as the season to start full-time in the top level of British speedway.

Whether that would be with Ipswich, with the likelihood that JB would be seeking to take the club forward, or with another club was something to be sorted out later.

I figured if I could continue to improve with Ipswich, take guest bookings in the First Division and win the Second Division Riders' Championship, there wouldn't be much doubt about my ability to be able to successfully step up in 1972.

All the British League clubs that spoke to me were told: "Thanks, but no thanks." I may be wrong but I think some of the promoters took this less well than others and they may have been behind the new rule brought in for 1971, barring riders from guesting for clubs they were not attached to or if they had a Second Division average over eight. I can certainly think of one promoter who, to this day, is very active in suggesting rule changes.

So in January, 1971, I signed a new Ipswich contract alongside newcomers Tony Davey and Clive Noy at an event organised by my fan club. The rest of the line-up was announced as skipper Ron Bagley, Ted 'Golden Boots' Spittles, Pete Bailey and Ted Howgego.

After attending Olle Nygren's pre-season training school, at Boston this time, to get myself sharp, I was ready for the new season.

However, in our first meeting, it was 'new boy' Tony Davey who grabbed the headlines with a 15-point maximum away at Boston, while I only managed eight. It was great to see Tony doing so

**Flying the national flag at Foxhall. Young England before facing the Swedes in June 1971. Standing, left to right: A distracted JB (team manager), Malcolm Shakespeare, Richard Greer, Kevin Holden, Pete Bailey, Malcolm Ballard. Kneeling in front of me, Shrimp and Geoff Bouchard.**

Ron Bagley was another who gave me lots of sound advice as well as practical on-track help in the early days. Here we are (below) team-riding in our successful defence of the Dave Bickers Best Pairs title in 1971 and, afterwards (top right), I'm taking Dave's wife Sylvia for a spin to celebrate our second victory in this event.

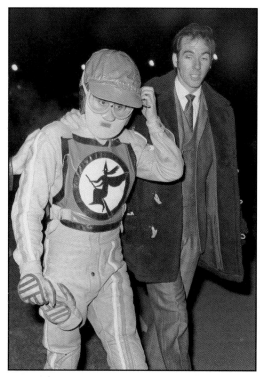

JB and I were good for each other for many years until it turned sour.

With Birmingham's Cliff Emms, who I beat to retain the Silver Helmet in July 1971.

Individual success in the Geoff Revett Trophy at Ipswich, ahead of Workington's Malcolm Mackay.

well though and it also helped encourage other scramblers to have a go at speedway as that made two of us doing well in a relatively short space of time.

Apart from that early 'hiccup', my plan for the season went well. I gained more trophies by winning the Eastern Counties Championship at Rayleigh in May followed by Ron and I successfully defending our Dave Bickers' Best Pairs at Foxhall in June (this time by a single point).

A few weeks after the win at Foxhall, Ron announced that he was retiring and I was given the huge honour of being appointed captain in his place. As mentioned earlier, Ron remained an important part of Ipswich as he was then appointed team manager by JB.

I also picked up the Geoff Revett Trophy in July and the end-of-season Evening Star Champion of the Evening Trophy.

I broke half-a-dozen track records up and down the country, held the Silver Helmet for most of the season, setting a record of 21 successive wins and overall won 26 of the 29 races I had in that competition. I also topped the league averages on 11.31. In all, I'm told I scored 21 full and four paid maximums.

To crown it all off, I won the Division Two title at Hackney, having dropped just one point to Peter Collins. I did have a minor panic in the last heat when my bike started to play up and I only just beat the two-minute time allowance but managed to nurse the bike round to win the race and clinch the championship.

Millicent Martin presented the trophy and cheque for £50. She was a well-known actress at the time, which all added to the glamour of the occasion. I remember my dad, mechanic John Bloomfield, JB and Ron Bagley all celebrating with me in the pits afterwards – definitely one of the best nights of my career so far.

Team-wise, we defended the Knockout Cup with victories both home and away against

**Me and Shrimp managed to grab a seat in this otherwise standing room only shot featuring riders from both teams in the Young England v Czechoslovakia Test at Peterborough in August 1971.**

Deep in thought during the Division Two Riders' Championship at Hackney, the personal highliight of the '71 season.

Victory over the cream of BL2 earned me a kiss from delighted Dad, Jack.

Actress Millicent Martin was at Hackney to present myself and runners-up Malcolm Shakespeare (right) and Hughie Saunders with our medals.

Peterborough, Rayleigh and Workington and then an aggregate success over Crewe in the final. We missed out again on winning the league title but had to be happy with third, which was the highest placing recorded by an Ipswich team since 1953.

On the international front, I was selected for the Young England side again against the Swedes, the Czechs and the Australians under a new team manager – JB himself! I was the only rider to earn five caps against Young Sweden and was captain for two of those meetings, retaining the captaincy for the other Test series as well. Two of my Ipswich team-mates, Tony Davey and Pete Bailey, also rode in all three series.

My best meeting was an 18-point maximum against Sweden at Ipswich, during which the track record was apparently lowered an amazing eight times. It was two seconds lower afterwards, but I was still the holder.

My worst moment was a fall in my first ride against Czechoslovakia, also at Ipswich, which resulted in a hospital stay with no solid food for a week after I injured my jaw.

Throughout the season, the support from our fans continued to grow. I've had numerous times to reflect on how fortunate we are at Ipswich with the following we get. First as a rider, and then as a

**Dad stands back as JB and Ron Bagley drench me in champagne in the Hackney pits.**

promoter, it has hit home on many occasions.

But it was around this time that it fully sunk in how lucky I was. They are the best in the land and, in my early days as a rider, there would always be a group of fans making a noise, which is great, especially when you are riding miles away from home.

Support had been fantastic at Foxhall that year and, allied with a great team spirit in the pits, made it a real year to remember.

By this time, I also had a fan club, which was run by Witches fanatic June Allum. She was a lovely bubbly lady who went on to become very successful in local amateur dramatics. Her husband Len was a second-half rider at Foxhall but unfortunately never progressed beyond that, partly due, I suspect, to the loss of two fingers in an early accident. My two-year-old son Chris was pageboy at their wedding that year.

I had managed a couple of open meetings at Division One clubs and finished on the rostrum at both Reading (beating Martin Ashby and Dag Lovaas in a race-off) and Wolverhampton. By the end of the campaign, I was 100 per cent confident that my career was ready for a move forward.

As I suspected (and hoped), my debut as a full-time top flight rider coincided with Ipswich making the move up in 1972. JB had taken over the West Ham licence when they closed at the end of 1971.

As an aside, in September I became the first English rider to attract sponsorship from major oil company Duckhams (they also sponsored Ole Olsen and Ivan Mauger, so I was in good company).

That Christmas, the *East Anglian Daily Times* and *Ipswich Evening Star* used Mick Mills (skipper of Ipswich Town) and myself on the sports pages. We posed in front of a decorated tree with Mick and his son Julian and me with wife Pat, along with daughter Joanne and son Chris.

Just before this, I had turned down the chance to ride in a 10-week long speedway tour of South Africa, representing Young England, at the invitation of Howdy Byford. It was a great opportunity but with the extra preparations required for the big step up into the top division, and a risk that I could pick up an injury, I reluctantly turned him down.

During the close season, I was pleased to find the speedway press had recognised my efforts in 1971:

*Speedway Star and News – Division Two Honours List – January, 1972*
*Mister Speedway: John Louis*
*This fantastic Briton dominated the whole league. He could have moved into the first division but decided to stay with the second for another season, improved on his already high standard from last year and led his home team to promotion. We are lucky he's English.*
*Mister Big: John Louis*
*He scored 450 points in league and cup matches and, with international appearances and individual meetings, was probably over the 600 mark altogether.*

These plaudits from the sport's weekly magazine all helped to boost my confidence for the big challenges to come.

We successfully defended the BL2 KO Cup by beating Crewe on aggregate in the 1971 final. Above: JB had the champers out again before (below) the two teams got together for the cameras.

First look at 'The Kid'. Billy Sanders (above) on his first laps of the Foxhall track after arriving from Sydney at the start of the 1972 season. Below: The 16-year-old Australian follows the old maestro Olle Nygren round his new home track.

Chapter 5

# On The Up With Witches

ONCE JB was given the all clear from the BSPA (British Speedway Promoters' Association) to take Ipswich into the British League, the make-up of our side would be largely decided by the Rider Control Committee. At that time, they had the power to move riders between clubs to 'balance the strength' of sides. He did, however, embark on a large amount of work to improve the track, pits area, etc. during the close season.

Regardless of who my eventual team-mates would be, JB had asked me to continue as captain and I went about preparing myself and my machinery to be in top condition for the start of the 1972 season. An extra incentive for ensuring my success in the coming months was the big decision I had made to become a full-time, professional speedway rider. I would no longer be working for Dave Bickers.

Behind the scenes, JB had been following the progress of a young Australian after hearing good reports about him. He took a big gamble in bringing over 16-year-old Billy Sanders to fill one of our reserve berths. There was an article in the local paper shortly after his arrival with a picture of Billy riding a moped with 'L' plates, highlighting that he was too young to ride a motorcycle on the road but he could ride a 500cc speedway bike at high speed around Foxhall!

In the big-time, the Witches team that took on the First Division elite at the start of 1972. Left to right: Alan Sage, Billy Sanders, Tommy Johansson, Sandor Levai, Tony Davey, myself, Olle Nygren and Ron Bagley, who hung up his leathers to become team manager.

Holding my own against Hackney's Swedish star and former World No.2 Bengt Jansson at the opening meeting of 1972.

Watching from the pits with Leicester's Dave Jessup, another product of the second division.

I first met Billy at the stadium when JB brought him straight from the airport to meet me and team manager Ron Bagley. I remember walking him around the track and wondering if perhaps JB was being a bit rash bringing such a young, inexperienced rider into the team. As history shows, JB's hunch paid off and Billy 'the Kid' was to play a huge part in Ipswich Speedway in the coming years.

Despite JB and Ron Bagley wanting to continue the plan of fielding mainly local riders, the Rider Control Committee allocated Olle Nygren, Alan Bellham and Alan Sage to us from West Ham. A Hungarian, Sandor Levai, was then allocated from Newport where he had been No. 1 and captain.

Huge interest had been generated in the town ahead of our opening fixture and an estimated 12,000 people turned up at Foxhall on Good Friday afternoon for a home meeting against Hackney in the Spring Gold Cup.

I think we may have tried too hard, resulting in several tapes exclusions in the first few heats. One of these gave Billy his first race in England, which he promptly won over Hackney's Swedish No. 1 Bengt Jansson, before winning the reserves' race as well. He ended up scoring eight points, the same as me. The fans had found another favourite.

Sadly, the afternoon was marred by an awful accident involving Tony Davey in which he got his left hand caught in his own machine. He lost a finger as a result and did initially consider quitting

Dave Jessup and I had to watch Wolverhampton's Ole Olsen collect the Golden Gauntlets at Leicester in 1972.

Dad and I listen to some pearls of wisdom from our Swedish veteran Olle Nygren.

Spreading the word . . . attending a shop opening in town with Ron Bagley, Tony Davey and Ted Howgego.

**Team-riding with Alan Sage to block out Exeter's Edgar Stangeland in our first top flight season.**

the sport. Fortunately, 'Shrimp' reconsidered and also went on to play a big part in Ipswich's success in the coming years.

The Mayor of Ipswich held a civic reception at the Town Hall in May to congratulate the team on its promotion to the top division. Several of us took trophies from the previous season to show what we had achieved already.

We lost nearly all of our Spring Gold Cup meetings but that period did allow us to settle down as a team and give everyone a chance to ride on some First Division tracks before the serious business of league fixtures started.

Alan Bellham was dropped after this and I think Mike Lanham may have replaced him for a while. JB also signed a young Swede, Tommy Johansson, who had to finish his National Service before making his debut in late April against Belle Vue. He made quite an impact, beating three- times World Champion Ivan Mauger twice and top scoring for us in the process.

We did have some excellent away wins but, in contrast, we let ourselves down a bit with some silly home reverses. But we coped well and I have to say what a big part Olle and Sandor played in the season. They helped the rest of us to settle in, being old hands at top level racing, and when the pressure was on, we could rely on them showing their class and also passing on what it was all about and what was needed.

Ipswich went on to finish sixth in the league table, which was creditable enough. We got as far as the quarter-finals in the Knockout Cup, losing at that point to Reading. I combined with Olle Nygren to keep the Dave Bickers Pairs Trophy at Ipswich for a third year.

The year had seen local lad Ted Howgego named as our official No. 8 as other young scramblers from the area began to follow myself and 'Shrimp' into speedway – encouraged all the way by JB.

Mike Lanham, Mick Hines and Clive Noy were made available for loan to Second Division outfits, with Mick brought into the 1973 side after his loan at Birmingham the previous season.

He replaced Tommy, who was suffering with a blood disorder and fatigue, which were not helped by his constant journeys backwards and forwards from Scandinavia.

Mike and Clive continued to ride on loan while another local rider Trevor Jones was now in the fold and he was also found a Division Two club – Canterbury.

On a personal front, I had started racing on the continent towards the end of April to expand my riding experiences further. More details of my exploits in Montagnana, etc. will be covered in a later chapter.

I finished fourth at my first attempt in the BLRC (British League Riders' Championship), scoring 11 points, ahead of experienced riders such as Anders Michanek, Ivan Mauger and Christer Loftqvist, so I hadn't done too badly for a 'new boy'.

My first senior cap for England came in September when I rode for Great Britain in the World Team Cup Final. This took place at Olching, West Germany. Our team of Ivan Mauger, Ray Wilson, Terry Betts and myself saw off Poland, Russia and Sweden to lift the trophy. I was pretty chuffed to finish on nine points, second highest behind Ivan, thanks in part, no doubt, to the excellent support from my 'pit crew'. Dad was mechanic, with Trevor Seymour and John Earrey coming over from Ipswich to cheer me on.

We all had quite a celebration afterwards and while individual success is always welcome, being part of a winning team, especially at international level, really is something else again.

The season ended on an unexpected high when I became the first Ipswich rider to qualify for a World Final since Ray Cresp in 1961. The final that year took place at Wembley and what a

King's Lynn team manager Alan Littlechild, Terry Betts and me listen as JB plots mine and Terry's progress in the 1972 British Final.

Rubbing shoulders with the best . . . finishing in the top four at the British Final, along with Ivan Mauger, Barry Briggs and the Boocock brothers, Nigel and Eric, was my ticket to a World Final debut at Wembley.

Rule Britannia! GB after retaining the World Team Cup at Olching, Germany – Terry Betts, Ivan Mauger, Ray Wilson, reserve Ronnie Moore and myself.

I had plenty to smile about in 1972, my first season at the highest level.

They got the GB World Cup-winning team together again before the BLRC at Belle Vue, where we put on specially made racejackets that looked much better than the bland ones we wore at Olching.

wonderful occasion it turned out to be – more of that later.

Statistics show that I got very close to 400 league and cup points with six maximums in 1972, ending the season with an average of nearly nine-and-a-half.

Another award came my way when I finished sixth in the *Daily Express* Sportsman of the Year poll (I think their readers voted for this). Ivan Mauger was third, behind Gordon Banks and Richard Meade, and I finished ahead of Jackie Stewart and Tony Jacklin.

It required a trip to London to a posh hotel where we all received our awards from HRH Princess Anne. I remember meeting shot-put champion Geoff Capes during a drinks reception beforehand and I watched amazed as he demolished a very large bowl of almonds. I had nibbled on a few before he caught sight of them and after that I never got a look in. I guess with his physique, you had to eat a large number of calories to keep your strength up!

I was invited to join a tour of Australia with the British Lions in the close season but turned the offer down. I wanted to spend some quality time with my young family after a very hectic first season in the top flight, although I didn't get a complete rest from speedway.

JB was always very keen to get us all involved in as many promotional activities as possible all year round and I was especially required to maintain a high profile in the local community. Looking at a newsletter sent out by my fan club that close season, I read a lesson at my local church to a packed congregation, opened bazaars, judged beauty competitions and visited local schools to give talks on speedway. I continued to take part in things like this for most of my Ipswich career. JB saw it as part of my role as captain – to be an ambassador for Ipswich Speedway, I guess.

At first, I struggled with public appearances as I wasn't sure what was expected of me and, yes, I was more than a bit nervous. JB told me to just be myself and the rest would follow. So that's exactly what I did and still do – what you see in public is me, nothing added by any PR agency or style guru (I think I would look slightly different if I had gone down that route…)

It makes it easier really as I rarely prepare for anything, I just go with the flow, answer people's questions and enjoy the occasion, whatever it is.

Before the new season started, I ran a couple of training schools at Scunthorpe with their promoter Brian Osborn, who was a former Ipswich rider. It was intended to provide a basic introduction to things such as track craft, gating and machine preparation for inexperienced young riders. As more and more scramblers in our area were showing an interest in trying speedway, this type of school would prove really useful for them.

The 1973 campaign started very well for me when I was named *Speedway Star and News* Personality of the Year, which was an honour I expected to go to the then World Champion Ivan Mauger. If I needed any extra encouragement after my first three years, this was it, and I went into Ipswich's second season in the First Division in great heart. TV personality Dickie Davies presented the trophy to me at a ceremony in London.

Team-wise, we had managed to retain all riders from the previous year, apart from Tommy Johansson who was still suffering from the blood disorder that was troubling him at the end of 1972. Mick Hines was signed in his place.

I was surprised, but happy, to accept offers of a column in the *Daily Express* and *Motor Cycle News*. JB obviously encouraged participation in anything like this as it helped promote the sport to a wider audience.

In early March, it was announced that the *Daily Mirror* were sponsoring a 'multi-national' speedway event to make up for the fact that all the other big international events were taking place abroad that year. Most countries would be involved in the qualifying rounds, culminating in a final at Wembley in July. England had just appointed their first permanent manager, Dent Oliver, who would be in charge for this tournament.

On my way to winning the 1974 British semi-final at Leicester, with Billy Sanders (outside) and
Sheffield's Reg Wilson in pursuit.

Not to be outdone, the *Daily Express* announced they were going to sponsor a big meeting called the Spring Classic at Wimbledon in mid-April. Barry Briggs and myself were invited to take part but all the other 14 places were to be voted on by the public from a list of candidates. It was certainly a different way to get their readers involved in the sport.

Unfortunately, one of the early Ipswich fixtures that year was spoiled by an incident involving me and Peter Ingram at the County Ground, Exeter. I was team riding with Billy in Heat 11 and we managed to finish on a 5-1. Ingram tried to go round me on the final bend and ended up in the fence.

This time, it was Ron Bagley and my mechanic John Bloomfield who 'saved' me, stepping between us before it all got out of hand with the unfortunate Ron ending up with a black eye. I was excluded after an Exeter protest and that probably cost us the meeting, although we did manage to claim a draw for our first league point of the campaign.

The Spring Classic at Wimbledon lived up to all expectations and provided a great spectacle for all those fans who travelled to Wimbledon. It was televised by ITV as well, so I got to watch myself ride for the first time afterwards. I finished joint sixth with Martin Ashby and, as the prize money extended that far down, we were both happy.

In early May, I was selected for a mini Test series in Poland, which required a very early flight from London to Poznan, then 120-plus miles by road to Wroclaw. The track was very wet, it was still raining, plus the Polish riders were using a different starting technique. The tapes rose at the same time as the green light went on and the Poles were trained to gate as soon as the light went on. In England, there was a pause between the light going on and the tapes going up, so the British riders felt they were at a disadvantage.

Not surprisingly, we lost heavily (76-31) with me top scoring for the British team on 11 points. We returned home very downhearted and disappointed at the Polish tactics. I was later reprimanded by Charles Foot of the BSPA for accusing the Poles of cheating – he explained that they just have different rules for starting. Perhaps some of this could have been avoided if someone had warned us before we set off, not when we got back.

The financial rewards were very poor – I received just £80 for my double figure score in Wroclaw and I had sustained £20 of damage to my bike from hitting large holes in the track. As a comparison, if I had ridden in Germany at an individual meeting, I could easily have earned £150-£200.

Some of the lads were talking about not doing the remaining two Tests because of the low pay rates and length of time spent travelling, etc. But to me, riding for my country was the greatest possible honour and things like money and conditions weren't going to prevent me putting on my English race-jacket. In fact, I am proud to say that during the whole of my riding career, I never turned down a chance to wear that red lion on my chest, regardless of where I had to travel or what I would receive in return.

The following Sunday saw another early start from London for a three-hour flight to Krakow, followed by a 70-mile road trip to Rybnik. Prior to this, I rode at Ipswich on Thursday (league), Wolverhampton on Friday (individual) and King's Lynn (World Championship qualifying round) on Saturday.

There was a much better result this time round for GB. In front of approximately 30,000 Polish fans, we won the meeting 55-53 with Reg Wilson getting the bumps after he won the final heat. Our hopes for a repeat the following month in Gorzow were in vain as the Poles thrashed us 75-33.

Seven days later saw a tough KO Cup affair for Ipswich against Newport at Foxhall. Tommy Johansson was back in the side temporarily for the injured Mick Hines and he helped build up a 12-point mid-meeting advantage. In the end, we won by just four points to take forward to the second leg in Wales.

However, it was a good night for me as I lowered the track record again; this time to 64.4 seconds and I won my first Golden Helmet match race by beating Reidar Eide (what a wonderful name for a speedway rider). In the return, he grabbed it back, but later in the season I won it again, this time from Arnold Haley at Sheffield.

I went on to defend the Golden Helmet against Pete Smith (Poole), Martin Ashby (Swindon), John Titman (Halifax), Malcolm Simmons (King's Lynn) and Ulf Lovaas (Cradley), to finish the season

Coatbridge and Scotland No.1 Jim McMillan chasing me in the 1973 British semi-final at Leicester's Blackbird Road.

The England team that beat Sweden at Sheffield in the 1973 Daily Mirror International Tournament. Standing, left to right: Martin Ashby, Eric Boocock, Reg Wilson, Len Silver (team manager), Terry Betts, myself. Kneeling: Doug Wyer, Peter Collins.

All smiles on the pre-meeting parade before we beat the Swedes again, this time in the final at Wembley. I wasn't smiling afterwards, though.

as holder. Ted Howgego, who was on loan to BL2 Birmingham, finished as holder of the Silver Helmet.

In July, Foxhall was chosen as the venue for an international meeting between England and Russia, which was a huge honour for the club. I remember it for one thing – and it wasn't that we crushed the Russians 56-21.

In one of the heats, Victor Trofimov, took a heavy fall and dislocated his shoulder. Obviously in a lot of pain, he got to his feet and walked over to one of the posts supporting our safety fence. He then proceeded to bang himself against the post until the shoulder popped back in. After swinging his arm round a couple of times, he calmly walked back to the pits. I was standing only yards away and couldn't believe what I was seeing – I had heard the Russians were hard characters but this was beyond belief!

I was also involved in the Daily Mirror International Tournament at Wembley, where England were victorious against Sweden after Peter Collins 'won' a race-off with Anders Michanek. When I say he won it, I mean he was awarded the race after 'Mich' took him a bit too wide and Peter ended up on the track. The Swedes weren't happy but the move was very hard in my opinion and there was only one decision the referee could make. Not the best way to win a tournament, but sometimes these things happen.

Although England triumphed, I had a disappointing meeting, scoring only two points, mainly due to bad gating. We had another match – GB v Rest of the World – straight after this, so I thought I would try my second bike. While I was warming it up in the pits, team manager Len Silver told me that I had been dropped from the team. To say I was disappointed was an understatement, but he wouldn't change his mind.

JB was absolutely furious and reported the whole thing to the SCB. He felt that not only had I been let down, but also all the thousands of Ipswich fans who had travelled to Wembley to watch me ride for my country. He argued that as I was booked and programmed to ride, it was too late to change the line-up and that if the roles had been reversed and I had failed to turn up, I would have been fined.

I'm not sure if JB got a response from the SCB but the incident certainly didn't improve the already tense relationship between him and Len Silver. I often wondered if Len held a grudge for not being able to sign me when I first started out in the sport, or if him and JB just didn't get on. Their notorious confrontations on the centregreen at Foxhall always provided great entertainment for the fans, although I do think that perhaps some of it was deliberately started by JB to inject some extra 'spice' into the meeting.

Len also tried to get a rule introduced when we were still in the Second Division that would force riders who were too good for that level to move up to the First Division. Apparently, he quoted me as an example of a rider who should join a top level club to avoid them having to import foreign riders and said that to let me stay in the second level was allowing me to take candy from kids.

This type of discussion still happens today when riders are perceived to be riding in a league below their abilities. At the end of the day, you can't force a rider to move up if he doesn't want to for whatever reason. Those of us who have ridden and managed to reach a good enough standard to move up are best placed to judge when that should be, not people who have never sat on a bike or perhaps just dabbled in the sport.

Len and I have continued our 'rivalry' to the present day as opposing promoters but we have never put on a show quite like the ones he and JB acted out at that time.

Ipswich finished their season off with their 25th consecutive home win and finished fifth in the table, so we were still going in the right direction. Sandor Levai announced his retirement from the sport and would be missed by us all. He had been a great team man and had given the fans a lot of entertainment during his time as a Witch.

My debut at Wroclaw, where England faced Poland in the first of the three-Test series in 1973. I'm on the inside, with Zenon Plech beside me and Ray Wilson in gate three. I was reprimanded for accusing the Poles of cheating.

I will never forget Sandor returning from a broken collar-bone after only two weeks and riding through the pain barrier. He was as hard as nails on the track, but a really nice guy off it, and we all enjoyed his company in and out of the pits.

On a personal note, I had upped my average to a fraction over 10 and came eighth in the British League Riders' Championship. I also retained the Dave Bickers Best Pairs Trophy at Foxhall with Olle Nygren again and came third, behind Ole Olsen and Anders Michanek, in a star-studded Golden Sovereign meeting staged at Foxhall in October.

During that year, the Witches brought other locals into the fold, with my old mate John Gibbons joining the likes of Dave Gooderham, Paul Clipstone, Ray Ball, Chris Ginn, Andy Sims, Denny Morter, Andy Stevens, Paul Mills, Paul Gilbert, Paul Davey, David Emeny and Philip Garneys in having laps around Foxhall. The majority of them fell by the wayside, despite the expert training from Clive Noy, and one other lad who so wanted to make a big impression joined them.

Action from the same meeting at Wroclaw and I've got two Poles in my sights.

Chasing Anders Michanek and Bob Valentine, with Jan Simensen behind, in the 1973 British-Nordic Final T Coventry.

Ipswich-based John Simmons was just 17 when he crashed in a second-half race at Peterborough in July. John had done enough to be invited by the Panthers for trials and so good were his performances that he was being tipped to go on loan to the East of England Showground-based club.

John was left paralysed and his injury put a big dampener on the whole season. It continued to be a constant reminder to the rest of us blessed with much better good fortune as, for many years, John would sit watching the action from his wheelchair near the entrance to the track in the Foxhall pits.

On a lighter note, another great character that could be found at Foxhall every Thursday was a lady affectionately known by most of us as 'Mother Witch'. Ruby Woods, or 'Mum Witch' as she preferred to be called, was an ardent fan and would always visit the pits before a meeting with a giant bag of sweets for us riders to throw to the kids on our lap of honour.

She was also responsible for me always turning out in spotless leathers. Every morning after a meeting (home or away), she would collect my boots, helmet and leathers and take them home. They

Despite the worried frowns, I had absolute faith in Dad to get my engines going good.

Keeping my Jawa engine warm on parade for the Witches during the 1973 season.

No disgrace to finish behind superstars Ole Olsen and Anders Michanek in the Golden Sovereign.

Aggro in Abensberg, where I was prevented from contesting the European Final. John McNulty of the SCB (far right) fights my corner with the FIM as Barry Briggs, Reg Fearman (BSPA) and I listen in.

were cleaned and polished to remove all traces of mud, etc. and she even polished my steel shoe with emery paper to a mirror finish. It was all returned the same day and this was repeated regardless of how many meetings I had in a week.

One thing I have only told a few people is that inside my neatly folded leathers, I would often find a Polaroid photo of Ruby wearing the leathers after she had cleaned them. I never mentioned it to her as I wasn't sure of the significance – I just hope she kept her undies on! She remained a faithful Witches fan long after I hung up my leathers and a few years ago I presented her with a bouquet on her 90th birthday.

Back to the speedway action, things continued to go well for both the Witches and me as we moved on to 1974. By this time, the heat leader trio of Louis, Davey and Sanders was beginning to cause others to seriously take note and we were rapidly becoming the best top three in the league.

John Berry even wrote in the *Daily Mail* that Tony and I were the best British pairing and that it would be a travesty if we were not selected for the World Pairs.

Mick Hines and Ted Howgego were now established members of our team and when injuries occurred, there was Trevor Jones, Mike Lanham or Dave Gooderham to fill in, so JB's plan of a locally-produced side continued to take shape (Billy was an adopted son of Suffolk).

In early April, we received the news that Pete Bailey, one of my very first Ipswich team-mates, had been killed in a road accident very close to Brandon stadium where he rode for Coventry. I was very saddened to hear that – Pete was a really nice bloke and I had missed his presence in the team when he left.

The Golden Helmet competition was changed this year. The *Speedway Star* came in to sponsor the

**Spring Gold Cup winners of 1974. Standing: Ron Bagley, Trevor Jones, myself, Alan Sage, Mick Hines.
Kneeling: Ted Howgego, Tony Davey, Billy Sanders.**

Public relations work wasn't always easy . . . but someone had to do it!

event, at £100 per month, and the once-a-match system was scrapped. It was now to be staged as the best of three races, by a nominated rider, on a home and away basis. The hope was that riders would take a greater pride in holding the title and that it would attract bigger crowds.

*Speedway Star* continues to come out every week thanks to fine people like Phil Rising, Richard Clark and Andrew Skeels. Many would say this is against all the odds with the electronic age taking over from the printed word in most people's affections.

Without the dedication of the three stalwarts mentioned above, fans would not have the pleasure of reading every meeting report and news items from every club, plus unparalleled coverage of the continental scene. Their love of the sport has shone through when no major publishing company would be backing the sport.

I started in April as the holder and managed to hold on to it until September when Phil Crump took it off me. So if it did bring in bigger crowds, JB must have done well out of it!

After beating Leicester's Ray Wilson in April, I was due to face Ole Olsen of Wolverhampton in the May challenge but the night before our meeting, he withdrew due to 'commitments in Denmark'. JB was not best pleased as obviously this had received top billing in the local press, etc. In the event, Peter Collins of Belle Vue was nominated to take his place and I beat him comfortably enough at Foxhall.

Soon afterwards, Peter beat me on his home track in Manchester where he won the first race. In the second, I spluttered to a halt within half-a-lap when I was in the lead and I was left shaking my head as to why I'd stopped. We later found out after stripping down the bike in my workshop that there was oil in the fuel tank, which I have been left to ponder over as we both used dope from the same source.

The decider was staged at Poole. Peter broke the track record in the opener, but the smile was

Leading Belle Vue's Peter Collins in our Golden Helmet decider at Poole in 1974.

removed from his face when I brought it down by a further four-tenths of a second to 66.2 seconds in the second race. The third and final race was another ding-dong affair between two riders at their peak, and it was not until I crossed the finishing line with my nose just in front that I was certain of overall victory.

In June, I faced Malcolm Simmons from King's Lynn, so East Anglian pride was at stake. We were even after two races and I had managed to squeeze past him on the last two bends of our third race when he clipped my back wheel and fell. Astonishingly, the race was stopped and awarded to him. The usual protests were made but to no avail.

The next leg at King's Lynn turned out very similar with Malcolm again coming to grief on the last lap. This time, the decision went my way, so we had to do it all again at Hackney the following night. I made no mistakes at Waterden Road and the helmet stayed in Suffolk.

In July, I stopped Hackney's Dag Lovaas from getting his hands on it and then in August Ole Olsen was nominated again. He did turn up this time but may have wished he hadn't as I took the first leg quite comfortably. He took the honours at his home track Wolverhampton, so we headed to Swindon for the decider. After thinking this was going to be one of the hardest three races so far, it turned out to be a bit of an anti-climax with Ole missing the gate completely in the first two races and it was all over.

Finally, in September, I met my match when a young Phil Crump beat me 2-1 at Foxhall and repeated it at Newport the next night. I seem to remember he took the Silver Helmet off me in Division Two. Oh well, it had been a good run against some of the top riders at the time.

At the end of October, I took part in the always hotly contested Pride of the East meeting at King's Lynn and tied on the same points as Ivan Mauger. I was fairly confident that I could win the race-off but, unfortunately, I never left the starting gate. In those days, riders were still allowed to move around at the start and touch the tapes as long as they didn't break them.

Ivan was very clever on the start line, moving backwards and forwards constantly and, like many other riders lining up against him, I allowed myself to be goaded into moving forwards as well. The inevitable happened and the tapes broke, with me being thrown out of the race and him picking up the trophy without any further effort. The biggest losers, of course, were the paying public who missed out on an extra race, which would have been fiercely contested right up to the finish line.

On the Ipswich team front, we continued our trend of finishing higher each year by taking third place in the league. My average went up to 10.79 and I passed the 1,000-point mark in British League meetings, but it was not all about me.

Tony Davey and Billy Sanders were also making big names for themselves as we continued to be known as one of the best heat leader trios in the country. I think one of the key factors to our success was that we all wanted the No. 1 race-jacket, so I had to keep improving to hang on to it with Billy and 'Shrimp' trying their hardest to catch me.

We were the greatest of friends off the track but when we were on our bikes, that was all forgotten in our quest to be top man. Despite this, we were even more competitive collectively against the opposition.

Team riding was what excited supporters as much as anything, particularly if you clinched a 5-1 that would win or turn a meeting. This was good for us and good for the club and as we got more experience of how each other rode, we became more adept at coming up with the goods when the chips were down.

Team riding is something that has gone out of speedway to a large extent since I stopped riding. And I think there are two reasons for this. One is that team managers and riders no longer see it as part of the entertainment provided in a meeting and, secondly, these days the machinery is different and bikes are not as controllable.

Saluting the Poole crowd after retaining the Golden Helmet by beating PC in 1974. I had a long run as the Helmet holder that summer, before Phil Crump took it off me in the last monthly challenge of the season.

With Hackney's Norwegian star Dag Lovaas before beating him 2-0 in both of our Golden Helmet match-race clashes.

Let's dance! Clive Noy and me enjoying a social function, rather than auditioning for *Strictly!*

A presentation from my hard-working fan club secretary June Allum.

A combination of having lay-down engines and improved silencers makes machines faster than ever. Nowadays, a bike wants to drive forward – they are built to have the power to get them out of the gate and down the straights at full pelt.

In my early days, they were easier to handle and more instant in their reaction. You could put into practice what you wanted to do when it came to getting into positions to hinder the opposition and help your team-mate. I can tell you from personal experience that when a vital 5-1 is required, shutting the opposition out gives you as a big a thrill on the track as you can find.

At one point in my Ipswich career, I was called in by JB and asked to slow down! He felt that I was winning races by too big a distance to make it entertaining for our supporters. He wanted to see more action on the track to keep his public happy, and to keep the turnstiles clicking.

Up to then, my thoughts were that if I gained my three points, it was going to play a significant part in the Witches winning a meeting. But JB had other ideas and perhaps because he could see I might need a bit of persuading, he offered me a four-figure bonus at the end of the season if I did as he wanted and did not go haring off into a 10-yard lead.

That was fair enough by me. He felt it would benefit the team and win us more matches, and in a more exciting fashion. The thought of a cash bonus didn't dim my enthusiasm either! Being faster, I always chose the best gate position and used to tell my partner that I would get him home as long as I got to the opening corner in front.

Once I arrived at the turn, I would judge what was best and would either block opponents or go wider to create an opening for my colleague to come through. As soon as we got ourselves sorted and were hopefully heading off down the back straight in the first two positions, I would look across and nod as if to say, 'now let's get on with it'.

Receiving the Speedway Star Personality of the Year award from the magazine's editor Paul Parish and ITV *World of Sport* host Dickie Davies.

Topping up Dave Bickers' wife Sylvia at another PR event, although her children look as if they think she's already had enough!

If we didn't 'do the business' on the first two bends, there would be seven other chances as long as my team-mate kept in touch. But to be honest, it was at the first corners where good team riding worked best and where it was crucial.

Over the years, I enjoyed good 5-1s with most members of the Ipswich side, but I was a big mate of Dave Gooderham and that made it even more special, while Mike Lanham and Mick Hines were also great at following me home.

And was JB grateful after I had changed my style to please him? I'm sure he was but he conveniently forgot about my bonus. That completely slipped his mind when the season ended.

But what didn't slip his mind was how to promote a winning club, and the next two years were brilliant ones for the Witches and myself.

A couple of other individual achievements that year were coming fourth in the World Final in Gothenburg and, best of all, leading England to World Team Cup glory at Katowice. We travelled to Poland with the experts predicting that we had little chance of beating the home team or finishing ahead of the Swedes. There were 80,000 Polish fans in the Slaski Stadium expecting their team to walk off with the title.

However, at the end of the meeting, England had finished 11 points clear of Sweden, on 42 points (their best-ever score in this competition), with Poland scoring only 13, just ahead of the Russians on 11. Peter Collins and myself both scored 12-point maximums, so we had to toss a coin to see who would take part in an individual final to be contested by the top rider from each team. I called it right and finished off a perfect day for England by winning the Victor Ludorum Trophy. The large glass

Another garage opening but it was good for the image of Ipswich Speedway and myself to be in such demand.

England were at their peak in the mid-70s when we had so many top-line riders to choose from.
Above: We've just won the UK round of the World Team Cup of a another huge Foxhall crowd of around 10,000.
With me are Terry Betts, Peter Collins, team manager Len Silver, Dave Jessup and Ray Wilson.
Below: Later in the season, Malcolm Simmons replaced the injured Bettsy and Reg Fearman took over Len Silver's role for
the WTC final at Katowice, Poland, where I scored a maximum and won the second-half as
the Lions roared to another triumph.

vase I received is one of the trophies I have kept to this day.

After the meeting, Polish star Zenon Plech told me he had no doubt that if the meeting had been the individual World Championship, I would have been crowned World Champion that day.

I certainly had a lot of speed and this was due to the gamble of using a long-stroke engine. It was really pulling away from the starts and then picked up speed quickly, which is just what you need on the large tracks over there.

In my third race, I was up against current World Champion Anders Michanek who was still unbeaten since lifting his world title. I again made a very good gate but I knew that he was capable of getting past me, so I rode extra hard in that heat. I watched it again recently and had to laugh at the way I was almost horizontal along the bike going down the back straight. At times, my rear end was almost past the back mudguard as I tried to get every ounce of drive I could out of the bike.

It was a great feeling standing on the rostrum with the rest of the team and Reg Fearman, our team manager, who had worked so hard that year to support and encourage us.

We had qualified for this event by defeating Australia, New Zealand and Scotland at Foxhall Stadium a few weeks earlier. I scored a 12-point maximum and England finished 10 points ahead of Australia, who included my Ipswich team-mate Billy Sanders.

In December, I was invited to test a new four-valve Weslake engine at Hackney. Why was I chosen? I guess the answer would be my progress at national and international level had been noticed by the late Don Godden, the international grass and long-track star who was involved with the project. And I also didn't live too far from thr east London track!

Weslake had been in the engine design business since 1920 but they had never before attempted to break Jawa's domination in speedway. Don Godden attended the Hackney trial, which went well and although there was the odd teething problem to overcome, everyone expressed themselves highly satisfied.

The Golden Helmet fitted me well. This time I'd just seen off Malcolm Simmons in a decider at Hackney.

The two-valve Jawa served speedway very well but big changes were in the air at the end of 1974.

If all went to plan, I would be using one for the next season and Weslake would be providing some sponsorship for me. Looking at a *Speedway Star* from that time, the cost of this revolutionary engine was £420 and Weslake were hoping for several orders over the close season.

I went on to become very good friends with Harry Weslake, often visiting his house on my way to the factory in Rye, Sussex. There, we would chat about engine development and he shared tales about when he worked for Volvo in Sweden, sorting out their cylinder head problems. He was very clever with engines and I owe a lot of my later success to being in on the Weslake revolution from the very beginning.

After another hectic but successful year, I was invited to join a tour of New Zealand organised by Ivan Mauger and Barry Briggs over the winter and this time I decided to have a go. I will talk about this and my other foreign excursions later in the book.

Chapter 6

# As Good As It Gets

**F**ROM virtually the first time I rode a speedway bike, I have been thankful for the grounding I experienced in scramble racing. **When you have been used to ruts that sometimes came up to your fuel tank, it was like Christmas every time I rode on a smooth, graded surface.**

Yes, there were plenty of tracks where conditions were not ideal but, having coped with the bumps and hollows on an undulating scramble track, it was nothing I could not handle.

By this time, I had moved on to ride regularly in long-track meetings in Europe where you were often motoring at 100mph, laying forward on the fuel tank and going flat out. That could be hairy; after that, speedway seemed easy at 'only' 60 to 70mph.

After five full years of racing, I had reached a point where I was confident of my abilities on a bike and had experienced many different tracks and conditions, so that I didn't get fazed by any meeting at any level. I felt more than ready to win some important trophies, both on the individual front and with Ipswich. Could this be our year?

JB was still following his policy of including as many homegrown riders in his team as possible. Like all successful businessmen, he had the knack of knowing what sold best. There was excited talk of Billy's Aussie mate Phil Herne joining us for a few weeks but, in the end, we took to the circuits with our 'local' side.

**Not much room on the line as I look for a gap inside Ole Olsen during the 1975 Wills Internationale at Wimbledon.**

One of the earliest photos of me riding the Weslake in 1975.

Having seven of the eight riders in the '75 squad that year born and living in the area was a masterstroke. I have been given the credit for setting the trend and, if so, it makes me proud that Tony 'Shrimp' Davey, Mike Lanham, Mick Hines, Trevor Jones, Ted Howgego and Dave Gooderham followed me - mainly from the scrambling circuit – into Foxhall Stadium. Billy Sanders completed the team (by now, it felt like he was a local as well).

I tried my new Weslake engine for the first time in match-racing conditions in the Spring Gold Cup at Foxhall against Hackney, at the start of the season. Despite the engine mis-firing slightly, I won my first race. I did later grind to a halt with an electrical problem but there was no doubt that the Weslake was quicker and was the engine of the future. I was further convinced of this when I equalled Ole Olsen's track record at Ipswich in June.

Fortunately, switching to the new engine had little or no impact on setting my bike(s) up for a meeting. Dad and I were still sharing these duties anyway, so we were able to adapt to any changes required quite quickly.

Our league campaign didn't get off to a good start when our opening two home matches were rained-off, leading to a lack of vital track time for the team. When we did get going, the track changes over the winter appeared to be working against us as visiting teams appeared more comfortable with the new shape than most of our team.

We were down in 13th place by the middle of May but our fans were right behind us and I had a feeling this could still be our year. It was not unusual to see three coachloads of Witches fans at away meetings as we gradually made up ground.

By the time September came round, we were simply flying and had pocketed 19 precious points out of a possible 20, including a 59-19 Foxhall thumping of Halifax. We went into our final match against Halifax at The Shay needing a win to maintain our chance of finishing above Belle Vue.

I took three bikes so that Mike Lanham could use one of them because he had been having a few problems with his own equipment and it gave him an extra option. In the event, Mike played his part to the full in our 43-35 win.

Now we had to wait while the Aces completed their fixtures, needing to collect a maximum eight points from four meetings to overhaul us by one point. Their toughest encounter on paper was their next match, at Exeter, and while we sat at home, fun and games were going on at the County Ground.

Scott Autrey rode out of his skin and Ivan Mauger dropped just one point to Peter Collins as the Falcons won 41-37. We were anticipating a Belle Vue victory, so when the call came through to JB from an excited Ivan Mauger – "We've just beaten 'em. You are the champions" – we were all initially shocked and then over the moon. The phone never stopped ringing after that as news filtered through. And then the partying began.

JB had achieved exactly what Howdy Byford predicted he would back in 1969 – win the Division One championship with a team of homegrown riders.

Ipswich had won the British League and I finished third in the World Final at Wembley (see chapter 14). I also helped England retain the World Team Cup at Norden in Germany, partnered Peter Collins to fourth place in the World Pairs at Wroclaw, Poland and finished fourth in the BLRC at Belle Vue.

I finally won the Golden Sovereign open meeting at Foxhall ahead of Dave Jessup and Martin Ashby and I finished my season where I started it – at King's Lynn – by winning the Pride of the East (after winning their season opener, the Dow Diamond). There was no race-off drama this year, as I scored a straight 15 points to win it.

I had a chance to get my hands on the Golden Helmet again in August when I challenged Dave Jessup. I duly won it back and managed to hold on to it until September, when Martin Ashby took it from me (think he was still smarting from the British Final).

Stats-wise, I recorded 22 full and two paid maximums in 50 meetings and finished on an average of just under 10.60.

The British Final was one of the hardest meetings of the year to win when I became national champion at Coventry in 1975.

Chapter 7

# Best Of British

THE 1975 season was a very good one for Ipswich and, in the midst of all the team successes, I achieved one of my main personal goals – the British Championship.

In those days, it was a very prestigious event with enough top-level British riders to make it very difficult to win, as pretty much anyone in the line-up was capable of doing so. Riders I would have to beat to lift the trophy included Peter Collins, Malcolm Simmons, Ray Wilson, Martin Ashby, Dave Jessup and my Ipswich team-mate Tony Davey.

The rules for World Final qualification had been changed that year and the top four places from the British Final would progress directly through to the World Final at Wembley, so it was extra important that I prepared well.

At that time, a man called Randall Bevan from Ipswich Borough Council was responsible for improving sports facilities in the town and he had already done a lot to help me on the training front by giving me a free pass to use the town swimming pools, which I took advantage of regularly to help improve my stamina. He then introduced me to a man who was to become my personal trainer for the two months leading up to the British Final. I was only ever given his first name and unfortunately I have no recollection of that, but the reason for secrecy was due to his previous career – in the SAS!

We were given access to a gym located at one of the town's swimming pools that was not yet open to the public. To say that he worked me hard is an understatement. After doing several circuits of the gym equipment, each time with the weights increased, I barely had time to get my breath back before we went out to the car park where a line of chairs waited for me. I had to run from one end to the other, swinging one leg over each chair as I passed it and then turn round and repeat with the other leg. This was repeated over and over again, until I could barely stand or breathe. Only then was I allowed to stop and go home to recover.

Sometimes, on the same day, I would get a call in early evening to go out for a run with him. This was several miles in length and included an activity halfway round that involved running up and walking down a very steep incline about a dozen times before running back home. This was repeated several days a week and my physical strength and stamina increased significantly as a result, although initially I was so exhausted afterwards I did wonder if he was trying to kill me.

We also used to have sessions where he coached me on how to prepare mentally for dealing with the 'enemy'. It was all based on the 'kill or be killed' approach, which is part of the SAS training he had received himself. I was also encouraged not to take 'phone calls and basically cut out as many distractions as possible (I can't imagine that happening today with the constant internet and mobile 'phone activity that goes on.)

By the time I lined up for the first race at Coventry, I had the firm belief in my head that I was going to win the battle and absolutely no one was going to get in my way.

I was in the habit of preparing an engine with the help of the Weslake engineers for big events and this was no exception. Peter Collins, Ray Wilson and Martin Ashby were also using Wessies for the British Final and, if any of us made it onto the rostrum, the factory in Sussex would probably be working overtime to cope with the extra orders.

Dad travelled with me to Coventry, along with JB, Ron Bagley and my mechanic Brian 'Brassy' Goodchild. Charles Ochiltree and his staff had prepared a perfect track and I knew by looking at it that gating would be very important. Although it was not always my strong point, on this occasion

I knew I was prepared both mentally and physically and that, even if I missed the gate, I could still beat the other three riders. It sounds arrogant but this was down to the training I had endured, which had made me sharper than ever and given me the confidence that I was going out there to do one thing – win the meeting.

I won my first heat comfortably and equalled the track record at the same time. After three more straightforward wins, I was on 12 points and only needed two in my last race to lift that coveted trophy.

Typically, I missed the gate and wasn't helped by Martin Ashby taking me out slightly but I watched him as he approached the next bend on the outside, leaving me a gap to dive through and take the lead, which I held on to until the chequered flag.

Martin refused to shake my hand after the race, which was a bit petty as, in a meeting of this importance, it's every man for himself and I had simply ridden through a gap that he left open. I'm pretty certain he would have done the same if the roles had been reversed. I remember the noise from the fans was deafening as I rode round on my lap of honour feeling on top of the world. I had finally done it – I was British Champion.

After the meeting, I found out that I had been fined £3 by the referee for delaying the start in one heat. I didn't have to pay though, as the travelling Witches fans presented me with a hatful of money they had raised from a whip round. It was just another reminder to me that they really are the best supporters in the land.

Big celebrations followed, of course, but I had a meeting the following night, so I had to hold back a bit. I paraded my trophy in front of my home fans, who gave me a fantastic reception. Then it was down to business as we faced Swindon in a league meeting – we beat them 47-31 with me scoring a 12-point maximum. I think I was still on a high from the previous night!

**Receiving the victory bumps at the end of a great night at Coventry.**

Chapter 8

# Witches' Special Brew

**W**HAT a great year 1975 had been for so many reasons. Put yourself in my position for a minute. You are captain of a successful team in the town that you were brought up in. One where you have your family, friends, work mates and know so many other people. Does it get any better than that?

British League champions for the first time in 1975. Standing: Billy Sanders, Mick Hines, Ron Bagley, Tony Davey, Ted Howgego, Trevor Jones. Kneeling: Mike Lanham, myself, Dave Gooderham.

Well, for me, it was the ultimate dream come true and out of everything I achieved in speedway, winning trophies with the Witches came top of the list.

JB's plan worked, both on the track and in his pocket, and it is remarkable to look back now and see that we only used the eight riders from our initial squad. Dave Gooderham was our official No. 8 and he came in on five occasions – four when Ted Howgego was injured and once when 'Shrimp' was riding in the British Semi-Final at Sheffield (who staged their home meetings on the same Thursday race-night as Ipswich).

There were no guest bookings or use of the rider replacement facility, although I have to say that good fortune smiled on us with the lack of injuries we suffered.

We had all become great mates and we were not just doing it for our supporters and our management team, but for each other as well. That side was special and we all got on well with no arguments, which led to a great team spirit where we all looked out for each other

It was all very special for me and with success came the fruits of our labours. We became celebrities and were entertained by the Mayor at the Town Hall. I think I speak for the other lads when I say we had the time of our lives.

We went through the season unbeaten at home and we were all still pinching ourselves somewhat that it was happening to us locals, as we had all begun life at Foxhall Stadium on the terraces and been fans.

'Shrimp' summed up the change that it all had made to our lives in an article in *Speedway Star* when he said he had never seen so much money. He was on £1.50 a point, plus £1.50 start money. As a mechanic, he was earning £3.80 a week, with £1 of that repaying the loan on his scrambling bike and £1 going to his parents for his lodgings!

As captain of the side, and by now a successful international rider, I perhaps received the lion's share of the acclaim. But the Witches would not be able to include 1975 British League winners (and 1976 double winners) in their roll of honour if it hadn't been for my superb team-mates.

Billy averaged a magnificent 9.78 that year, while Shrimp rose to great heights as well, with his huge talent shining through on numerous occasions, often away from home. He was such a super guy as well.

Although we were both from scrambling backgrounds where track conditions were often far from ideal, Tony and I were different in many ways. I was not put off by any track but Shrimp would rarely walk the track before a Witches meeting. He preferred to keep the same mindset that he

Let the celebrations begin . . . drinking to our league title win in 1975.

Cool and calm, team manager Ron discusses tactics with me and Mike Lanham.

entered the stadium with and didn't want to have his thoughts swayed by any possible concerns about the conditions.

In fact, throughout my career, I made a point of treating all tracks the same – there were no favourites or those that I didn't like. They were all there to be raced on, regardless of the weather, shape of the track, etc. If you let tracks worry you, then you are already half-beaten before you start.

I have always believed that a positive attitude at the start of every meeting is an absolute must. In fact, before home meetings, my preparations started before I left home. If possible, I would do something simple, like mow the lawn, and at the same time rehearse in my head the preparation I would go through leading up to each of my starts. This helped get me in the right frame of mind before I even got to the track.

When I did arrive, my mechanics had the same instructions every week that I insisted on them following, without exceptions. Their first job was to keep everyone away from me so I could focus on the meeting ahead and nothing else. The only people I talked to were my team-mates but no-one else got a look in. After all my heats had been completed, I was more than happy to talk to fans, sign autographs, pose for photos, or give interviews for as long as anyone wanted.

At this time, I was predicting that Mike Lanham could become the 'next Peter Collins'. He was a promoter's dream, creating so much excitement on the track after working his way to the front, head down, after missing a gate or three.

Mick Hines provided a steadying influence and clocked up many a vital point after a sticky start to the campaign, while reserves Ted Howgego and Trevor Jones came good just when it mattered most.

At one time, JB gave trials to Les Rumsey and Keith Anderson as he wanted more firepower from the bottom end but, while form may be temporary, class is permanent and it was Ted and Trevor's return to form that, in the end, won us the title.

Okay, we were all-conquering at Foxhall, but championships are often won on opposing tracks and I found that if you won the reserves' heat, you were usually well on your way to an away win.

After the British Final, the Weslake engine became very popular and orders began flooding in to the Rye factory. Having been 'on the inside' right from the start, I was able to set up the 'Wessie' exactly right and this may well have contributed to my success.

There were some who said the advent of four-valve engines was not in the best interests of the sport but I was all for trying something new and I had great faith in Weslake.

As I said, it was the best time of all and there were some nice words from JB in his programme notes: "Congratulations to John Louis, British Champion, British Match-Race Champion, third in the World Final and skipper of the League champions. With less than six years riding under his belt, John is the senior team man, and his single-minded dedication, when at times even my enthusiasm has sagged, has kept us pushing further and further forward."

Still no sign of that bonus, though!

After a great trip to South Africa in November, it seemed no time at all before I was preparing for the 1976 season.

Ted Howgego, Mick Hines and I definitely look unhappy about lack of horsepower during the end-of-season donkey derby.

Artist Steve Irving drew this picture of me racing in 1975.

Chapter 9

# Champions At The Double

THE die had been cast in 1975 – now could we do better? The answer was an emophatic 'yes'. Not only did we retain the league title, the Witches also won the Knockout Cup for good measure to emulate the previous year's achievements.

Speedway being speedway – and I can understand why, because a rout can be boring and you want teams to be of a similar strength to give fans entertainment on the track – we had to weaken our team on paper.

This was done through the Rider Comntrol Committee Mick Hines moving to Wimbledon. He had dug his heels in and refused to consider a forced move 12 months earlier but this time he reluctantly accepted his fate, which meant Dave Gooderham moved up into the team proper to replace him.

Dave and I struck up a good understanding on-track, with me being able by now to control races (providing I was in the lead at the first bend). I would either look for him to go round while I held the opposition back on the white line, or guide them towards the fence, opening up a gap for him to go through on the inside. After that, I simply tucked in behind him and made sure no-one got past. We enjoyed many 5-1s together and I like to think I helped him progress as a rider.

For the second season running, we remained unbeaten racing on the heath at Foxhall, a sequence spanning 44 home meetings going back to 1974.

We would arrive at the stadium every week confident we were going to do well and send the opposition home disappointed. It was also great for our fans as they were getting one excellent display after another, week in, week out.

Mick Hines had gone but (at the far end) Kevin Jolly, Andy Hines and Colin Cook made up the 1976 double-winning squad.

Leading from Ted Howgego at the 1976 pre-season practice.

At home with the family – first wife Pat, daughter Joanne and son Christopher.

We were giving the supporters of other clubs plenty to watch at their tracks as well, because we were usually very competitive and made most meetings close and interesting. We won nine matches on our travels for the second year running.

Rivalry was, and still is, intense between Ipswich and King's Lynn and it is still fresh in the memories of many the abuse that we got when Kevin Jolly hit the deck without too much apparent cause in the final and deciding heat during our 1976 league meeting there.

Kevin and I lined up at the tapes knowing that we needed three points to win and we both missed the gate. I don't know whether Kevin had been asked to 'drop it' by the management if we were in trouble but it certainly did not please the Lynn faithful when the race was stopped with the home pairing in front and set for a match-winning 5-1. Kevin was, of course, excluded from the re-run . . . but a re-run meant a second chance for me to get the better of the Stars duo.

I screamed back into the pits to get my other bike ready and I was 'winding it up' for all it was worth, right up to the tapes, to get it warmed up before the re-start.

Through my goggles, I could see fans hurling abuse at me from the terraces. And it was even worse after I took the chequered flag, much to the delight of the travelling section of the Saddlebow Road crowd.

Having recently discussed the controversial incident with Kevin, I can now reveal that he was given very clear instructions by JB and Ron Bagley on what to do if we missed the gate. I'm not saying anymore apart from, I'm sure that other teams have employed similar tactics when a result is on the line.

Lynn fans were certainly in a hostile mood that night and, apparently, Stars' general manager Martin Rogers tried to get Kevin removed from the pits a few weeks later when he turned up there

On top of the world . . . Malcolm Simmons and I stand on top of the rostrum after winning the 1976 World Pairs Final ahead of Ole Olsen and Finn Thomsen and Bengt Jansson and Bernt Persson.

as a mechanic for another rider. In years to come, however, things were to change and I would look upon Saddlebow Road as one of my favourite venues, a welcoming home track where the fans actually cheered me on as one of their own.

An exceptional away run followed and, coupled with our consistent home form, it saw us go into a match at Cradley Heath needing victory to retain the title. By this time, Andy Hines and Kevin Jolly were making appearances in the team, with Trevor Jones initially taking a break after a loss of form and then out through injury, before he joined Mildenhall in a swap deal involving Kevin Jolly.

But after suffering a shed-load of misfortune, we lost 45-33, putting Belle Vue in a position again where they could overtake us if they won their meetings in hand.

Ironically, our final away trip was to Hyde Road, where we were involved in an epic encounter with the Aces. We were six points down after six heats but a brilliant fightback saw us go into the final race two points in front.

I had beaten Peter Collins by a tyre's width in Heat 11 and I won another battle royal from the start again, and managed to hold off Peter's relentless challenge.

We were the champions again and ended up finishing seven points in front of Belle Vue. But it could have been so different if we had lost in Manchester.

It was a night when our team spirit shone through. If you really want to be the best, you have to believe – and believe hard! And we did just that on a big Hyde Road track that was super-quick and enabled riders like Peter Collins to win a hatful of races without necessarily making good starts.

Foxhall Stadium is a much different circuit with sharp corners and long straights. We had to adapt to come home with the goods and I salute all the riders who wore a Witches race-jacket that night.

John Berry was there, spurring us on, showing that he was as much a hands-on promoter as an office-based one while, as I have mentioned before, team manager Ron Bagley supported us in a quieter but just as effective way.

The *Speedway Star* KO Cup saw us beat Cradley after pipping them by just one point at home – it was 44-34 away – and then nail-biting two-point and four-point aggregate successes against

**Friends and rivals . . . handshake with Terry Betts before the 1976 KO Cup Final, first leg, at King's Lynn.**

They're off! The tapes go up on the 1976 KO Cup Final between bitter East Anglian rivals Ipswich and King's Lynn at Saddlebow Road. Stars' teenage sensation Michael Lee is on gate one, I'm on the outside, with Ian Turner and Dave Gooderham on the middle gates.
Below: I'm ahead of Lee with Mike Lanham typically battling as hard as ever for a crucial point.

Another hard, but fair, duel with Terry Betts.

Swindon and Belle Vue set up a final with our old rivals King's Lynn.

Winning the cup would be the icing on the cake and we managed to silence the Norfolk club's supporters with a 41-36 win at Saddlebow Road before we ended powerfully and decisively with a 50-27 home leg bonanza. I scored a maximum in each leg, which felt very good against the local 'enemy'.

It was not a successful British Final for me, though. I managed only fifth place at Coventry on the night Malcolm Simmons won the title. I finished third in the BLRC, so on the rostrum at last, and I also lifted the Southern Riders' Championship at Reading.

A new event was staged at Foxhall in October, the Gauloises-sponsored British League Pairs Championship. Seven pairs contested this, including names such as Zenon Plech, Ole Olsen, Malcolm Simmons, Dave Jessup and Peter Collins, with Billy and myself riding for Ipswich.

It was very closely fought, with three teams finishing on 21 points, but Billy and I went one better and took the trophy on 22 points. Ole Olsen and Mitch Shirra finished as runners-up, with Chris Morton and Peter Collins third after a three-way race off. We won £250, plus a large wooden plaque, and were also presented with a large carton of Gauloises cigarettes each. I don't think that would happen now!

So, there were double celebrations at the end of the season as we had two major cups to parade. Our total trophy haul for that year was: Division One title, Knockout Cup, Spring Gold Cup and British League Best Pairs. Ipswich was the place to be in the speedway world at that time and being able to sample the delights of success for a second year running was brilliant.

As I keep stressing, this was a team effort from John Berry downwards but, personally, I had to be over the moon with an average of 11.08 to see me top the British League averages.

I had mixed fortunes on the international front. Earlier in the year, I had been appointed England captain and my first meeting was a World Team Cup qualifier at Foxhall against Australia, Scotland

**Pride of East Anglia . . . the silverware is mounting up after emphatically beating King's Lynn in the 1976 KO Cup Final.**

With Brian Lovell, technical manager at Weslake. He was one of a number at the factory who helped me to get the best from the engine.

As captain, I was asked to perform many duties in and around town. As this photo with Miss Ipswich Julie Snell suggests, being a beauty contest judge wasn't a chore!

For some reason artist Mick Prodger and his version of Peter Collins seem amused by the shoulder injury that disrupted my '76 season. I certainly wasn't laughing at Kevin Jolly.

and New Zealand. Before the meeting, I was pretty confident I could lead the team to a win.

However, after hitting the fence in my first ride, I was left with a bruised thigh, which hampered me in my remaining heats. Dave Jessup was also in the wars after hitting the deck in Heat 11.

The round was won by Australia, led by none other than a certain Billy Sanders on a 12-point maximum. They went on to win the World Team Cup for the first time that year.

In June, things looked up when I partnered Malcolm Simmons in the World Pairs competition. We cruised through the qualifier held in Miskolc, Hungary, both scoring paid 18-point maximums. Two weeks later, we lined up at Eskilstuna in Sweden knowing the opposition would be much stronger.

This meeting proved to be another big highlight in my career – I scored paid 18 points again and, with Malcolm contributing 10, we took the title ahead of Denmark and Sweden. We both received a small glass trophy, which was a bit different to the usual cups, etc. It turned out to be a replica of a famous rune stone near Eskilstuna called the Sigurd Dragon Slayer Stone.

I was a bit surprised to hear Malcolm tell Dave Lanning after the meeting that he hadn't brought his best bike, as he had left them back in England ready for use in an important meeting for his club Poole the following night. But, as it happened, he had still scored enough on his 'second best' bike, so there was no harm done.

The biggest low point for me that year came at the start of July when I was injured by one of my own team-mates. In fact, it turned out to be one of my longest injury spells, which didn't go down well with me at all.

I initially tangled with Chris Morton but, while I was sitting on the track still a bit dazed, Kevin Jolly hit me in the back, dislocating my shoulder in the process. I still can't believe he didn't see me. When I fell off between the third and fourth bends, he was still coming down the back straight but I guess he must have been concentrating on his line and not really looking ahead.

According to a press report at the time, I had this to say: "Every British League match is important now but I can't kid myself. I've been told I should be right in a month. And I've also been told that if I take a chance before that time, the shoulder will simply come out again. If it comes out once, they can fix it. If it comes out twice, it will need an operation. I'm going to ride again but I owe it to myself, and my family, not to finish up permanently injured by trying to skimp on a few weeks.

"My left arm is in a sling and I've got no feeling in the fingers at all. That's a relief in a way. When it happened, the pain was agonising. I can't begin to describe the absolute agony in the hour-and-a-half before they put the shoulder back in. No way could I lay to get any comfort at all. Then they put it back in, the pain went down and I started to joke and laugh.

"I'll be back in a month and that will give me another month to get racing fit for the World Final. That's the one I really want. For Ipswich. For England. And for me. Meanwhile, I'll supervise the installation of a swimming pool in my garden and generally moan so much and be such a nuisance that they'll all be glad when I go back to work!"

During this time, I was having some intensive treatment from Brian Simpson, a local physiotherapist who is known nationwide for his ability to accelerate the healing process with his laser techniques. Initially, I had no feeling in my arm or hand at all due to a trapped nerve but, eventually, a small tingling came back in my fingers so I knew I was on the mend. This spurred me on to get movement back as soon as possible and, when I considered I was ready to get back on a bike, I went to Brian for a check-up.

He wasn't as convinced as I was about my fitness to race and made me do 10 press-ups in front

**Introducing the Witches . . . one of the proudest moments on the steps of the Town Hall after we had won the double in 1976.**

Billy Sanders and I with the BL Best Pairs shield we won to complete a memorable Witches treble. Now what have I done with those flared trousers and platform shoes . . .

Dave Gooderham, Ted Howgego and Tony Davey join Billy and me in saluting our fabulous fans.

of him before he would sign me off. They were the most painful exercises I have ever done in my life but I was determined to ride in the World Final, so I gritted everything and went through the pain barrier and then some. It was just over a month before I rode again but, fortunately, it didn't impact too much on my league season, although it probably affected my World Final performance in Poland that year.

In October, we were invited by Ipswich Town FC to do a lap of honour at Portman Road, with very strict instructions not to stray onto the actual football pitch. It was a bit surreal, motoring round the outside of the football pitch, holding up our trophies to a large crowd of football fans, but they gave us a great reception.

We were also invited back to the Town Hall in Ipswich for a civic reception where large crowds greeted us as we paraded our trophies. The Mayor of Ipswich, Hugh Davis, and the Ipswich MP, Ken Weech, gave speeches about us bringing great credit to the town and that we had shown outstanding sportsmanship as well. They also praised our supporters who had behaved with 'exemplary conduct'.

To cap a brilliant season for the team and me personally, I was handed the *Evening Star* Sports Personality of the Year award.

Chapter 10

# A Chat With The Queen

**A**FTER all the achievements, both on a team front and a personally, in the previous two seasons, 1977 would have a lot to live up to – would we be able to maintain the momentum?

Fortunately, there was no intervention from Rider Control this time, so we were able to field an unchanged line-up. Not that we were short of possible replacements as we had the likes of Jeremy Doncaster, Tim Hunt, Andy Hibbs and Carl Baldwin waiting in the wings.

I had taken delivery of two new Weslakes and was planning to have one machine kept for individual meetings. The previous year had seen most of my efforts directed towards Ipswich and helping them win as much as possible, with any individual meetings used mainly to try out different engines and set-ups.

One development that could only be good in raising the profile of the sport was that Anglia TV got interested after our success in the previous two years. They sponsored a second-half pairs trophy for a few weeks at the start of the season and began to show regular clips of meetings on the local early news programme.

We took a knock in confidence when we lost for the first time in 58 home meetings – against Reading in the Spring Gold Cup – and followed that up with a 40-38 defeat against Belle Vue in the KO Cup at Foxhall.

In the return in Manchester, we were thrashed out of sight, suffering a debilitating 59-19 reverse when everything that could have gone wrong did. It was a real blow to lose our hold on the cup competition so early.

**Witches of 1978. Team manager Olle Nygren with (left to right) Mike Lanham, Shrimp, Kevin Jolly, Ted Howgego, myself, Billy Sanders and Colin Cook.**

Our early league meetings were not helped by silencer problems and a serious shortage of Weslake spares. The engine was now being used by most of our team members as well as riders throughout the country, at both British League and National League level. Its popularity had led to the factory being unable to keep up with demand.

I suffered badly through not getting all the engines promised by Weslake in my contract and this led to me reluctantly withdrawing from riding for England in May, as I felt I was likely to let the side down. I believe Peter Collins, another Weslake-sponsored rider, had similar problems – I guess the English engine manufacturer became a victim of its own success.

I can usually manage when things go wrong but the ongoing problems with my engines, and the impact it had on my points return, really got to me this time. The euphoria from being at the top of my game seemed to have disappeared in an instant, to be replaced by a sense of hopelessness.

I decided to get away from everything and everybody by booking a short notice trip to a Greek island for a few days. I hired a 50cc moped and spent every day just riding around and swimming at a local beach, trying to put everything in perspective.

When I returned home, I felt much better about everything. It wasn't long before things started to improve and was hitting double-figure scores again.

**How I promoted my SIM 50cc bike aimed at young kids.**

**SUFFOLK ENTERPRISE**

The Queen
in Suffolk
July 11 1977

1977

**Mum and Dad at home where they decorated their back garden to commemorate The Queen's Silver Jubilee celebrations in the summer of 1977. Sadly, it was only seven months after I had the honour of meeting Her Majesty when she visited Felixstowe Docks that Dad died.**

The rest of the team also got their engine problems sorted out after JB funded a trip to the Weslake factory to get everything checked over and repaired/replaced as needed. Although we only finished fourth in the league, we still managed to remain unbeaten in the BL at home for a third season.

I had a very busy month off-track in September. First, I was involved in a charity football match at Foxhall Stadium with local and national celebrities taking part. I can't remember all the names involved but Ipswich Town boss Bobby Robson and Radio One DJ Dave Cash were on one team and I was on the other with comedian Lenny Henry – I let him take any headers for obvious reasons!

Later that month, I took part in a Festival of Sport held in a large park in Ipswich. The main attraction was the Ipswich Superstars competition, which required us to compete in eight events, including sprinting, a 400m cycling race, target golf, archery, gymnastic events and football shooting.

A selection of top local sportsmen from football (ITFC), swimming, athletics, karate, rugby and speedway took part. To be honest, looking at the line-up, I wasn't expecting too much but, after a recount, I was announced as the winner. My fitness levels were still quite high but to beat Ipswich Town footballers and Mick Blackwell, a local karate expert, among others, felt good. I'm pretty certain they all followed regular training programmes, whereas mine was a bit more ad hoc and fitted in around my racing schedule.

There was some silverware, however, as we got through to the final of the Inter-League Cup where we beat Cradley Heath in a two-legged final, 81-75 on aggregate. This had been the one trophy that had eluded us in the previous year, so we had added something new to the Foxhall trophy cabinet.

Billy Sanders and I retained the Gauloises British League Pairs Championship at Foxhall, ahead of David Gagen and Michael Lee (King's Lynn), with Gordon Kennett and Steve Weatherley (White City) completing the rostrum.

It turned out to be the last year this competition was staged and the large wooden shield we received still hangs in pride of place on the wall of my office at Foxhall Stadium. Two more names were added in 2010, Rory Schlein and Davey Watt, when they won the Billy Sanders Memorial Pairs

Billy Sanders and I retained the BL Best Pairs title at Ipswich in 1977, ahead of Michael Lee/David Gagen (King's Lynn) and Gordon Kennett/Steve Weatherley (White City).

Billy and I accompanied by a 'bunny girl' at a London speedway press function.

An unusual overhead view of Malcolm Simmons and me racing at Poole in our identical Weslake/Gulf Oil-sponsored leathers.

staged to mark the 25th anniversary of Billy's passing.

Billy won the Golden Helmet for the first time during the 1977 season against fellow countryman Phil Crump and defended it against Peter Collins, before losing to Gordon Kennett.

He also finally overhauled me as top Ipswich rider and qualified for the BLRC. I had enjoyed a long time in that No. 1 race-jacket and it felt strange handing it over but Billy and Tony (Davey) had been challenging me for it for almost as long as we had ridden together, so it was inevitable that one of them would finally succeed. I still managed a 9.50 average that year, which isn't bad for a No. 2!

After he returned to Australia, Billy won his first Australian Championship, demonstrating that he really was starting to hold his own among the sport's top names.

Outside of speedway, 1977 saw The Queen celebrate her Silver Jubilee Year and, as part of its journey around Britain, the Royal Yacht Britannia docked at Felixstowe (about 12 miles from Ipswich). I was very honoured to receive an invite to go aboard and be a sports representative for Ipswich. Compared to today's cruise ships, it was not a big vessel but, as I lined up on deck along with local dignitaries and other sportspeople, it seemed huge to me.

Down one flight of steps came The Queen and down the other flight came the Duke of Edinburgh. I was standing next to Mick Blackwell, who is well known for bringing karate to Suffolk, and we were having a bit of banter, all dressed up in our finery.

We were positioned near the foot of the steps and were the first people Her Majesty came to.

"What do you do?" she asked.

"I ride speedway for the local club at Ipswich," I replied.

"What is that?" she asked.

I explained: "Ma-am, motorcycles with high power engines travelling as fast as they can around a cinder track for four laps."

"That sounds very exciting," Her Majesty added, as she moved graciously on to the next in line.

Our brief exchange probably only lasted a few seconds but it seemed longer and I felt very privileged to be picked out from 'the crowd'. We mingled, as you do, for some while and enjoyed a couple of drinks and a buffet. It was a day I will never forget.

It made me realise how much of an impact I had made in my hometown, that I had done enough to be included at the front line in what was a huge day for Ipswich and the surrounding area. That felt very special indeed.

Surprisingly, I won the *Evening Star* Personality of the Year award again but couldn't collect it as I was in the Canary Islands on a family holiday. Billy Sanders was runner-up and he, too, was absent from the ceremony because he was back home in Australia. I did a phone link-up from my hotel in Tenerife while JB accepted the awards on our behalf. I hadn't expected to win it for a second year after dropping my average and struggling with mechanical problems.

Just after the end of this season, Ron Bagley announced his retirement from speedway to concentrate on his photography business. He would be sorely missed, having done so much for the team and me, both as a rider and as our team manager. It was going to feel strange without his presence in the pits, for sure.

Early in 1978, I claimed a victory without turning a wheel when the BSPA agreed to limit the size of carburettor a rider could use. This was something I, along with JB, had been campaigning for all winter. We felt some of the more inexperienced riders couldn't cope with them, which raised serious safety concerns. On top of that, riders that were already at the top of their game, like Ivan Mauger and Ole Olsen, were winning races by a country mile, making the racing a bit processional. These top riders weren't happy with the decision but they would still win when using a standard carb, just not by as much. My fellow England internationals Peter Collins and Malcolm Simmons also supported my stance on this issue.

**Action from our 1978 home league match against Belle Vue shows me leading down the back straight from Peter Collins and Mike Lanham.**

Olle Nygren was appointed as the Witches' new team manager, with JB stating that the veteran Swede was potentially the best team manager in the world. He was still riding for his Swedish club Vargarna and also heavily involved in his very successful training schools for young riders, which I had benefited from in the early days.

JB also announced that I would play a part in the club's management by looking after public relations work and planning tactics before each meeting. This didn't really change my day-to-day role much, though. I was already doing a lot of the PR work and, as captain, was involved in discussing the approach to meeting with the lads.

My dad's health had been deteriorating for some time, mainly due to the years he had spent in a foundry, where he inhaled black sand from the moulds he worked on, and the fact that he had always smoked heavily. He hadn't helped with my engines for a couple of years and I had been doing them myself since then. His breathing had become so bad that even walking short distances became difficult, but still none of us expected to lose him at such an early age.

In early February, he passed away suddenly, aged just 58. Apart from the normal grief associated with losing a parent, I also missed his presence in the pits and my workshop – he had been alongside me since my early scrambling days and had supported me in so many ways when I first ventured into speedway and then shared the successes I had enjoyed up to this point.

He left a big gap in my life but I had to be happy that we got to spend so much time together throughout my career, which had been started by his passion for all things to do with motorbikes. He may not have taken up any motorsport himself but he was in every race with me, even after he had gone.

Around the same time, I started a new business called John Louis Racing. We made frames for speedway bikes that allowed the use of a straight carburettor (as developed by Otto Lantenhammer, a well-known German engine tuner at the time).

We also came up with the idea of creating small speedway bikes for youngsters to use and help encourage them into the sport. These were known as SIM (Speedway In Miniature) bikes. I was mainly involved with the promotional side, appearing on flyers advertising the bikes, etc, so I'm not sure how many were sold.

I also decided to help a young rider, Tim Hunt, through a bit of sponsorship from my new company, having spotted him in local grass-track events that I attended with my son Chris. Tim seemed to have the right attitude, was sensible and very keen to break into speedway. I agreed to give him some personal tuition and he also attended several training schools.

He was also an ex-cycle speedway rider from Kesgrave Panthers (the same team my brother Tony had ridden for) and I believed that he had a bright future in the sport. Little did I know that later on we would have a couple of 'incidents' on-track when racing against each other!

When reading through a meeting report from that season, I was reminded of a very funny incident that happened to one of my mechanics, Colin Robinson, when we were staying overnight at Glasgow. While getting ready for bed, he couldn't find his glasses and mistakenly put some cream intended as a treatment for piles on his toothbrush. We all laughed about that for weeks.

Towards the end of the season, a German long-track rider called Georg Hack joined the team – he worked for Otto Lattenhammer and came highly recommended. I was selected to mentor Georg as, apparently, due to my visits to his homeland for long-track meetings, I knew a bit of the language. Hmmmm, while I might have learned how to order a beer and a steak in broken German, I wasn't sure if that would help me communicate with Georg!

In the event, it worked okay. What I couldn't get over with sign language, I explained in diagrams

**More from the same Belle Vue match, as I pull clear of Aces' Alan Wilkinson, with Mike Lanham looking for a way past 'Wilkie'.**

Many years before air fences were introduced to reduce injuries, Sheffield's Reg Wilson and I tangled just before putting the collapsible wood and wire mesh safety fence at Foxhall to the test.

and, within a few days, had struck up an understanding with the Bavarian, which quickly produced dramatic results. As he knew little of English conditions and could so easily have been beaten before he started, this early pairing with me prevented that.

Soon afterwards, Georg top-scored in the KO Cup Final against Belle Vue at Foxhall and beat Peter Collins . . . without realising the importance of the occasion. He finally caught on when we were presented with the trophy!

After 74 meetings, we finally lost our unbeaten home record in the league to Coventry (who went on to win the '78 title) whose skipper Ole Olsen scored the only maximum by a visitor all season. We finished sixth in the table, dropping two places.

Myself, Billy and Tony continued to be the top heat leader trio in the league, with Shrimp now getting a chance to challenge for the Golden Helmet. We were the only club to have all three heat leaders selected to compete for it. I think we had endured for as long as we had because of mutual respect and wanting to do the best for the team. Although now third in the Ipswich averages, I still scored 400-plus points during the season and had passed the 100 maximums mark in league racing.

One thing I haven't mentioned before, and many fans still remind me of it, are the 'theme tunes' that we all had in those days. These were played over the PA system whenever we won a race. Mine was *I'm A Tiger* by Lulu, Tony's was *Nice One Cyril* by Cockerel Chorus and Billy's was *Billy Don't Be A Hero* by Paper Lace. All of them were a bit corny but no-one ever got tired of listening to them because if one of the tunes got an airing after a race, it meant we were doing rather well!

We also won the Anglian Cup against our old arch-rivals King's Lynn, so even in a quiet year by our standards, there was still some silverware to display. Shortly after we won the KO Cup, Billy dropped the bombshell that he wanted to ride for a new club in 1979.

JB announced that 1979 would be my testimonial year, to mark 10 years as a Witch. Some people then asked if this was likely to be my last season, to which I responded that I would ride until I was too slow and/or no-one wanted me!

It was strange welcoming Billy Sanders back to Foxhall as a member of the opposition but that's what happened when Birmingham came to Foxhall in 1979. Naturally, this son of Suffolk received a tremendous reception from the Foxhall crowd who had seen him rise from unknown 16-year-old rookie to world class. Below: He was back at Ipswich again that season for my testimonial meeting.

Chapter 11

# Honoured By Bobby Charlton

**B**EFORE the start of the 1979 season, JB appointed an Australian, Paul Johnson, as Ipswich's commercial manager, a new full-time position within the club.

One of Paul's innovations, and he had several, was to go for some glamour by bringing in 19-year-old Barbi Jones to act as start marshal. We were the first club in the UK to use a female in this role.

She did well enough and certainly stood out in her white trouser suit at the start gate, although her cleaning bills must have been sky high. Paul was a flamboyant flag-waver himself who went on to take charge of the tapes in several World Finals, including the last at Wembley in 1981.

In fact, there was a great deal of showmanship about Paul but I expect that's what JB wanted to keep fans coming through the turnstiles after the inevitable drop in interest following the club's dominance in the mid-70s.

It was Paul who first brought the 16-Lap Classic to Foxhall, based on something he had seen in Australia. Often described as the most gruelling speedway race in the world, the final produces the unique spectacle of eight riders, off two starting gates, all heading towards the first turn at the same time. An extra challenge often missed by the crowd at the start of the final is posed for the start marshal on the first grid, who has to be very quickly off the track before the riders from the second grid reach him!

Before this, riders compete in 12 qualifying heats and, if they fail to reach the grand final, they compete in a six-lap consolation final.

As well as organising the first staging of this event, Paul wrote all the supplementary regulations for the meeting, which are still used today. For as long as I can remember, it has been staged as our season finale but in that first year, it took place in June. Joe Owen from Hull won the inaugural staging, which was sponsored by the *Daily Mirror* and Weslake. Phil Collins from Cradley Heath and Gary Guglielmi from Coventry completed the rostrum. I came in fifth after qualifying well in the heats.

There still appears to be no shortage of riders who want to sign up and pit themselves and their machines against the stresses and strains of the unique final. The roll of honour includes such big names as Billy Sanders, Phil Crump, Kenny Carter, Hans Nielsen, Jason Crump and the rider who has won it a record six times, my son Chris.

In last year's programme, he had this to say about the meeting: "I know from my own experiences that I faced the 16-lap final with dread and excitement in equal measure, a real mental and physical battle that can really only be attacked with one tactic. Qualify well, race from the back grid and attack from the off! So many times I've heard riders tell me how they're going to pace themselves, ready to attack when everyone else is tired. The one big flaw with that is I can guarantee you will also be far too tired to launch any sort of attack and start riding in the deep dirt!

"Speedway is raced over four laps and that's how you get conditioned, so it's really quite amazing how tough it becomes when you change that and each rider taking part on Thursday will be feeling the effects after just six-to-eight laps. It becomes a mental battle and mind over matter from that point on. The event has a reputation for being hard on the machines, although it's normally just a fuel issue, with the extra fuel system not operating properly, leaking out or, of course, just not carrying enough!"

It was an event I never won, although I think I came third one year. And there was the year when

Action against Belle Vue again, this time from 1979, shows me ahead of Peter Collins, with Mike Lanham looking
to surge through on the inside.

Jeremy Doncaster rode over my head (1984) after I had fallen in front of him – I've never been quite the same since!

The fact that JB could employ full-time staff showed that he was not only getting it right on the track. His bank manager must presumably have been pleased as well and when the time comes to list the best-ever British speedway promoters, his name deserves to be right up there, if not at the top, then certainly not far off.

Another first that year followed at Foxhall in July, when the Ipswich Evening Star newspaper sponsored a prestigious individual event called the Star of Anglia. The line-up was better than many World Finals and included the likes of Michael Lee, Phil Crump, Malcolm Simmons, Hans Nielsen, Bobby Schwartz, Dave Jessup, Bruce Penhall and Ole Olsen. Kevin Jolly and I represented Ipswich.

It attracted the biggest crowd of the season and for once on a Thursday the weather was perfect. Cheered on by my home fans, I scored 13 points from a possible 15 to lift the trophy before Ole Olsen won a race-off against his fellow Dane Hans Nielsen to finish second.

The Ipswich team that year was very different from the previous one for several reasons. Billy Sanders left for Birmingham at the start of the season and was replaced by young Dane Preben Eriksen. Georg Hack could only ride until the end of April due to his long-track fixtures and employment commitments in Germany with Otto Lantenhammer, which would leave another space to be filled.

More problems were to follow when Tony Davey suffered a horrific crash at Leicester and was out until mid-September with a broken thigh.

Former World Champion Anders Michanek was drafted in as a temporary replacement for Tony, who prepared and maintained Anders' bikes for him. Unfortunately, he didn't last until Tony was fit again. He broke his arm in August and was replaced by ice racer Milan Spinka.

Ipswich fans were relieved in early September when, not only did Tony return, but Billy came back to Foxhall as well. Their team had a familiar look to it again after all the 'foreign' arrivals that year.

JB had done well to retain a team of local riders for as long as he had but with the likes of Ted Howgego, Andy Hines and Dave Gooderham moving to other clubs, it couldn't be sustained into the 80s.

Not surprisingly, with the team line-up constantly changing, we finished a lowly 15th in the league with five Foxhall defeats. Personally, I was back at the top of the pile with an average of 9.33. I had enjoyed a hugely successful testimonial year, plus I really finished off my season in style.

My testimonial year started with the usual social events and a large booklet was launched called *The Year of the Tiger*. Mike Horne produced it, with Dave Kindred providing most of the photos. I don't know if other riders read their own testimonial stuff but I didn't take much notice at the time, as I was far too busy riding and getting ready for all the extra events that had been organised. I have now finally read it and I thoroughly enjoyed revisiting so many highlights that I had achieved up to that year.

On the night of the 16-Lapper, I was honoured to receive a House of Commons goblet from Ipswich MP Ken Weetch to mark my 10-year anniversary. I took him round for a lap of honour on the back of my bike afterwards and, although we were only pottering along, he seemed to be hanging on rather tightly!

In early August, we had a Saturday meeting and somebody thought it would be a good idea to have another donkey derby. This time around, it was mainly sponsors who were brave/foolish enough to volunteer as jockeys – Andy Archer of Radio Orwell, Bob Shelly of the Nippin Café and Ken Bean of the Chevalier Club being among them. The usual mayhem ensued, with Ken especially finding it hard to stay in the saddle. I'm not sure what came over me, as my past experience on four-legged animals wasn't good, but I leapt on to Ken's donkey and rode it across the finishing line with Paul

Ahead of Anders Michanek, one of several short-term foreign imports in 1979, in front of Belle Vue's Robert Maxfield.

Mechanics Colin Robinson and John Bloomfield share in my 1979 Star of Anglia victory.

Bobby Charlton tests my heading skills. I was honoured that one of England's World Cup legends got involved in my testimonial year.

Johnson waving the chequered flag as only he could.

My testimonial meeting took place on Sunday, August 19 and the main event saw a current Ipswich team, led by me, take on an ex-Witches team headed up by Billy Sanders (it still seemed odd to think of him riding for another team). We beat them 42-36 but that afternoon it wasn't all about the result, more about entertaining the huge crowd that had turned up.

There was loads of entertainment laid on, including stunt riding, space hopper racing (anyone still got one?), a wheelie competition and I think some of us put on funny big heads and had a cycle race of sorts. It was a great afternoon and I hope everyone enjoyed it as much as I did. Even after 10 years, I was still amazed that so many people continued to support me (and the team) and it was great to meet and talk to so many of them that afternoon.

A couple of weeks later, I had another exciting afternoon, this time at a football match. It was organised by Micky Smith, who worked for one of my sponsors, Willhire, and also played in goal for Bury Town FC. He contacted the manager of Ipswich Town, Bobby Robson, and asked for some help in arranging a very special guest to take part in the match.

The big day arrived and I could hardly believe my eyes when I saw who this guest was. The hairs on the back of my neck stood up as Bobby Charlton walked through the gates of Ram Meadow, the home of Bury Town.

This was the man who had played such a big part in England winning the World Cup in 1966 when former Ipswich Town manager Alf Ramsey was in charge. He was known throughout the world, yet he had given up his time to help me.

It was a wonderful gesture and I can still picture him now, walking out of his taxi and into the ground with his kit casually held over his shoulder and slung down his back.

There was a great photograph taken that appeared in the *East Anglian Daily Times,* which I managed to find recently. Bobby is holding a ball at arm's length with little old me jumping up to try and reach it with my head. As you can imagine, there was a bit of a height difference.

I had played football at school but nothing serious and for 90 minutes, in the presence of such a legend, I was in soccer heaven. Other local celebrities, including Bobby Robson himself, Bobby Ferguson (ITFC coach), Mel Machin and John Benson (Norwich City FC) also kindly gave up their time to take part and they were great, but it was Manchester United and England hero Bobby Charlton, knighted in 2011, who made my day.

He wanted to know how my career was going and, although he was not a speedway fan as such, he showed a huge amount of interest and was impressed with the size of the crowd that he had helped to attract.

In September, I travelled with the Ipswich team and a very large group of fans (there were 90 of us altogether) to Landshut in Germany to race against Georg Hack's team. We were all in high spirits and very much looking forward to the meeting but the weather had other ideas. Unfortunately, we never turned a wheel after a heavy downfall caused the track to become waterlogged.

However, we did get to enjoy the Bavarian evening they had organised for us. The beer flowed, there was lots of dancing which, of course, I had to get involved in but I didn't get so carried away that I tried on any lederhosen (not with my legs!).

Back in England, my testimonial year was drawing to a close but I had one last challenge before the end of the season . . .

Bruce Penhall's face says it all after our brilliant deciding race in the 1979 BLRC. I don't suppose he was amused either that Belle Vue spelt his name wrong!

Chapter 12

# My Greatest Race

**I**HAD experienced a wonderful 10 years at Ipswich but there was one thing that was **still bugging me, nagging away in my mind. Many regarded the British League Riders' Championship as being the one meeting to win in England and it had managed to elude me so far.**

Winning the British Final in 1975 had been huge but to get the better of the top riders in the world would be another proud feather in my cap. The field for this annual end-of-season classic held at Belle Vue was regularly better than the World Final, featuring all the top riders from each of the British League teams. Just qualifying for the meeting as your club's No.1 riders, based on averages, was an achievement in itself.

To give you an idea of how competitive it was, there were 18 teams in the senior British League in 1979. The top 16 number one riders – my qualifying average was 9.04 – would start the BLRC but the two lowest qualifiers had to settle for the reserve slots.

I'd previously represented the Witches there from our first season in the top flight (1972) until 1976, when I came third behind Ole Olsen and Peter Collins. Billy Sanders had worn Ipswich colours at the 1977 and '78 BLRCs, so this was my chance to have another good crack at a prestigious title all the top riders wanted on their CV.

Time was not on my side, though. I was now 38 and among the world class line-up assembled for the '79 BLRC, only Ivan Mauger (at 40) was older – and he'd just won his sixth world title! I travelled to Manchester to ride at the superb, but now-demolished, Hyde Road stadium determined to give it what might well turn out to be one last shot.

Having prepared as best I could, I was perfectly happy with my equipment and it was a case of gritting my teeth and putting in a performance that would give me a chance. I was so happy with my Weslake that I gambled on taking just one bike.

I did have one slight doubt after doing my usual casual appraisal of the opposition, when I noticed that everyone else was using Pirelli tyres while I was on Dunlop. I quickly made a decision to switch and asked my mechanic, John Bloomfield, to get one from the spares van. He replied: "That tyre has served you well all year, what on earth do you want to change it now for?"

I had always trusted his judgement, so the Dunlop stayed.

After dropping a point to my old World Pairs partner Malcolm Simmons in my first ride, I reeled off four consecutive wins and by the time I lined up for my final outing, my heart was pounding.

Two-time World Champion and top-rated American Bruce Penhall stood in my way as he had also dropped just one point – beaten by Michael Lee. We lined up against each other for our final outing, Heat 18, with Swindon's Phil Crump and home track idol Peter Collins. Twice BLRC winner and never off the rostrum in the previous five years, PC lined up on the inside, Crumpie in gate two, me off three, with Penhall on the outside.

I think Bruce and I must have passed and re-passed each other five or six times. It was either him hurtling round the boards and me hugging the inside white line or vice-versa for the first three laps. It felt like we were the only two riders on the track.

Nothing had been planned, of course; it was just that we both thought the other had found the best line as we kept switching back and forth from inside to outside. By the time we got to the last lap, Bruce was about six bike lengths in front of me going down the back straight at the big, fast 418-yard

**Bruce had recaptured his smile by the time he and Michael Lee joined me on the rostrum.**

Manchester raceway.

I was calling myself all the names under the sun as I had failed to cover his move when I came out of the second turn. But I knew from how the race had gone so far, and on that wonderful circuit that offered so many different racing lines, that all was not lost.

Bruce decided to hunt the dirt going into the third bend and I thought it would be best to follow him to try and extract at least as much traction as he was getting. I didn't want to gamble on being too far behind before making a last-ditch charge to the line. He went deep and I took the same path until I met the pits gate halfway around the wide, sweeping bend.

Bruce continued his move around the outside to try and get the last bit of dirt available but I then came hurtling down the banking, clipped the inside white line with my front wheel and held on to win by just inches.

The adrenalin had helped to get me home and having at last won the BLRC – and after such an amazing race – it is still one of the most vivid memories I have of my riding career.

It was, in many ways, my proudest moment. And that last ride at Belle Vue was certainly my greatest-ever race. Beating Bruce, who was at the top of his game at the time, destined to win the 1981 and '82 World Finals, was something to shout about and I have to say the way I beat him only adds to the pride.

Cradley's 'golden boy' Bruce was not too happy and called me a 'British so and so' afterwards. I think the defeat really hurt him and he needed time to come to terms with it. He was a truly great rider and a colourful, flamboyant star of world speedway and he showed all his skills as he refused to go away in our four laps of full-throttle action.

Bruce reflected on his defeat when contributing to the *John Louis – Celebrating 40 Years* website. He also has a vivid recollection of that magnificent night in front of a big crowd. "It came down to the last lap, last turn after I thought I had the race and the meeting won," he wrote.

"John came under me at Mach 9 and moved me quite hard. It was a perfect pass from 'Tiger' and very hard.

"It was good for him but not so good for me! That was the closest I came to winning the BLRC.

"Many have said the BLRC was the hardest race of the year. I believe the same. 'Tiger' was one of the hardest racers I have met. A true ambassador for the sport of speedway."

They were kind words, indeed, and only added to my frustration at not being able to get my hands on a video recording of that race. I have numerous others in my collection but this one omission stands out like a sore thumb.

The event was going to be televised but the original meeting was rained-off, and the television company was not in a position to reschedule for the new date. Otherwise, I would have been able to lay my hands on a recording long ago. I have been asking around for ages to see if anyone has film of the race and I am happy to pay if necessary. I'd really love to re-live the action.

Standing on the rostrum at Belle Vue, and holding aloft the coveted trophy won by most of the British League greats, was a dream come true and a very fitting end to a very special year.

Obviously all my friends and family were very pleased with my success and my mum was moved (as she had done in the past) to write a poem on the 'congratulations' card they gave me, which I still treasure to this day.

I'm not sure how long it took me to come down to earth again but it was a while. I later learned that I was the first rider to lift the Riders' Championship in both leagues, which made me extra proud.

One last trophy came at the end of the year when I was voted *Evening Star* Professional Sportsman of the Year for the third time. I beat Ipswich Town's Dutch midfielder Arnold Muhren and hot-rod driver Nigel Murphy.

I met up with Geoff Capes again when I attended the awards ceremony at the Corn Exchange in Ipswich. We had a laugh about our previous meeting at a fundraiser a few years earlier at a school in Ipswich. He had mentioned that he was a bit peckish during the evening, so we sent out for a few burgers. A stack of six arrived in a brown paper bag and we all watched in awe as he devoured the lot without pausing for breath!

After all the action, I needed a rest but nonetheless I was pleased to hear that I had been selected for a Middle East Masters Tournament in November. Another overseas adventure to enjoy.

**Looking for Bruce . . . Phil Crump, me and Peter Collins about to be pushed off for the start of my dramatic final race of the 1979 BLRC.**

In Renfrew Road you will find a place,
Where once there lived a famous face,
Amid oil,grease,bikes and a car
He was destined to become a star.

Never mind his age,
In the,'Evening Star',he captures apage.
His entertainment caused him to tour
The World over for all who saw.

He's Captained England and the'Witches',
Along with his fooling he's had us in stitches.
In those ten years I've had my fears
But to him they were his best years.

This fighting 'Tiger' went to Lancashire
With one bike only and no fear,
And he showed them all he's no has bin'
He went and won the blinkin' thing!

A local boy,but he's my son,
With a family so proud of what you've done.
Dad helped you in your rise to fame,
Speedway Star,'JOHN LOUIS',that's your name.

From,

Mum,Sister Pat,Brother Tony.

Chapter 13

# Bitter Betrayal

**I**DID consider retiring from British speedway after the 1979 campaign and there was an offer of a move to Brokstedt in the German League that would have seen me combine speedway with long-track and grass-track.

I decided to stay in Suffolk because, after my BLRC triumph, I felt I still had what it takes to compete against the best in this country. Another incentive to continue in the British League came straight after my triumph at Belle Vue, when I was named as the first challenger of 1980 for Bruce Penhall's Golden Helmet. This demonstrated that others had confidence in my durability as well.

But if I had known what JB was already planning for 1981, I may well have taken a completely different path.

Billy Sanders also took a bit of persuasion before he finally returned to the UK in May, so Ipswich's preparations that season were not ideal. I found out afterwards that if Billy and myself had not returned to the Witches side, Hans Nielsen and Bobby Schwartz had been mentioned as possible replacements but, in the end, we still had the basis of our side filled by locals, with Tim Hunt the latest to make the team proper when he replaced Milan Spinka.

Olle Nygren had missed a number of meetings in 1979 after being appointed Sweden's national coach and he was replaced as team manager by JB, who himself had stepped down from the England team manager's position. Ted Howgego was appointed JB's assistant and I was named as the team's rider-coach.

In March, I took part in one of the traditional season openers, the Daily Express Spring Classic, in which, but for a very harsh tapes exclusion, I think I could have lifted the trophy. I still finished third, scoring a maximum 12 points from my remaining four rides.

The April Golden Helmet challenge against Bruce didn't go to plan when I suffered engine problems while leading in three of the four races – bad luck or what! I especially hated losing to a Yank and I wasn't best pleased that I had been robbed of a second chance to beat him.

Ian Thomas and Eric Boocock took over the management of the England team and I was chuffed to hear that not only had they selected me to ride, but had appointed me as skipper as well. Our first Test series was against the USA, so I was more than pleased to have a chance to lead my national team against them.

I was starting to feel sharper and more focussed again after taking up yoga. A few aches and pains had started to creep in, reminding me that I wasn't as young as I used to be, and I found the stretching exercises helped sort this out. It also taught me how to relax, which is not something I had ever consciously tried to do before.

Ipswich started the season well enough, winning eight successive league meetings and were at the top of the league table at one point. But it all started to go horribly wrong on the track when Kevin Jolly broke his thigh in two places while guesting for Hackney at Waterden Road.

Just before Tony Davey's testimonial meeting, he was involved in a collision with Belle Vue's Louis Carr, hitting the fence hard and breaking his thigh for the second time. It brought an abrupt end to his career, which he definitely did not deserve, and Shrimp spent his testimonial night in the Bell Jones ward at Ipswich Hospital.

One of the fastest gaters in the sport, Tony was a loyal club man who played a huge part in all the successes we enjoyed and, as everybody who knows him will testify, he is one of the nicest men you

I might have been getting on but yoga kept me supple and I was still collecting sponsors' awards. In the 1980 season I earned a recall to the England World Team Cup squad. As captain, I was an unused reserve for the Overseas qualifier at King's Lynn, where the Lions beat USA, Australia and New Zealand.

could wish to meet. He is now a successful garage owner with his brother Jim and still living in the tranquil Suffolk village of Framsden.

We covered for the absence of Kevin, who had been riding brilliantly, and Tony by using our own resources – Nigel Flatman, Andy Hines and Kevin Teager.

I missed my first-ever Ipswich meeting, for reasons other than injury, in August due to a long-standing promise I had made to my 11-year-old son Christopher. I told him that if he got through to the British National Junior Grass-track Championship, I would go and watch. It was scheduled for a Sunday, which was a rare speedway race-day, so I thought I was pretty safe.

JB was fully aware of this commitment many weeks before and I know that he did try to get the league match at Eastbourne re-arranged without success. He put a lot of pressure on me to back out but a promise is a promise and on this occasion, for the first time in many a year, I put my family commitments ahead of speedway. I've read JB's thoughts on this and all I will say in response is that he was not pleasant to be around when he didn't get his own way.

For the record, Christopher came very close to winning the championship. After four wins, he was leading his final race when he hit a hole and went over the handlebars. I think he finished seventh after that. It was great sharing this event with him and my only regret was that I couldn't have gone to more of them.

Preben Eriksen was also missing from the visit to Arlington because of the Danish Championship but the spirit that remained in the camp shone through with a narrow 40-38 defeat. With all the bad luck we suffered, we did well to finish in seventh place and I dropped below nine points a match for the first time since my first year in 1970, ending on 8.80.

Was there a whiff of change in the air as the curtain came down on another campaign? Although I was supposed to be part of the management team, I had no idea of JB's plans for the next season. If I had, I would have handled things VERY differently over the close season.

As early as November, 1980, I was asking him if there was still a place in the team for me. He replied that he had a lot to consider but that he would let me know as soon as his team plans were complete. I kept in touch with him and when January, 1981, arrived, I started to worry and also get a bit annoyed that he wouldn't give me a straight answer.

Finally, towards the end of February, he broke the news that I didn't have a place. I was initially shocked and then very, very angry. The decision left me with almost no time to find another team place, especially as most teams were pretty much complete. JB would have known that and, after

Making plans . . . JB issuing instructions as we are about to go on parade for the 1980 Star of Anglia.

**My last Star of Anglia as a Witches rider, leading American Scott Autrey.**

I had finished letting him know in no uncertain terms what I thought of him leaving it so late, he admitted he had done it deliberately.

He wanted me to carry on riding but as far away from Ipswich as possible, so there was no danger of fans following me to my new club. If that had happened, he was pretty sure that his turnstile receipts would have been adversely affected and that was not allowed to happen under any circumstances.

I'd served Ipswich Speedway as well as any rider had served any club and had been at Foxhall Stadium for over a decade. The club was based in my hometown and I'd never thought seriously about riding anywhere else. Now I was expected to transfer to another club, possibly at the other end of the country, with all that entailed and almost no time to do it in.

As I have written before, I always had a great deal of respect for John. He played a big part in my life and also played a big part in my career blossoming as it did. But it worked the other way as well – he put in print more than once how I had been the catalyst for Ipswich Speedway's success over the years, how my rapid progress in the sport had encouraged so many others to follow in my footsteps and that, without me, things could have gone very differently, etc, etc.

I fully appreciated that he had a business to run and that he needed to do what was best for his interests. He was a businessman first and foremost and the money he made out of speedway proved how successful he was. However, the way he handled this particular 'business change' was completely wrong and I felt betrayed by the way he did it.

In his book *Confessions of a Speedway Promoter,* he actually tries to defend himself by suggesting that I was no longer focussed on speedway due to things going on in my personal life. He must have read too many trashy tabloid newspapers to come up with the ridiculous story that followed.

Yes, I had split up with my wife Pat and I had moved to a small bungalow in Bramford (on my own) and she had moved to Ipswich, with the children. This obviously caused some upheaval, as it would in anyone's life, but not to the extent that it affected my racing.

I seem to remember that JB went through a few changes in his personal life as well but I wouldn't stoop so low as to suggest that it affected the way he ran his business. I was pretty disappointed that he felt the need to do it to me.

Even after 11 years of riding, my sport was still my No. 1 priority and any change in my domestic arrangements would not be allowed to affect my preparation for the next season. Anyone who thought otherwise clearly didn't know me very well at all.

The bottom line is that after all the years I had given to him and the club (and all the associated turnstile receipts that had gone into his bank account), he was callously throwing me out in the worst possible way to protect his business.

I had always known that he was a bit of a cold fish when it came to personal relationships but I thought, foolishly, that when the time came for me to leave the team, it would have been done out in the open and handled in such a way that it would have given me time to plan ahead for the next stage in my career. How wrong could I be.

Instead, I was faced with a mad scramble to find a team with the 1981 season starting in less than a month. I had enjoyed a very happy time at Ipswich but, to this day, I can never forgive JB for the way he treated me over it.

My anger increased when I read in the *Speedway Star,* dated March 28, 1981, that JB had been planning to discard me for some time. He was quoted as saying: "This year will see us track the side I had in mind for last season."

Me winning the BLRC in 1979 had obviously ruined his original plans. He must have known all along that, as far as he was concerned, 1980 was going to be my Witches swansong but he just couldn't bring himself to do the decent thing and let me in on what was going on. It kind of contradicts his book's version of why I was dropped as well.

My words when I found out that a Yank had replaced me were unrepeatable, especially as I knew it would have cost JB a very large sum of money to bring it off. It was money that had been generated by having a succession of very good years with a team led by a captain who was asked to put his own ambitions behind team aspirations, while being promised end-of-season rewards for the sacrifices made that never materialised.

Bitter? Yes, I was VERY bitter and it would be a long, long time before I spoke to JB again.

**A quick start in the Commonwealth Final at Wimbledon, with Mitch Shirra on the inside and Phil Collins and Larry Ross behind us.**

Tense, pensive moments in the Wembley pits before the 1972 World Final. I was too focused to realise my best bike had gone missing.

Chapter 14

# Down Wembley Way

**B**EFORE reflecting on the period after I was forced out of Ipswich against my wishes at the start of 1981, it's about time I took a chapter to look back at my various attempts to win the individual World Championship during the 70s. It was an eventful journey that took in two Wembley finals, Sweden's Ullevi Stadium in Gothenburg and the vast Katowice bowl in Poland. I should have contested two finals in Chorzow but as you'll see, officialdom had other ideas . . .

## 1972

I'd only been riding speedway for three years when I made the World Final at Wembley in 1972. Reaching this level after such a short period on the shale was completely off my radar when I was riding a scrambles bike, virtually as a hobby, and working in the stores at Dave Bickers Motorcycles.

As a Second Division rider, I never had a chance to qualify for the championship, so with Ipswich moving into the top flight, this was the first year I was eligible.

Now there I was, a new recruit from the sticks, locking horns with 15 of the best riders in the world at the iconic twin-towered stadium.

As we drove down the A12 bound for Wembley, it seemed like every other car, van or coach had a Witches scarf or banner hanging from the windows. The sight of all those hundreds (possibly thousands) of fans making the trip made me extra determined to do well, both for myself and for them.

The plan was to start well by winning my first qualifier at Foxhall but I was denied by a harsh exclusion. Referee Lew Stripp threw me out of Heat 18 when eventual winner Dave Kennett came hard under me and hung me out to dry on the fence. The conditions were very wet that night and it only took the slightest nudge to unsettle even the best riders, but the referee wouldn't take any of that into consideration, despite protests from myself, Ron Bagley and JB.

In fact, JB was so incensed that he wrote to the SCB telling them that he didn't want Lew Stripp back at Foxhall ever again. I eventually finished fifth on 10 points but still had two more rounds to go.

My next qualifier was at Hampden Park, Glasgow, which was rained-off after I had got there. So it was straight back home with nothing to show after 13 hours behind the wheel.

I scored 12 points in what became my second round at Coventry, so I was looking for at least 10 from the final round to secure my place in the British semi-finals. In the re-arranged Glasgow meeting, I did just that, scored 10 and qualified.

The semi-final was held at Leicester and my hopes took a knock when I found myself getting passed too often after making good starts. However, I finally managed to get dialled in and scraped together eight points. It was not a very good score by my standards but enough to get me through to a coveted British Final berth.

Dad Jack was still in charge of my engines and, after we had struggled a bit in the early part of the season, everything was looking much rosier by the time the British Final came around at Coventry. In those days, British Final night was a very big occasion, always held on a Wednesday, and there were enough top riders of a similar high standard to make it very competitive and difficult to pick a winner.

**Emerging from the famous Wembley tunnel with Bernt Persson and Nigel Boocock for the pre-meeting parade.**

**Watching Heat 1 with Barry Briggs and Nigel Boocock, with Dad behind me.**

Five-figure crowds were the order of the day and, with the pressure off as no-one expected me to finish in the top five and book a place at Wembley, I was up for a good night in front of so many fans.

Nerves did not hamper me, having sneaked in under the radar so to speak, and the 11 points I collected was good enough to qualify. I finished fourth after a race-off with Barry Briggs and, but for my bike playing up after I had led him for three laps, I could have got third.

It didn't sink in until I was halfway home to Ipswich that I had qualified from Brandon along with some of the sport's greatest names in meeting winner Ivan Mauger, Briggo and the Boocock brothers, Nigel and Eric, and was going to ride in the biggest meeting of the year, having qualified at my first attempt.

There was about a six-week break before the Wembley final, so I purchased a new two-valve Jawa bike and spent hours with Jack also making sure that my other machine would be in tip-top condition as well.

There were doubts about whether the meeting would take place because of a financial dispute involving the British qualifiers and the BSPA. Being the relative 'rookie' of the British quintet, I didn't really get involved in the negotiations – I think they were arguing over an extra £5 a point or something silly like that. This was unsettling but sometimes a stand has to be made. Deep down, though, I never really expected the sport's showpiece event of the year to be cancelled and, in the end, we agreed to ride.

Apart from one previous visit, I'd had little experience of the Wembley track, so I took my time on practice day and learned as much as I could. Having not been used all season after Wembley Lions closed at the end of 1971, the track was a bit rough but it didn't concern me. I'd seen a lot worse and I always felt I had a bit of an advantage if conditions were tricky.

We arrived at the Empire Stadium in plenty of time on Final day after a drive down from Ipswich and even at 4.00pm, you could sense what a huge night it was going to be. For many fans, it was their big outing of the year and they arrived in their thousands by train, coach and car. A large contingent of Witches fans – believed to be around 5,000 – were there among an estimated near-80,000 crowd and I went there determined to give them plenty to cheer about and make their trip to north-west London as enjoyable as possible.

The noise in the pits tunnel area when warming up the bikes was always deafening but, by this time, I was in a world of my own, making sure my concentration was at the right level.

Ole Olsen, Christer Lofqvist and Bernt Persson were my first opponents and I came third in a dramatic race, assisted by Ole falling when trying to pass Christer on the final bend. This mistake by Olsen ultimately cost him the title, because he went on to win his other four rides.

Before the meeting, the party of six Russian riders had mysteriously 'lost' two bikes along with various other bits of equipment and now it was my turn. At first, with everything going on, I thought my machine had been mistakenly taken out on to the track, ready for the pre-meeting parade. Dad and my mechanic Brian Goodchild had not seen anything untoward, so the security guards and then the police got involved, checking all the other machines.

Where had my £400 bike gone? Funny things have been known to go on at big speedway meetings and this was one of them. What happened, I will never know, but presumably someone wanted my No. 1 bike out of action.

I still managed two wins riding my second bike and finished joint fourth with Christer Lofqvist on 11 points. As the highest-placed British rider and the only one in the whole field not to have been capped by his country, I was pretty happy with that result.

Luckily, my missing bike was found, albeit two hours after the end of the meeting, virtually untouched, propped up beside a hot-dog stall outside the stadium. How bizarre is that!

When I arrived home in the early hours of the morning, I found my house draped with streamers and 'well done' messages scrawled across a lot of the windows. It was great to see how much my efforts had meant to the Ipswich fans. I found out later that it had been the best World Final performance by a British rider for 10 years – since Peter Craven won the title in 1962, which made me extra proud.

It didn't matter to me at all that our 'reward' for performing in front of the biggest crowd in world speedway that year (plus a national TV audience of millions – highlights were screened later that night on ITV) was a paltry £5 a start and £5 a point.

## 1973

The following year, things again got off to a bad start when I was injured at Wolverhampton just before my final British qualifying round at Ipswich. I was advised to rest for two to three weeks but I needed three points to get through to the British semis, so I wasn't going to miss out on another chance to ride in the World Final, even if I did have cut tendons in my left foot.

With my foot bandaged and plastered, I managed to score the required points at Ipswich and then withdrew from the meeting. I must mention how impressed I was when 'Shrimp' Davey firstly beat Ivan Mauger in the heats and then almost got the better of him in the race-off for first place – another ex-scrambler making his mark in the sport and an even greater achievement considering that awful hand injury he sustained in the first meeting of the previous year.

My foot was still troubling me when I arrived for my semi-final at Leicester but, again, I gritted my teeth and scored 13 points, finishing runner-up to Ivan Mauger, and broke the track record as well. Tony also qualified on eight points.

I struggled in the British Final at Sheffield with two pointless rides before switching bikes and scoring two wins, plus a third, to finish on seven. That would only see me go to the British-Nordic Final at Coventry as first reserve but, at the last minute, Rick France withdrew, handing me a place after all. Perhaps my luck was finally changing for the better.

The 10 points I scored at Coventry got me through to the European Final in Abensberg, Germany – or so I thought. At the time, there were concerns about the quality of the fuel being used at Foxhall Stadium, so I went down to the outskirts of London and brought back a 25-gallon drum of what I thought was pure methanol.

My fuel was randomly tested after the Coventry meeting and it was a huge shock to me when I was told they had found an additive in the fuel. I was summoned to appear at an ACU tribunal in London where my fate would be decided.

Several fuel experts were present and one of them explained that the additive – propylene oxide – had been put in to help multi-cylinder stock cars fire-up faster. He went on to say that no advantage would be gained when used in a single cylinder speedway engine. It was enough to convince them that I had done nothing wrong.

The fuel supplier also admitted full liability, stating that I couldn't have known about their error.

Every person at the tribunal stood up and shook my hand after I had been cleared and, to a man, they wished me well in Germany. 'Go out there and do well again for Britain', was their message.

So off I went, relieved that I had been cleared of any wrongdoing, and in practice I was absolutely flying using standard methanol bought in Germany, recording the fastest time of the session.

The FIM had appointed the SCB to decide my fate but at the 11th hour the FIM decided, in its wisdom, to overturn the verdict. I was warming up my bike for the meeting – the penultimate round of the World Championship – when I was told I would not be allowed to ride after all.

John McNulty, the manager of the SCB, was at the track and he gave me the bad news. His explanation was that someone had brought to his attention that the rules regarding fuel had been altered recently, and these hadn't been taken into account at the tribunal in London.

If this was true, why had they waited until after practice to inform me? I think someone very close to the rider who took my place in the meeting, Bernt Persson, had raised an objection and they had talked the SCB into throwing me out.

**Dad gets down to business in the pits.**

**Shrimp shocked Ivan Mauger in the Ipswich round.**

In my career, I cannot remember ever being so disgusted and disappointed as I was that day. After all the pain I had endured to qualify this far, and having done nothing wrong, I was being denied a chance to take part in the sport's showpiece event.

I left the stadium in Germany as fast as I could, completely shattered, and drove straight back to England. I initially thought of quitting for the rest of the season but loyalty to my club and the Foxhall fans stopped me from throwing in the towel.

As an aside, I do know for a fact that some riders, even in international meetings, added water to their fuel, as their engines were too strong. In my mind, this is also an additive but no-one ever got thrown out of a meeting for doing it. Perhaps they weren't tested?

Nowadays, I don't think as many tests are carried out and to my mind that's a mistake. I believe both man and machine should be randomly tested at both league and international meetings throughout the season. The small amount of time spent conducting these tests would deter riders from using equipment that gave them an unfair advantage or turn up for a meeting with any illegal substances circulating in their blood.

During my time, and for several years afterwards, all riders knew they could be tested after any meeting to check they hadn't taken a banned substance. We were also aware that at any meeting our bikes could be checked for over-sized carburettors, etc.

It took a long while for my faith in the authorities to be restored but, at the end of the day, I had a career to pursue and had to put it behind me.

The ACU later handed me a token one-month ban from international racing, effective in March 1974, which had no effect, as my World Championship qualifiers didn't start until May that year.

# 1974

Qualifying went a lot smoother this time. I won all three of my qualifiers, at Ipswich, Hackney and Swindon, and two of them with a 15-point maximum. I also won the semi-final at Leicester with 14 but came across something that, frankly, I wouldn't have believed if it hadn't involved me.

Part way through the meeting, I was approached by a rider's representative and asked if I could help said rider in my next race, as he was struggling for points. It took a split second for me to say 'no', before adding that I wouldn't be helping anyone gain points, as I had always got what I achieved by my efforts alone and his rider would have to succeed (or fail) by his own efforts as well.

I don't know if anyone else in that meeting was asked to do any favours of this nature but, to be honest, I was pretty shocked. Although I had heard the odd rumour about it going on, and one or two well-known riders have since revealed their involvement in the buying and selling of World Championship points, or 'doing people a favour', I had never been approached before and never was again.

I went on to come third in the British/American/Nordic Final in Fredericia, Denmark and qualified for the 1974 World Final in Gothenburg, where I won two heats, scored nine points and again finished fourth. The night belonged to the Swedes, with Anders Michanek unstoppable on 15.

There was a bit of controversy after this World Final, when Ivan Mauger's machine was found to be one or two ccs over 500 and the Swedes were very vocal in calling for his second place to be taken away from him. The fact that their man, Soren Sjosten, would then move up from third had nothing to do with it, of course!

The objection was thrown out and Ivan retained his place, which was the right decision in my opinion. I would have loved to finish on the rostrum but not in those circumstances. Ivan had supported me in Abensberg in '73 and at least this time common sense prevailed.

Whenever you are ready . . . I wait patiently on gate three while Ivan Mauger goes through his usual pre-race shenanigans before our Wembley run-off.

## 1975

Just missing out on a rostrum place for the second time spurred me on even more and when I fought my way back to Wembley for the final in 1975, I was in the right frame of mind to earn myself and my small army of wonderful supporters something concrete to remember the night by. I had got there by winning the British Final (see chapter 7) and I felt it was time for me to climb onto the World Final rostrum as well.

There was a crowd of around 90,000 packed in that night but, unfortunately, track conditions were not what are expected for meetings at the highest level. A lack of watering created very dusty conditions and the track was very patchy, too. However, it was the same for all 16 of us. Good gating definitely helped and this was borne out by Ole Olsen winning every one of his races from the gate and taking the championship.

Every time I went out on track, the noise from the crowd was deafening, which really lifted me. With wins in my third and fifth outings and second places in my other rides, I totalled 12 points and earned myself a run-off with multiple World Champion Ivan Mauger for third place, behind Olsen and Anders Michanek.

I was obviously aware of Ivan's ability to outsmart most referees with his starting technique. At that time, we were allowed to move at the tapes and he got this down to a fine art – he would constantly move backwards and forwards, managing to nearly always be going forward when the referee hit the start button.

The referee, expecting Ivan to pull back the same distance each time, would release the button, perhaps trying to out-think him or punish him for trying to gain an advantage. But Ivan was very clever at not going as far back the second time . . . and away he would go, having gained yards on his opponents.

Ivan was the ultimate professional and gained the sponsorship necessary to be on the best equipment available. He also prepared his own bikes, was totally dedicated to speedway and was someone you couldn't help but admire.

However, I had to believe it was possible to beat him – the track was a bit grippy at Wembley on this occasion and I knew it was not up Ivan's street. I kept a level head and was prepared for whatever he got up to at the start.

As already mentioned, Ivan had previously tricked me into breaking the tapes at a Pride of the East meeting at King's Lynn and I wasn't about to let him do that again. He did try to unnerve me by lining up at the tapes, only to turn round and head back towards the pits. But I didn't look back, just kept my Weslake engine ticking over on the footrest and focussing on my own start.

It worked. I reacted quickest from the gate and soon pulled away, beating Ivan by a clear 20 yards in the fastest time of the night. Ivan had been in the top three every year since 1967 and I had been the man to break his run.

The first Englishman for 13 years to stand on a World Final rostrum since the late Peter Craven – and I was that rider. Brilliant, just brilliant!

## 1976

After collecting a bronze medal at Wembley, there was only one more World Final for me – at Katowice in 1976, when I scored nine points, winning one race and coming second twice and third twice.

I was still suffering with a shoulder injury in Poland that year and it probably cost me a couple of places on a day which saw my England team-mates, Peter Collins and Malcolm Simmons, finish as the world's top two in front of a reported 100,000 crowd.

## World glory with England

While I did not conquer the world on an individual basis, I did win gold at both Pairs and World Team Cup levels, which more than made up for not getting to the top of the individual World Final rostrum.

**Congratulating Ole Olsen, while Anders Michanek looks on, after climbing the World Final rostrum.**

Looking calm on parade with Hackney's Dave Morton before the 1975 British Final.

Not one to lavish praise lightly, JB was one of the first to congratulate me at Coventry.

My brother Tony looks startled by all the fuss after I won the 1975 British Championship.

The large contingent of Brits in the vast Katowice crowd at the 1976 World Final. I wish I could have given the Ipswich followers more to shout about.

Riding for my country meant a great deal to me and standing on top of the podium after World Team Cup success in 1972, 1974 and 1975 gave me great pleasure. I also felt that it rewarded in some way my family and my fans for all their support.

If I did badly in an individual meeting, the only person I let down was myself, and I would be left to deal with that. In the World Pairs and Team Cup, I felt that if I had not done enough, I would be letting down my team-mates and my country.

England had a great crop of top riders during my time and we went on to win the World Pairs again in 1977, 1978 and 1980 but, such was the quality of competition, I wasn't selected for any of those finals.

It was disappointing for me but understandable, because there were so many other good riders around. There was a great competitiveness between us and we all wanted to be selected and to ride for England as many times as we could.

Of course we helped each other during Test match and World Pairs races but the bottom line was not to do anything silly, not to lose your hard-earned position in any heat, as we were up against the very best who could, and would, capitalise on any errors.

Peter Collins was very competitive and very good at coming from the back, having been brought up on the Hyde Road circuit in Manchester with its multiple racing lines. He was a great rider at his peak and thoroughly deserved his individual world title. PC and I got on well.

Malcolm Simmons and I were always having fun together. I remember one occasion at Foxhall when he played a joke on me. He told me that his engine was playing up and prone to stopping suddenly. Simmo went on to say that if this happened during a race and he was ahead, he would put up his hand to signal me past.

So we lined up, he managed to out-gate me but I was in hot pursuit. Down the back straight, his hand shot up and I backed off a bit, as I was right behind him. Instead of slowing to a halt as I expected, he then wound it on and left me for dead! I quickly recovered, though and, approaching the finish line, we were neck and neck but I think he just beat me on the line.

Simmo was laughing his head off as we headed back to the pits but that was the first, and last, time he pulled that stunt on me.

Terry Betts was always hard to beat, so strong if he got out in front of you, but 'Bettsy' was another good friend. I had some great battles on the track with Ray Wilson but I never got to know him that well, even though we once rode together in a 1975 World Pairs qualifier at Maribor in Yugoslavia. Dave Jessup, who started out in speedway not long before me in 1969, was also very easy to get on with and a great little racer.

Basically, they were a great bunch of lads and we had some wonderful times riding around Europe in our combined pursuit of glory for Britain.

To captain your country in any sport is a great honour, and some might have thought I could have felt aggrieved when John Berry, who had succeeded Len Silver as England manager, chose Poole's Malcolm Simmons to replace Ray Wilson as the national skipper in 1977.

I was just happy to be working with JB for the collective good of both club and country. It did not worry me in the slightest that Malcolm got the plum job. For one thing, I had captained my country previously.

It was generally expected that perhaps JB would show bias towards me but he picked who he thought was the best choice for the job and I respected that. The object of the exercise was to win Test matches, World Pairs and Team Cup titles and to all try and help each other. I felt just as important as I previously had and, to be honest, I still had just as much input as Malcolm anyway.

In fact, JB was lucky enough to have several riders in his team capable of being captain. At that time, we had a lot of talented riders who rode well together and we all knew there were more waiting to step up when we retired from international riding, or lost form. What a shame that today we almost struggle to find enough riders to complete a team from the whole of Great Britain while the sport in this country struggles to produce enough riders of the right calibre.

Since 2000, when Mark Loram lifted the world title, only Tai Woffinden has made any real impression on the world scene for Great Britain – and the double World Champion learned his craft in Australia. This points to there being something fundamentally wrong with how we bring on riders in this country and I think it is great that Tai has said he wants to be part of any initiative to encourage more young riders to strive for the top in the sport.

Wouldn't it be great to have a British Final with 16 riders from the Elite League, as opposed to having to make up the field with almost two-thirds from the Premier League (second tier level)? In my day, any of the riders taking part were capable of winning it but for the last 10 years at least, the winner is only likely to be one of three or four of the riders taking part.

Has this been caused by the top league using foreign riders to win the league at any cost, leaving many British riders stuck in the Premier League? Or is it a lack of ambition or funding on the riders' part that they don't want to go up to the top level?

The new fast-track system may be helping National League riders gain experience at the top level but I'm not sure if this is preventing Premier League riders from progressing quickly enough.

Something does need to change, although it won't happen quickly. But when I see someone young and talented like Robert Lambert, who had to ride abroad to get enough track time when he was younger, I agree with Tai that we need to do more to encourage and support our young riders in this country.

Powering ahead of Belle Vue's Alan Wilkinson on the
Weslake. It revolutionised speedway in the mid-70s.

Chapter 15

# Four-valve Revolution

**IT goes without saying that success in any motor sport is highly dependent on having reliable, fast machinery. You might be the best racer in the world but you're not going to win the World Championship unless you are riding the best equipment there is.**

Having inherited a sound mechanical awareness from my father, I made sure I always tried to have the fastest and most reliable engines available.

I was lucky enough to be at the centre of a revolution that hit speedway in the 1974-75 close season. Up to that point, riders had always used two-valve engines – with Czechoslovakian company Jawa at the time ruling the roost. Previously, the British-built JAP engine had monopolised the sport, but the Jawa had virtually replaced it.

So it was good that another British company, run by Harry Weslake and based at Rye in Sussex, decided to develop a four-valve engine. As I have already said, I was chosen as the Weslake factory's test pilot.

They had built a relatively simple, but still highly efficient, four-valve unit and after a series of test-bed runs at Don Godden's works, it had a more professional look and, by December 1974, was ready for a private track-trial at Hackney.

This went as smooth as silk . . . the Weslake had begun its journey to the top.

What the four-valve engine provided for me was more instant power. Straight away, as soon as you turned the throttle at the tapes, you were away – no messing.

The conrods were made of aluminium, to make it all as light as possible. But they used to break and cause an enormous amount of damage as bits flew everywhere. Later, they used steel conrods, which were stronger and developed so that they did not add undue extra weight.

I used to spend a lot of time at Rye and the lads on the Weslake factory floor often asked me to go for a drink – just to leave them in peace. This was because I was always bothering them, wanting to know what was going on behind the scenes and what they were doing to improve the engine.

If Harry was there, he was happy to make me a cup of tea and we would sit chatting in his office. He had found a niche in the engine manufacturing market for producing the most efficient fuel flowing systems. He told me once that he started out by utilising a gas meter and working forwards from that. I didn't fully understand everything he mentioned but enough to know that he was very clever when it came to engines.

Don Godden continued to be heavily involved in the engine development and he enjoyed a good working relationship with one of Weslake's brightest brains, Ron Valentine.

I became a Weslake works rider for a number of years and knew that I always had enough power – not only to get out of the start as fast as possible, but also to come out of a broadside at just the right time for maximum effect. The two extra valves made it naturally easier to ride a bike because of the extra power and, of course, new track records were set all round the country. Riders everywhere were gaining from the instant power that Weslake engines provided.

The four-valve revolution actually began in Australia the previous winter, when Newport rider Neil Street teamed up with mechanical boffin Ivan Tighe to build a four-valve conversion for a Jawa engine.

Neil's son-in-law and Newport team-mate Phil Crump took Australia by storm in the winter of 1974-75 riding one of his engines and 'Crumpie' continued his success when he arrived in the UK

**New beginning . . . with Don Godden before my private test session aboard the Weslake engine at Hackney in December '74.**

at the start of the '75 season.

Jawa had little option but to join the party and they eventually brought into production their own version of the now much coveted four-valve, in the form of an overhead camshaft engine.

Former European Grass-track Champion Don Godden also developed frames that could be used with the new Weslake engines but I kept my standard Jawa frame, as did a lot of riders.

From his base at West Mailling in Kent, Don went on to make his own GR500 four-valve engine in 1979 which utilised a single overhead cam design, as opposed to the Weslake's pushrod system. I found this was a bit uncomfortable to ride – it became hot just where my knee touched the engine and I preferred the unit developed at Rye.

Someone who did take to Don's design, and went on to win his first three World Championships with it, was Danish superstar Hans Nielsen. He became the first renowned Godden works rider and used it to great effect, becoming the best rider of his era. Simon Wigg, Shawn Moran, Kenny Carter, Phil Collins and John Davis also used the Godden to great effect.

Another great engine expert was German Otto Lantenhammer, who experimented with a four-valve, two carburettor engine.

He had lost the tops of four of his fingers when he caught them in a primary chain while working on a long-track bike he used to ride but that did not interfere with his ability to be an ace tuner.

I went over to see him after my Weslake sponsorship had ended and he did a new engine set-up for me using twin carbs. I used it to great effect but, unfortunately, at the end of that season, the authorities banned twin carb engines, so I had to adapt my prototype back to a single carb, which had worked for me before.

Over the years, I have often been asked if the introduction of four-valve engines was good for the sport. Understandably, there were those who said the change from two to four-valve in the mid-70s damaged speedway because of the extra costs enforced on riders and, ultimately, their employers. These new engines were more expensive to produce and, consequently, riders were going to their clubs and asking for more points money.

In my opinion, you can't stop progress. And it is the same in all motorised sports from Formula One downwards. Everyone wants to be on the fastest equipment and it is wrong that there should be any attempts to deny you this.

Another big change in speedway came with the arrival of the lay-down engines in the mid-90s. I was retired from competitive racing by then but I rode my son Chris' machine and have to say that I did not get on with it.

This was in the early days of their introduction and I found it slower to build up speed and, for me, it drove too hard and was pulling me towards the outside of the track. In contrast, the good, old uprights of my day gave you instant power and easier handling.

I guess it also had a lot to do with what you were used to. Of course, modifications were later made to silencers and the efficiency of getting the exhaust gases away increased dramatically.

Like all speedway riders, I was always looking to go faster than everyone else and a gentleman called Mike Erskine tuned one of the fastest speedway engines I ever used.

He had been a World Finalist in 1950 after a career stretching to both sides of the Second World War, but retired the following year due to injuries. He was well spoken and I found out later that he was an Old Etonian who took up an engineering career in both bikes and cars once his riding days were over.

At the time, I was suffering a drop in form and, unbeknown to me, it had not gone unnoticed by Mike, who lived in Dorset and was an avid reader of *Speedway Star*.

Out of the blue, my telephone rang one day and it was Mike on the other end: "I see your scores have dipped in recent weeks," he said. "You appear to be struggling a bit. I think I can help you. I have worked on machinery for Barry Briggs."

The Street-Jawa conversion that Phil Crump used to such great effect in 1975 before Weslake monopolised the market for a while.

To be honest, I had never heard of him but following the death of my dad and one or two other things, I was not doing as well as I wanted to and not enjoying life so much. There were thoughts starting to creep into my head that it was my age, as I was getting on a bit by now, so perhaps it was that rather than my set-ups or engines not being right.

Having thought about it, I had nothing to lose, so I took one of my engines down to Mike, more in hope than expectation. He asked me what the most important aspect of a race was for me. My reply was: "To get to the first corner and around the first two bends in the lead. I am light on the bike (around nine stones in those days), so I can deal with the rest."

Mike was a typical highly-intelligent boffin-type and his house was piled full of technical books and stuff, while his workshops were immaculate with his lathes spotless and backed up with all the latest equipment.

It was a while before the engine was ready to collect but once I had fitted it and had a ride . . . wow!

Seven meetings passed before I tasted defeat again, such was the power and performance of the engine Mike had created for me. It was one of the best speedway engines I ever rode. It was a shame I was past my World Final days by then, because I am sure I would have cleaned up everywhere.

By this time, I often stayed at Mike's house and he was at Wimborne Road to watch me ride against Poole on one occasion. I can still see the look of satisfaction on his face when I won my first four races.

Sadly, the engine seized during my fifth heat and although I continued to work with Mike for two years, we never quite reached those heights again. I do believe that Mike's call picked up my career and probably extended it.

One day, I was looking through some of his bits and pieces and saw this Offset JAP engine laying there that had been earmarked for Barry Briggs. At the time, I had no idea what an Offset engine was but around 2010 – many years later – GM brought their first one off the production line.

Mike, who died in November, 1985, was a pioneer and I owe him a big debt.

Speed was my business and I had to get a hurry-on before a meeting in Germany after being held up while driving back from Italy. I had already put my leathers on and mechanic John Bloomfield quickly worked on the bike to get it warmed up and ready to race.

The first part of the meeting was what they called the Bahnrekord, where you did a lap as fast as you could. I went past the start-line on full gas and carried on round at top speed to clock the fastest time.

It was less than half-an-hour since I had arrived at the stadium, yet I had already won myself a trophy! Everything continued to go well and I went on to win the meeting as well. It was a strange track, having sand laid on top of tarmac.

I may have been fast that day on the track but what made me go fastest in my whole life, without the aid of machinery, was a bungee jump. Gravity took a hold as I travelled downwards so fast – and back up again at almost the same speed.

There was a fete taking place in the village of Great Blakenham, just outside Ipswich, where they have a cycle speedway track. At the centre of the field was a giant crane with a basket attached to the end of the arm.

A couple of hours must have passed as I wandered about plucking up enough courage to have a go.

I was not keen and I admire anyone who can jump out of the sky with hardly a care in the world. They have more courage than me. However, would I ever get another chance? Most probably not – and it was for charity.

What didn't help was that the person ahead of me chickened out when they reached the top. Everybody else I had watched before then had jumped. So I was even more nervous when they closed the gate on the cage and lifted me up.

Looking down from the cage is completely different to looking up at the top of the crane. It felt as though I was in the clouds and, in fact, I'm sure I passed right through one!

However, once I decide to do something hairy, I just want to get on with it – the more I mess about, the worse it gets. So as soon as the crane stopped lifting me and it was almost perpendicular, knowing that the rope had been safely fastened around my legs before I left the ground, I went for it.

Only I'd forgotten to open the gate and cracked my body against the frame. Oh dear! By this time, my head was spinning but I was going to do it, so I opened the gate and dived out as though I was diving into a swimming pool.

Down I came at a rate of knots and just when I was about to bump my nose against the inflated airbed on the ground, whoosh, I was zipped back up again at virtually the same supersonic speed.

This upping and downing continued for some while as I hung like a rag doll until, slowly but surely, I found myself back on terra firma – amazingly, in one piece.

Riding a 500cc motorcycle with no brakes at 70mph around sharp bends with three others for company would scare most people but I never thought about the dangers involved in that. Unlike jumping out of the sky – my heart is still pounding!

Ready to try out the sand-track bike with a JAP
engine that Don Godden built for me in 1972.

In action at Romford in 1970, my first full season on the shale. I remember that concrete wall!

Winning the 1971 Division Two Riders' Championship, my first major title, at Hackney in 1971, with runners-up Malcolm Shakespeare (left) and Hughie Saunders.

The 1971 Witches. Left to right: Ron Bagley, myself, Ted Spittles, Clive Noy, Ted Howgego. Kneeling: Tony Davey, Pete Bailey.

The 1976 league and cup double squad and management with the BL1 championship trophy:
John Berry, Mike Lanham, Tony Davey, Billy Sanders, Kevin Jolly, myself, Dave Gooderham and Ron Bagley,
with Ted Howgego, Andy Hines and Colin Cook in front.

1978 KO Cup winners. Olle Nygren (team manager), Kevin Jolly, Colin Cook, Tim Hunt, Mike Lanham, Georg
Hack. The heat leader trio of Billy Sanders, myself and Tony Davey messing around for the camera.

Practicing with Ted Howgego (outside) and Tony Davey at Foxhall in 1978.

Son Chris posing with me for one of his first pictures in the pits in 1978, although many more would follow.

A sight to delight all Witches fans . . . Colin Cook and me beat Stars' duo Richard Hellsen and Michael Lee to the first corner in 1979.

THE JOHN LOUIS TESTIMONIAL

OFFICIAL PROGRAMME/SCORESHEET

Sunday, 19th August, 3.30 p.m.

Admission by programme £1.50

Past and present favourites and popular visitors to Foxhall turned out for my testimonial meeting in 1979. Standing: Colin Cook, Terry Betts, Ted Howgego, Phil Herne, Peter Prinsloo, Preben Eriksen, Tony Davey, Milan Spinka, Kevin Jolly. Kneeling: Dave Gooderham, Nigel Flatman, Mike Lanham, Andy Hines, Billy Sanders.

Not sure that Young England was the appropriate team name given some of our ages in 1971 but here we are at Bradford ready to face Czechoslovakia. Stan Holey (team manager), Arthur Price, Dave Baugh, Paul Tyrer, Dave Kumeta, Doug Wyer and Alan Knapkin. I think the JAP that Tony Davey and me are sitting on must have belonged to local star Alan.

Before the Test against Sweden at Ipswich in 1971.

Billy Sanders and I were opponents when England met Australia in front of 10,000 fans at King's Lynn in the 1973 Daily Mirror International Tournament.

When England ruled the world. It's 1974, the year the Lions whitewashed Sweden (5-0), Poland (7-0) and USSR (5-0) in home Test series before retaining the World Team Cup. Happy days! This was taken before we thrashed the Poles 78-30 at Foxhall. Left to right: Len Silver (team manager), Dave Jessup, Malcolm Simmons, Terry Betts, Barry Thomas, Peter Collins. Front: Tony Davey, Ray Wilson and me.

Another big international night at Ipswich, this time the 1977 Test against the Rest of the World. The BSPA couldn't find a single country strong enough to take us on that summer! As you can see, I was captain before our team manager John Berry handed the job to Malcolm Simmons on a full-time basis that year. Left to right: Dave Jessup, Michael Lee, Simmo, JB, Gordon Kennett, Peter Collins, Terry Betts.

On parade at Wimbledon before the historic first Test against the USA in 1980 which ended in a thrilling draw.

My last-ever World Team Cup appearance, alongside Dave Jessup before the qualifier at my home track King's Lynn in 1984.

Me and Peter Collins find ourselves behind Hans Nielsen and Bo Petersen in the 1982 Test against Denmark at Halifax, where I was spending my second season with the Dukes.

Pensive in Poland. Me and Peter Collins before the 1975 World Pairs Final at Wroclaw.

WORLD FINAL '72

Practice prior to the 1976 World Final at Katowice, Poland. I started wearing glasses full-time in the mid-70s and following a problem where I had to remove my goggles during a race (think it was the 1984 race at Oxford, which I was falsely accused of 'throwing'), I then had a pair of glasses made especially for riding, with larger lenses, and would have been difficult to spot behind my goggles.

An unusual shot of the 1976 World Finalists waiting around for the post-meeting presentations after PC, Simmo and Phil Crump had finished in the top three at Katowice.

Speedway riders are more used to breaking (track) records, not making them, but it was fun and something different being among representatives of British League teams in October 1973 who attended the Decca recording studio in West Hampstead, London, where – under the guidance of BBC Radio 1 DJ's Ed Stewart and 'Diddy' David Hamilton – we cut a 45-inch single which came out at the start of the following season.

Speedway being what it is, however, we couldn't manage without a guest rider – or, in this case, singer. As there was no-one available to represent Sheffield, they called up Bert Harkins who had ridden for the Tigers in 1972, while five clubs – Hackney, Halifax, Oxford, Cradley and Newport – sent no-one at all. How many do you recognise? I'm obviously at the front flanked by Martin Ashby (Swindon) and Nigel Boocock (Coventry), and the others are (left to right) Dag Lovaas (Reading), Malcolm Brown (Leicester), Graeme Stapleton (Wimbledon), Scott Autrey (Exeter), George Hunter (Wolverhampton), Terry Betts (King's Lynn), Jim McMillan (Coatbridge), Peter Collins (Belle Vue), Pete Smith (Poole) and Bert Harkins (declining to wear Sheffield colours again!).

Our group was named The Rivals for the purposes of the Decca record label and the song on the A-side was titled simply 'Speedway'. On the flip side, as DJs used to say, was 'Hoskins Still Rides', a reference to the late, great Johnnie Hoskins who is credited with bringing speedway to England from Australia in 1928.

It couldn't exactly have taken the charts by storm, because I'm still waiting for my share of the recording royalties!

I enjoyed contesting the Silver and Golden Helmet match-race championships in the 70s. This was taken before me and Malcolm Simmons went for gold in 1974.

One of my proudest moments as a rider was lifting the British League Riders' Championship at Belle Vue in 1979. In Chapter 9 I recall why the race in which I beat main rival Bruce Penhall to clinch the coveted title was my greatest ever race.

Despite all the travelling involved, I enjoyed my two years with Halifax. Here are the Dukes of 1981 (left to right): Craig Pendlebury, Dennis Gavros (team manager), Doug Wyer, Ian Cartwright, Ian Westwell, Steve Baker, Kenny Carter and me.

I had reservations about joining King's Lynn but was pleased to enjoy two happy seasons there at the end of my career. I was captain of this 1984 Stars team (left to right): Kevin Jolly, Richard Hellsen, Martin Dixon, Dave Jessup. Kneeling: Steve Regeling, Keith Bloxsome. I was still on Weslake after 10 years.

Back at Ipswich as promoter, the club has never known another year quite like the one we had in 1998, when we won the treble with arguably the Witches' greatest-ever team. Myself, Mike Western and Mike Smillie join (left to right) Savalas Clouting, son Chris, Scott Nicholls, Tony Rickardsson and Toni Svab after victory over Coventry in the Craven Shield.

It's always great to see familiar old faces back at Foxhall. See how many you recognise from our 60th anniversary reunion in 2011. Left to right: Tony Davey, Ted Howgego, myself, Rod Laudrum, Olle Nygren, Jeremy Doncaster, Ron Bagley, Dave Gooderham. Sadly, Rod, who was one of the original Witches in 1951, passed away in 2013.

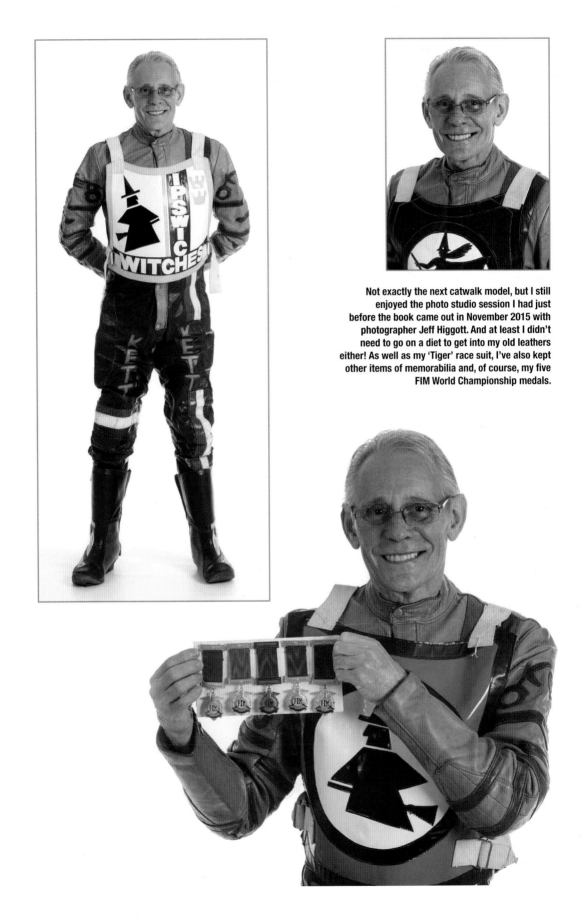

Not exactly the next catwalk model, but I still enjoyed the photo studio session I had just before the book came out in November 2015 with photographer Jeff Higgott. And at least I didn't need to go on a diet to get into my old leathers either! As well as my 'Tiger' race suit, I've also kept other items of memorabilia and, of course, my five FIM World Championship medals.

**Hopefully there's still plenty of life in Tiger Louis! A different kind of 'action' shot here showing me on the dance floor enjoying Ceroc, a form of modern jive.**

Chapter 16

# On The Road

**W**HILE I had plenty of thrills (and close shaves) on a speedway track, there were also some extraordinary episodes on the way to and from meetings, both at home and abroad.

This went back as far as my early days in Division Two when I was guesting regularly for First Division Newport and made many 500-mile-plus round trips from Suffolk to South Wales. We all moan about the M25 today but it would have been nice to have had it available at that time.

Instead, it was a drive down the A12, navigate through the City of London (without a TomTom) before picking up the A4, which led to the M4. Then we had some decent motoring conditions past Reading, Swindon and Bristol before finally reaching Wales. It used to take around four-and-a-half hours but longer if weather conditions were not perfect.

One night, fog came down after the meeting at Newport and we were undecided as to what to do. Do we stay the night and risk missing Ipswich's meeting the following evening at Rayleigh? Or do we take it steady all the way back to Ipswich, even if it takes a lot longer than usual? I knew JB would not be impressed if we failed to turn up for a meeting, so we set off for Suffolk.

I shared the driving with my mechanic and, as expected, it was a horrendous journey. I don't think we managed to get above 20mph. We eventually drove into my drive at Ipswich having been on the road for more than 12 hours.

Dad got to work on my machinery and I managed to get a couple of hours' sleep before we set off for south Essex and the meeting against Rayleigh Rockets.

Sitting in the pits between races, I could not stop myself dozing off but every time I went out onto the track, I was fully awake (probably helped by the adrenaline). It certainly didn't slow me down as I broke The Weir track record and then equalled the new time later on.

This type of exhausting schedule was by no means unfamiliar to me or many other riders at that time. With between 17 and 19 tracks operating in both divisions throughout the 70s, we often raced four or five times a week, the length and breadth of Britain, plus international meetings. On top of that, we spent hours in the workshop cleaning and/or preparing the bikes. Sleep was something that just had to be fitted in around everything else.

At least Sundays were usually non-race-days and most riders took advantage of that to take a break. However, there were a few of us who did exactly the opposite and travelled even further to race on the continent at places such as Montagnana in Italy.

In 1972, I decided to have a go at some of the lucrative sand-track meetings being staged most weekends and take on the likes of Ivan Mauger, Ole Olsen, Don Godden and Egon Muller.

I took delivery of a brand new 500cc sand-track bike, specially designed by Godden (who built bikes for many of the aforementioned riders). The bike was basically a JAP-powered speedway bike with modifications to reach top speed quicker and the ability to cope with a bumpier track surface. It had a gearbox, 22-inch rear wheel and rear suspension but, as in speedway, no brakes.

I had gained some new sponsorship from Trevor Seymour, who was clerk of the course at Foxhall and ran Britannia Stores in Ipswich. I used it to help purchase a brand new Ford Granada (signwritten with his company name) that I intended to use for my long distance journeys.

Sand-tracking was much harder than speedway and not easy to break into. Tracks were a lot longer – between 600 and 1,000 metres – and the racing was much faster, with riders reaching speeds of around 90-100mph. There could also be six riders in a race and the track surface would vary between

**With sponsor Trevor Seymour of Britannia Stores and the three-litre MkI Ford Granada with its V6 engine.**

excellent and so bad that large stones could fly up, causing cuts and bruises and even smashed goggles if you were really unlucky.

The riding technique also had to be different because of the higher speed. When going down the straights, you had to keep your head down, tuck your left arm in and trail your left leg back for maximum streamlining. I was going to have to learn as I went along, as it was very different to my usual riding style.

I only had a few practice sessions with my new bike and the only place available to me was some local field covered in grass, which was far from ideal preparations for what lay ahead.

Towards the end of April '72, I took part in my first sand-track meeting. I left Ipswich with my mechanic, Brian 'Brassy' Goodchild, on Thursday night straight after a Witches meeting for the 1,000-mile journey to Montagnana in Italy. We caught the ferry from Harwich and then drove through Holland, Germany and Austria to reach the track at 5.30 pm on Saturday, just in time to watch the last practice session of the day. After seeing some of the other riders practice, I almost had second thoughts about taking part. I had never seen motorcyclists go so fast.

To save money, and because I wasn't expecting to earn anything from the meeting, we decided to sleep in the car, so I woke up aching all over. My first practice went quite well, apart from some clutch trouble, which we worked on for a couple of hours but ran out of time. Luckily, I had no further trouble in the actual meeting where the bike performed very well.

I was the only Englishman in a field of 16 riders and, unbelievably, won all of my five races and then beat my top three rivals to record the fastest lap time from a flying start. The result of the meeting depended on the last race and I was up against Gianna Pizzo (the Italian Champion), Alois Wiesbock (Germany) and Fritz Knening (Holland). The 15,000 fans were all behind their local hero but I won by almost half-a-lap.

I was presented with two huge trophies and was chief guest at a reception afterwards. I then received an invitation from the local promoter to return in June for another meeting, which I won as well. I became quite popular with the Italian locals and banners started to appear with 'Tiger for King' on.

Despite the long distances being travelled, we enjoyed visiting this northern part of Italy where the long-tracks were situated. With Lake Garda just down the road, the scenery was spectacular. On one trip we also got to see the famous Romeo and Juliet balcony in Verona. However, as every tourist knows, visiting a new country always throws up a few things that are different from back home.

In Italy, the toilets came as a bit of a shock. Having been brought up with flush systems and a seat, it was bewildering to be confronted with a pair of footprints either side of a hole in the ground! The first time we ordered coffee caused confusion as well. Not only could I not get my finger in the handle of the tiny cup, just one gulp and the lot had gone. And it was so strong as well – nothing like the Nescafe I was brought up on!

We travelled there on a regular basis and used to see progress being made on the Brenner Pass as we made our way through the Alps on the final leg of the journey. We always aimed to reach Italy in 13 to 14 hours after getting off the ferry, and the only stops we made were to re-fill with fuel.

With the bikes in the back, the Granada used to resemble a ship with the front up and the back weighed down but we aimed to travel at 100mph whenever we could. The autobahns in Germany were excellent for that and we made the most of there being no speed limits.

John Bloomfield was often my mechanic on the trips and we shared the driving, having two-and-a-half hour stints at the wheel. We may have been mad but, in our eyes, there was no time to stop when we switched over. We did it on the move. Firstly, we slowed down to around 70mph with the driver reclining his seat, so that it was virtually flat. Then, whoever was passenger would climb in behind and take the wheel, allowing the driver to slip over onto the passenger side – simple!

Don't try that on the A12, folks, as the local police may have something to say! But at that time, we thought nothing of it and anyway, us speedway riders always like to be on the edge.

I remember one time when an Italian policeman, on a motorbike, stopped us. After a few minutes of arm waving and hand gestures, we realised he didn't like the bike wheel slightly sticking out at the side of the car. We used to have one bike in the boot and the other on a rack with the front wheel slightly turned. I had travelled many times in the UK like that and never had a problem but in Italy, apparently it wasn't allowed.

So we took the front wheel off and re-positioned the bike, so the engine was resting on the rack. Not ideal but it seemed to make him happy as he waved us off. A few hundred yards down the road, we went round a corner, stopped the car, put everything back as it was and continued on our way!

The next time when the police in Italy stopped me, I was told in broken English that my foot was too heavy. After a few exchanges, we finally understood that he meant we were going too fast. I tried to explain we were late for a meeting and, in frustration, pointed at my bikes saying: 'Tiger Louis, Montagnana'. By now, I was starting to have a bit of a following over there and the penny quickly dropped – he immediately escorted us to the track before shouting what turned out to be 'Good Luck' in Italian as he left.

After my first meeting in Italy, I visited two long-tracks in Germany. The first was in Norstadt, where track conditions were deep and very bumpy – completely different to the one in Montagnana – and I wasn't helped by an engine failure in my first heat. After missing out on the final, I realised I had been using too high a gear, so made a note for my next visit.

Next up was Elmshorn, where I went much better, finishing as top scorer and breaking the track record. The previous holder was none other than Don Godden, who had built my bike.

Back to Italy, and I completed three more meetings over the summer of '72, winning two of them. In one, I finished ahead of Barry Briggs and Garry Middleton but in the last one, I had engine problems while leading one race and could only manage fourth, although I was the only rider to beat eventual winner Ivan Mauger.

In later years, there wasn't always time for me to drive back and I had to take to the skies to get to a meeting in the UK. When that happened, mechanic John Bloomfield would find a cheap hotel and find things to do until I returned the following weekend. He was a taxi driver who, luckily for me, was able to take plenty of time off. Sometimes we reversed the routine – he would take the bikes by road while I flew out on a plane to meet up later.

I had several close calls when flying out to Italy and, on one occasion, I was with Barry Briggs at Heathrow waiting for our flight to be called. Bad weather had delayed it and, as more time went by, I started to panic that we would miss our meeting. Barry didn't seem too bothered, saying that it would all be okay in the end, but even he couldn't have predicted how hairy our journey would turn out.

We finally took off and landed just as the meeting was due to start. The only problem was that we still had 70 miles to cover by road. An Italian driver was waiting for us in a very small Fiat and it was at this point that I wished I had stayed in Ipswich. He covered the 70 miles in under an hour, some of it along country lanes, screeching around corners while his hand managed to constantly hit the horn and at the same time wave to any young ladies we passed.

When we got to the track, he still didn't slow down but went straight through the pits, finally coming to a halt in the middle of the centregreen. They had delayed the start and we were able to join the riders' parade – I even managed to win another trophy but that journey was far scarier than any speedway race I've ever been in.

During one of my Italian visits, we had time to spare before catching our flight back and Briggo suggested we went for a swim in the pool at our hotel in Venice. The trouble was, I had not brought any trunks but Barry said I could borrow a pair of his.

I was at my best 'fighting weight' of around nine stone, dripping wet, and Barry was a fair bit wider than me. It was hot and I was desperate for a cool-off, so I put his trunks on and tied the cord as tight as I could.

Being me, I didn't make a measured entrance down the steps and into the shallow end. Instead, I ran along the side and leapt in at the deep end. It was not until I came back up to the surface that I realised I was naked! After what seemed like ages of diving down into the depths of the pool, I found the trunks and eventually managed to twist them back on. I then climbed out of the water looking as nonchalant as I possibly could, but cringing inside.

Don Godden was a great long-track exponent and one meeting that we were both involved in still sticks vividly in my mind. It was another one at Montagnana and I was having a bad time, with my machine packing up regularly during practice.

What made it more of a worry was that I wouldn't get paid if I didn't ride. I approached several of the other riders to ask if I could borrow one of their bikes. Luckily, Briggo and Alois Wiesbock lent me one for a couple of races and then I approached Don Godden.

He initially said no, and I walked off trying to think of someone else to ask. Soon afterwards, Don tapped me on the shoulder and offered his bike. I said I would be gentle with it, as I was just happy to be in the race and pick up my start money.

"No," he boomed. "I want you to win. You are using my bike, so I want it to come first."

It was then a big rush to get ready, with the race about to start. I had never sat on the bike before but, to my great relief, it was the fastest thing I have ever ridden. The extra speed caused my helmet peak to lift up and my helmet straps were tight against my throat.

After a lap, I got it under control by dipping my head down towards the track and beat Mauger, Briggo and Wiesbock. The local fans were delighted with the result and there were shouts of 'Luigi, Luigi' from all quarters as I went back to the pits.

**Flat out at the Montagnana sand-track circuit in Italy, where we reached speeds of up to 100mph.**

Don had certainly put together something special and I'm sure I clocked my fastest-ever two-wheeled speeds in that race. Don kept himself apart from most of us and was quite difficult to get to know but he certainly knew his way around a motorcycle engine.

Journeys home could also be eventful and after one tiring rush back to Zeebrugge, my mechanic and I fell asleep while our car waited in the lane to board the ferry. The loading crew must have thought it funny that we didn't move and they left us there while everyone else boarded. When we did come to, we were the only vehicle in a huge car park and the boat was sailing off into the distance.

I was riding for Ipswich at Reading the following night, so I had to act fast as ferries from Zeebrugge were not as frequent as those from Calais. We rushed off down to Ostende, where we were told that we couldn't use our original ticket. So it was a rapid reverse and on to Calais, where they said we could use it.

The ferry was ready to leave but we burned some rubber and we made it on to the boat just in time. Ironically, we arrived in Dover before the ferry from Zeebrugge we were scheduled to be on.

Soon after I had purchased a sparkling new Peugeot, I set off for a meeting in Rodenbach, Germany, with Olle Nygren and my mechanic Brian Goodchild. We left straight after a meeting at Swindon, catching a late night ferry from Dover.

Olle and I decided to sleep on the boat but 'Brassy' got talking to some lorry drivers and may have had a drink or two. When we got there, we set off in the dark and were in the middle of Belgium somewhere when Brian must have fallen asleep at the wheel.

He woke up as we were starting to go down a grass verge by the side of the road. He tried to get it back but we turned 180 degrees before rolling over two or three times and ending upside down by the central barrier.

I finished up on the driver's side and Brassy had taken my place in the passenger seat. All the

'Luigi, Luigi!' . . . the Italian crowd were very supportive after I won their big sand-track meeting.

windows were shattered and we managed to climb out through one and run up the road, leaving the car 'parked' in the fast lane.

Several cars screeched and swerved to avoid it, as they couldn't see it. A car then stopped, the driver jumped out shouting and waving his arms at us and, although we had no idea what he was saying, we got the gist. He then went to his boot, got his red triangle out and placed it several yards back and drove off.

We then looked at each other to ask the same question: "Where's Olle?"

We looked inside the car and there he was, still in the back seat, lying on the roof, slurping straight from a bottle of duty free whisky. We helped him out and, even in the dark, could see the car was completely wrecked and the handlebars of our bikes in the trailer had been bent so they faced down to the front wheel forks.

I'm not sure how he knew but a breakdown truck then pulled up. The driver gave us a rope to tie the doors shut before towing us back to a garage. After we had been there a while, the garage owner was trying to tell us the car couldn't be driven because it was too dangerous.

I wasn't ready to write it off, so I thought I would see if the car would start. After wiping some oil off the top of the engine, I leaned in and turned the key and, at the second attempt, it started.

There was still a big problem in that the roof was touching the steering wheel but, using all my strength, I managed to push it up using my back, so that I could sit in the driver's seat. The garage owner was still dead against us leaving but after getting me to sign some paperwork, he reluctantly let us go and we set off back towards the ferry port.

Thankfully, they let us on the boat, although we got a few strange looks from some of the other passengers, and it was a relief to reach Dover. We travelled up the A2 and, at Canterbury, a police car waved us down.

"I've had reports of a stock car being driven out of Dover," he said. There I sat with my crash helmet and goggles on in a very dented, windowless car held together by rope and no lights.

He then walked around the whole car, checking it out, and spotted Olle flat out on the back seat.

"Is that man in the back okay?" We put the policeman's mind at rest by saying that he was still a bit shocked. The truth was, his Scotch bottle was nearly empty!

The policeman asked us to change a wheel, which he said had buckled, but I knew that the half shaft was bent. After the wheel had been changed, it seemed to satisfy him as he said there was an improvement. I also told a white lie by saying we were only going to the other side of the Dartford Tunnel, so he reluctantly let us go.

"But don't tell anyone that you've seen me and please go very carefully," were his parting words.

I didn't want to leave the car, valuable equipment and riding gear behind, because we had no other way of transporting it all home. By the time we reached Colchester on the A12, it was starting to get dark and, of course, we had no lights.

Hardly surprisingly, we were stopped again, this time by a motorcycle policeman. He could see the bikes, he knew who I was and, after hearing our sob story, he let us go.

"The best thing is for you to get home and off the road as soon as possible, but please take it steady," he said.

"By the way, please don't tell anyone you've seen me," was his parting shot, and I have never been more relieved to reach anywhere than my drive in Glencoe Road, Ipswich.

John Ford, from Knodishall, near Aldeburgh, bought the 'wreck' and restored it so professionally that when I saw it four years later being used as a taxi, I hardly recognised it. The driver said he had not had a moment's trouble from it and had done over 250,000 miles. That Peugeot had certainly been through more than the average car and lived to tell the tale!

Ole Olsen made a fast start in this German sand-track meeting, with Barry Briggs (6), myself (2) and the partly hidden Egon Muller leading the chasing pack.

Leaving home bound for New Zealand in early 1975. Yes, they did allow me through customs in those trousers!

Chapter 17

# Around The World

**B**EING involved in the Ivan Mauger/Barry Briggs World Series Troupe was one of the highlights of my career. It allowed me to see the world during the British close season, gain experience racing on unfamiliar tracks and pit myself against some of the best riders.

My first trip was to New Zealand, Australia and the USA at the very start of 1975. I was the only English rider in the group and, after spending Christmas and New year with my family, I joined up with reigning World Champion Anders Michanek (Sweden), Great Dane Ole Olsen, German long-track superstar Egon Muller and the top American, Scott Autrey, along with Kiwi legends Ivan and Barry.

My trip got off to an eventful start when the plane developed a fault during a refuelling stop in San Francisco en route to Auckland.

Ivan had arranged for someone he knew to ensure my engine made it onto the flight, as it was heavy and would normally require a surcharge. All was going well until we had to switch planes, at which point I was told there was no paperwork to cover the engine and I had to pay £200 before they would transfer it to the new flight.

I had about £250 in cash on me, so this unexpected bill left me short of money before I had even got anywhere. The resulting delay caused me to miss my connection in Fiji and I was told it could be up to 24 hours before another flight became available.

I slept in the airport at San Francisco with my head resting on my engine in fear of losing it until, eventually, a kind lady at one of the check-in desks arranged a flight for me.

I had a stroke of luck when I arrived in Auckland, too. Ole Olsen was at the airport with his young son Jacob. He said that if I didn't mind having Jacob on my lap, I could use his seat on the internal flight to Christchurch.

Not having slept properly for three days, I have no recollection of that opening meeting of the tour. I was straight off the plane and on to the track.

We went on to ride at Invercargill, New Zealand's most southernmost city on the South Island, and I recall some good days among the hot springs at Rotorua in the North Island, as well as riding in Auckland itself. But it was Christchurch where I have my best memories. I shared a room with Egon Muller at a house that had a swimming pool and where we were perfectly looked after.

Egon referred to me as 'Churchill' and I jokingly called him 'Hitler'! We got on like a house on fire – even though he would get up at 6.00am most mornings to go for a run, despite not having gone to bed until the early hours after a night on the town.

Never slow to push himself forward, Egon would take me into various shops and say: "Hi, this is the British Speedway Champion and I am the World Long-track Champion. What help can you give us?"

Sometimes, we would be given stuff for free and sometimes we wouldn't. But we did enjoy a great deal of success at Tommy's Suzuki Centre, a huge motorcycle dealership in Christchurch city centre. Egon persuaded them to let us borrow a couple of trail bikes, which we used both on and off-road.

When we took them back, the owner said he had had reports of two riders doing wheelies riding away from traffic lights. We just smiled and left the shop quickly.

We had made our own track in a big field that had a dry stream running through it with small banks. Because both Egon and I hated to be beaten, we used to go round and round this course for what seemed like hours as he tried to pass me. He never did, though. I picked out a circuit that included potholes and tree roots, as well as the banking by the stream. He wasn't so good on this type of rough terrain, not having had any scrambling experience. Anyone watching would have thought we were crazy but, to us, it was simply great fun.

Then it was off to Australia, where we rode in three meetings at Mildura, Bundaberg and Liverpool, near Sydney. There was less time to let our hair down as we spent a lot of time travelling, although we did fit in some sightseeing as well.

Last stop was California in the US, where we were due to ride at Costa Mesa, Houston Astrodome and Irwindale. Egon took one look at the tiny Costa Mesa circuit and announced that "the German boy will NOT be racing on such a small, dangerous track". He promptly took himself back to the hotel while the rest of us sorted out our equipment and had a few practice skids.

Being used to riding on tracks up to 1,200 metres long back home, I could understand where he was coming from. Shame that he didn't give it a try, as we did all eventually adapt to racing on one of the smallest speedway tracks in the world.

I'm certain Egon didn't think he was missing out, however. When I returned to our room later, I found he had made friends with some locals!

We had to learn new techniques to master tracks that were very short with extremely tight corners. It is little wonder that when the Americans come over to the UK, they can learn new tracks very quickly – anything is easier than what they are used to.

While in California, I stayed with engine tuner George Wenn and his wife Frieda for part of the time. He showed me around his workshop and explained about his engine tuning, which was proving very successful since his move out there. I found it funny that his wife had picked up an American accent and sounded like she had always lived there but George still sounded like he came from the East End of London.

George's pride and joy was his Corvette sports car, which he showed off to me. He said that if I came out again, he might allow me to drive it.

I also got to meet one of the managers at Wynn's Products in Los Angeles, based on an introduction sent over from the agent I used in Ipswich. He took me out in a huge American car to sightsee around Hollywood and also took me to Dino's Lodge on Sunset Boulevard (owned by Dean Martin). Although I didn't see anyone famous, we had a very enjoyable lunch.

Towards the end of this trip, my wife Pat and kids flew out for a few days' holiday and we did the usual Disneyland, Universal Studios and Hollywood visits.

In November 1975, Ivan and Barry arranged a tour of South Africa, which I was only too happy to join. Another new country to experience. We started in Johannesburg, where I qualified for the individual WCSS (World Champions Super Six) Final and went on to beat Ivan, Ole and Barry. The next day saw us race in Durban, where I could only manage third behind Ivan and Ole.

After a few days, we drove to Rhodesia (now Zimbabwe) for meetings in Salisbury and Bulawayo. Both were run as Best Pairs events, with each of us teaming up with a local rider. Scott Autrey won the first one with his partner Dave Hemus, breaking the track record three times during the meeting. I was runner-up with Zak Koekemoer. In Bulawayo, I was reunited with a former Ipswich team-mate Peter Prinsloo and, again, finished in the runners-up spot (by a single point), this time behind Ivan and Dave Hemus.

Poor Egon broke a bone in his foot and had to spend a few days in hospital before flying back to Jo'Burg. He missed our trip that had been organised after the racing was finished – and what a trip it was. We had two days at a first class hotel at Victoria Falls that was spectacular to see, plus a sunset trip up the Zambesi river.

I had a very close encounter with a crocodile at a farm we visited. There were several of them dozing behind a fence and I thought I would give one a gentle prod with a stick to wake him up.

A rare shot of me racing in Australia. This was taken at Jerilderie Park, Newcastle, New South Wales.

Ole Olsen leading the way from 'Hitler' and 'Churchill' at Christchurch.

No sooner had the stick made contact than he reared up, snapped the stick in half and then looked straight at me, possibly viewing me as his next course. I won't be going near any crocodiles again in a hurry!

We returned to Johannesburg to catch a sleeper train to Cape Town, a journey that took an incredible 28 hours. I saw more local wildlife from the train when I was idly leaning out of the window as we travelled very slowly through a dense forest. A rather large, yellowish snake slithered from under the carriage, over the line that ran alongside and into the undergrowth. I quickly checked there were no holes in the floor in case he had any friends with him.

In Cape Town, I again qualified for the WCSS Final and finished second behind Ole and ahead of Ivan and Scott. Ole went on to win the overall WCSS title at the end of our four-week stay.

One other memory I have of that incredible trip was our visit to the Kruger National Park. A small group of us drove there with me at the wheel and when you reach the park, you have to go through a large gate, which is then shut behind you before a further gate is opened, allowing you into the park.

We made a typical tourist's mistake by stopping to watch a group of small monkeys. Predictably, they all leapt onto our car and, after a few minutes, our aerial was in bits and being thrown down the road. At this point, I decided enough was enough and I let out the clutch a bit sharpish, which resulted in monkeys flying off in all directions.

After that, we kept on the move and were lucky enough to see all the big animals –elephants, lions, giraffes, hippos, etc, at quite close quarters. It was a great day out and one we would all remember for a long time. In fact, the whole trip was brilliant from start to end.

The following winter, I headed back to New Zealand and Australia (no USA this year) with Ivan and Barry again but my travel was much more organised this time. I did, however, have another plane-related incident while travelling across New Zealand on an internal flight. I was sitting at the back when what looked like smoke started drifting into the cabin from the overhead lockers. I was terrified.

I jumped up and screamed: "Look at all the smoke, are we on fire?" Other people jumped up and more than a few started to look worried. A stewardess came rushing through the mist to ask me to quieten down and stop causing a panic. It turned out to be a small fault with the oxygen supply. I can look back on it now and laugh but, at the time, it was 'change of pants' time!

Unfortunately, I damaged a knee in Invercargill and, despite trying all sorts of treatment like acupuncture and physiotherapy, it was still giving me trouble when I got back to the UK.

JB was not impressed to hear I was injured before the season had even started. After watching me struggle for several meetings, in which I improvised a metal splint to pull the front part of my foot upwards so my knee wasn't jarred when it touched the ground, he took matters into his own hands.

He took me to a doctor in Valley Road, Ipswich and I was told that what he was going to do might or might not succeed. He hadn't used it on a knee joint before, mainly on back injuries, but thought it should work in the same way.

It was a cortisone injection but, first of all, he had to give me a local anaesthetic. I had injections from this very long needle in several places around my knee joint. The doctor then unscrewed the handle to the needle and filled it up with some new liquid . . . leaving the needle in my knee!

After about 10 minutes, by which time my knee was completely numb, he injected the cortisone into my knee joint several times. I was then sent home after being told it would either work within three or four days, or not at all.

Three days later and it felt better. A day or two after that, I was riding without any pain whatsoever. And it has been no trouble ever since.

I returned to the States in February, 1979, for another trip with Ivan Mauger and Barry Briggs. After the other successful tours I had enjoyed with them, I expected this to follow the same pattern

The wide open spaces of Christchurch, where I had my most memorable times in New Zealand.

but, sadly, it didn't.

I travelled out with Malcolm Simmons but confusion reigned from the first night when our hotel booking appeared to have been overlooked. An old friend, George Wenn, helped us out, otherwise I'm not sure where we would have ended up.

The next problem came when we saw the equipment we had been promised. It had definitely seen better days and, although we had taken our own engines, we had a lot of bike problems. The final straw came when Malcolm's van was broken into while he slept in a hotel and the thieves took a lot of his spare equipment and his ignition box.

As we still had one more meeting to complete, he approached Ivan and Barry to ask them if they knew where he could get a replacement. I'm not sure exactly what went on between them but they couldn't help him and he was less than happy when he came back.

He decided there was no point in staying any longer, as he needed to sort out some replacements for the start of the British season. As I also hadn't done very well, I said I would travel back with him – even though we had to pay for new flights home.

The only enjoyable thing that came out of that trip was a Weslake engine that George Wenn did for me when I paid him another visit. George used to stamp his surname onto his engines and they were unique in that he used to hard-chrome the moving parts to make them rev faster. I watched him test it on a speedway bike connected up to a dyno in a special test room at his workshop. He was revving it so high that the back tyre started to break up and the rubber was burning off, went up the wall and along the ceiling. The engine ran very well for a couple of months but when the chrome started to wear off, it wasn't as fast.

It was good to meet up with George again, though, and he kept his promise by allowing me to drive around in his Corvette during the few days I stayed with him.

Another trip that was both unusual and unforgettable was when Reg Fearman, one of the most prominent British promoters of his era, took a troupe of riders to Kuwait in the late 70s. The trip certainly opened my eyes to Middle East customs. We were looking around the speedway track, built inside a football pitch, when suddenly most of the players stopped their training, went down on their knees and started praying. After a while, we got used to the fact that this happened at regular intervals every day.

One of the football team's trainers ran over to me and said: "Hello John, how are you?" It was Ian Collard, a former FA Cup finalist with West Brom who had moved to Ipswich Town and knew me as a Witches rider. He was coaching in Kuwait at the time and he invited us out for a drink that night.

Knowing it was a dry country, we wondered what was in store. He took us to a house where there were a lot of British airline staff staying over before their next flight. There was beer fermenting in the bath and the bathroom cabinet was full of spirit bottles with optics on them. Reg joined in as well and we had a load of laughs.

We had also managed to 'smuggle' some alcohol through customs while being pushed through a fast-track system, meaning none of our luggage was checked when we arrived. I assume this was because we had been invited over as guests and were being treated as VIPs. If anyone had seen us out in a restaurant, they would have thought we all liked lemonade but, in fact, it was a bottle containing a certain Russian spirit that could be added to a bottle of coke to liven it up a bit.

I was with Peter Collins in a minibus on the way to the track when we pulled up next to a big American-style car with two females in the back. They were wearing the traditional veils over their faces, so you could only see their eyes. PC said: "Come on, let's have a giggle." We stuck our tongues out at them to see what reaction we would get. When we pulled up at the next lights, we knew they had seen the funny side. They pulled up their veils and stuck their tongues out at us!

The local organsiers clearly had not prepared many speedway tracks before, because it was too sandy and soon developed deep ruts after only a few laps of practice. It looked more like a moto-cross circuit.

Although far from ideal, we managed to put on a good display. It was mainly exhibition stuff, so we didn't have to go flat out. The football stadium was only about half-full and I don't think they attracted as many fans as the authorities had hoped for.

In the pits in Kuwait during our Middle East adventure in 1979.

Chapter 18

# Long Road To Halifax

**H**ALIFAX isn't the other side of the world but in British League terms it can seem that way when you are based in Ipswich and have to travel 200-plus miles each week to work.

It goes without saying that once the shock of John Berry dropping me from the Ipswich team had worn off, I was very keen to get a new team place sorted for 1981 as soon as possible and not have to deal with JB any longer than I had to.

He had circulated my name to other British League clubs knowing full well that only a few were likely to have a space to fit me in and that most were many miles away from Suffolk.

Soon afterwards, Eric Boothroyd from Halifax enquired if I would like to join them and, although one of the last places I wanted to travel to for my home meetings was The Shay, I had enjoyed some success there and always found Eric to be a very likeable, friendly person to deal with.

Unbelievably, even at this late stage, JB was denying in public that he had already dropped me from the team and was quoted as saying: "The biggest consideration must be John. He has been the backbone of the Witches for so long and given wonderful service."

What an absolute load of rubbish. He had shown me no consideration at all and was probably already planning how he was going to spend my transfer fee.

On February 28, it was finally announced that I had signed for Halifax. Eric Boothroyd said: "Louis will fit the bill for us very nicely – he has the experience and has been one of the top three

**Me and Ian Cartwright had to settle for the minor placings behind Kenny Carter in the 1981 Dews Trophy meeting at The Shay.**

Kenny Carter displaying some of his impressive machinery outside the farmhouse where his life and that of his wife Pam ended tragically.

British riders in recent years. He is the third most successful visiting rider at Halifax, behind Peter Collins and Ivan Mauger, averaging 10 points a meeting."

A couple of weeks later, the last piece of JB's plan fell into place when it was announced that Billy Sanders was moving to Hull in a move that would see the Vikings' American duo of Dennis Sigalos and John Cook join Ipswich. They went on to become big stars at Foxhall and I'm sure this maintained JB's turnstile numbers as per his business plan.

To be honest, I had no time to think about what was happening at Foxhall. I now had far more important things to do, like preparing for a new season at my new club. It all seemed a bit unreal but here I was, at the age of 40, starting afresh, riding for the furthest club away from my hometown (so JB definitely got his wish) and a four-hour journey just for my home meetings. My life was definitely going to be different from the previous 10 years.

My average with Ipswich in 1980 was 8.80, which was still a creditable figure, and I was to go on and average 7.82 and then 7.52 in my two years with the Dukes. To prove my fitness and reliability, I rarely missed a meeting, even at my advanced age, riding 45 meetings in my first season and 42 in my second.

Eric Boothroyd became a good friend, he was very genuine and a real character. He did all he could to help me settle in at Halifax and I shall never forget the way he used to suddenly do back-flips and somersaults on the centregreen whenever he got excited about something. Considering he was in his mid-50s, I have no idea how he managed such acrobatics!

Doug Wyer joined Halifax (from Sheffield) at the same time as me and he also became a great friend. In fact, he still calls in at Foxhall whenever Sheffield are racing against Ipswich and we reminisce about the 'good old days'. I also got on well with our skipper Ian Cartwright.

The other person who made a big impression on me during my two years in West Yorkshire was the late Kenny Carter, who had just turned 20 when I signed. I was one of the few riders in the Halifax side that Kenny regularly talked to. He didn't have much time for engaging in friendships with much of the team, such was his singled-minded attitude towards racing.

He was a very determined character and a succession of injuries that would have badly affected many a rider did not faze him in the slightest. Early in my first season, we were up against Birmingham with new signing Hans Nielsen in their ranks. Kenny suffered an engine failure while leading Nielsen in Heat 1. A few heats later, they faced each other again and Kenny was chasing the Dane hard, trying to pass him and join his team-mate up front. This went horribly wrong when, at the end of the first lap, Kenny clipped Nielsen's back wheel. He was thrown from his bike, face-first into the fence on the home straight at The Shay.

The St. John's staff went over to him straight away and immediately called for the ambulance, so it wasn't looking good. I wasn't prepared for what happened next. Kenny jumped straight to his feet and started to take his helmet off as he walked towards the pits on the entry to the first bend. As a couple of us approached him, we could see that he was spitting into his helmet – spitting his teeth, that is, as several had been knocked out in the fall.

It was later confirmed that he had broken his jaw in eight places and it had to be wired back together. That meant he couldn't eat solid foods for several weeks – his only meals were pureed and sucked through a straw. A measure of the man was that he was back riding just over a month later, scoring 17 points against Cradley Heath who included his greatest rival Bruce Penhall in their line-up.

Kenny often used to insist that I left Suffolk in plenty of time to call in at his place on meeting days. Before I got to know him, I thought of him as a bit of a tearaway but couldn't believe how organised and dedicated he was.

**Still life in the 'old dog' . . . leading for the Dukes ahead of King's Lynn's Dave Jessup and Melvyn Taylor (right) at Saddlebow Road in 1981.**

**I found Kenny Carter talkative and friendly during our two seasons together at Halifax.**

He had converted a derelict pub into a farmhouse perched at the top of a steep hill in Bradshaw, a rural village about five miles outside Halifax. There was a starting gate at the top of his garden and some moto-cross bikes he used for practice. It was just as well they had brakes because the circuit went downhill from the gate and, after making a start, he needed to be able to slow down before he went round the bottom of the garden and then rode back up to repeat the exercise.

But what impressed me most was what I was to find inside the very big Anderson shelter he used as his workshop. It was immaculate from the moment you walked in. First, on the right, was his office, which had a big desk and chair with everything he needed to manage his racing commitments. Everything was filed away neatly.

Next came his spares department where everything he might need – and more – could be found. Every type of spare part you could think of was there, neatly arranged and all in perfect condition. Further along were five or six speedway bikes, ready to race, all lined up in a perfect line, with all the front wheels turned at exactly the same angle. On the opposite side was his workbench and tools where he used to prepare his bikes. It was very impressive and I haven't seen many other riders in this country with that type of professional set-up.

Kenny came from a motorcycling family. His father Mal had been a club road-racer, while younger brother Alan was a highly successful international road-racer who went on to win the 250cc French Grand Prix in 1983.

Before I joined Halifax, I thought, like many others, that Kenny tended to over-ride and was a bit wild but after riding with him, I soon recognised that he had a lot of control and was far more intelligent a rider than people gave him credit for.

His wife Pamela, who was a lovely lady, helped him to keep everything so pristine, and the farmhouse they shared was a credit to both of them. All the improvements had been carried out to their specifications – they even had a sauna, which was a bit unusual for this country in the early 80s.

Kenny used to ask me to go back and stay at their place after meetings but I always wanted to get the journey back to East Anglia completed as soon as possible, so I would turn down his invites. We never had a cross word and he used to stress time and again that he was always there to help if I needed any assistance.

We did get in each other's way once, in a race-off to decide the British Final at Coventry in 1981, when we lined up against Steve Bastable after the three of us had tied on 13 points. Kenny and I were so intent on beating each other to the first corner that we forgot about Steve, who had made a flying start and left us standing, going on to a well-deserved win.

From Brandon we progressed to the Overseas Final at White City and then on to the Inter-Continental Final, held on a typically very wet Vojens track in Denmark. Kenny relished the poor conditions but, once the rain had set in, I struggled and failed to qualify for what would have been my third Wembley World Final appearance.

Kenny often felt that he was the victim of dirty riding because people resented his success. One

It said something for the mutual respect Kenny and I shared that he asked me to be in his pit corner for the 1983 World Final.

such occasion was a meeting at Ipswich, where the home team were missing their captain, Dennis Sigalos, who had sustained a broken ankle in an incident the previous week while riding against Kenny.

The crowd gave him a lively reception, as expected, but he just shrugged it off. Unfortunately, he ended up in Ipswich Hospital after a pile-up with Witches' Preben Eriksen left him with a badly bruised chest and lung. When I visited him, he was convinced it had been deliberate on Preben's part but I tried to assure him that it was just a racing incident. I don't think he believed me, though.

He did have very strong, single-minded views, he was his own man, but you had to respect him as a rider. He was always superb around The Shay and most other tracks as well.

Even after I had left Halifax at the end of 1982, our paths continued to cross for a couple of years. I was at Kenny's side in the pits at Norden, Germany, for the 1983 World Final, when he equalled the fifth place he achieved in the previous two finals. Little did I know then what he was going to get up to the following year.

The Kenny Carter injury that everyone remembers most is when he broke his right leg at the start of 1984, soon after being named England captain. Most riders would have accepted their fate and waited for the leg to heal before getting back on a bike. But Kenny was not a normal rider. In his desperation to have another crack at the World Championship, he had a special over-sized boot made which was reinforced with a steel panel for extra protection.

For the British semi-final at Oxford he had to be lifted on and off his bike by two men and I don't think any of us thought he would get very far with such a bad injury. But he proved us wrong by qualifying for the British Final at Coventry.

I'm sure everyone remembers Kenny arriving in the Coventry pits in his motorhome. He emerged on crutches and, as at Oxford, was helped onto his bike before each of his five races. It was

Dark day . . . the funeral of Kenny and Pamela was a deeply upsetting experience.

unbelievable to watch and showed his determination and bravery. He showed me the wound on his thigh, which was still oozing a bit, and he had to have it re-dressed a couple of times during the meeting.

The track was in a pretty bad state following afternoon rain and referee Lew Stripp was called down to inspect it after only three heats. I fell off on the slimy outside part of the track around the first turn in my opening ride and agreed with the 13 other riders who were asking for the meeting to be abandoned, because we thought it was too dangerous to continue. Kenny had a very heated exchange with Peter Collins and at least one other rider in the dressing room as riders said their piece.

History shows that the meeting did continue, with a fired-up Kenny riding through the pain barrier and winning the championship for the first time. I still can't believe the bravery and sheer bloody mindedness that it must have taken to ride in such bad conditions with a broken leg – he really was one of a kind.

Despite their behind-the-scenes fracas on the night, Peter Collins later admitted: "To win that British Final with a broken leg was unbelievable stuff, a super-human effort, and you can't knock it."

I never saw any malice in Kenny, so it was a terrible shock when, in May 1986, I heard the tragic news that he had shot dead his wife and then turned the gun on himself. It was such a waste and came just a year after Billy Sanders had also committed suicide.

I was one of the coffin bearers at Kenny and Pam's joint-funeral and found it deeply upsetting. In fact, I think everyone there found it highly emotional as Kenny and his wife were laid to rest side by side in a shared grave at their local church.

My time at Halifax was enjoyable and despite a round trip of 400-plus miles from my home to The Shay, I have to say that the fans up there were great to me. They were easy to get on with and I used to enjoy a quick drink with some of them at a country pub on my way home from The Shay.

The local dialect was a bit difficult to grasp at times and once I was stopped just as I was about to join the A1 by a policeman because I was going too fast while towing a trailer. He had a broad Yorkshire accent and I thought I would make it as hard for him to understand me as I could him.

Name? "John Louis." He understood that. Address? "98 Renfrew Road, Ipswich." I mumbled as quickly as I could, mistakenly giving my mum's address.

"How do you spell road?" He meant Renfrew, but I shouted out: "R-O-A-D!" He didn't take too kindly to that and promptly handed me a speeding ticket (another one for my collection).

I loved riding the big, banked Shay circuit. The outside line was one I used to really enjoy, placing my footrest an inch or two from the boards. Riding the inside there rarely worked for me.

The fans seemed to take to me as well, voting me 'Favourite Duke' at the end of my first season and the supporters' club gave me a 'Mr. Value For Money' award.

I didn't finish my time at Halifax as I would have liked, though. I broke my left arm towards the end of the 1982 season in a crash with Leicester's Mark Courtney. He dived hard under me coming into the third bend, causing me to be thrown off my bike, and I landed awkwardly.

It required an operation to pin my arm back together and I also had to have skin grafts to repair the damage to my hand. It was probably the worst injury I had during my whole career and was the result of someone else riding recklessly. I had always tried to ride fairly and may have moved people over on occasions, but had never gone in full bore with no thought of the other rider's safety.

It seemed strange captaining the 'enemy' but I enjoyed my time at King's Lynn. The 1984 team: Kevin Jolly,
Richard Hellsen, Martin Dixon, Keith Bloxsome. Kneeling: Dave Jessup, Steve Regeling.
Promoter Martin Rogers was one of the shrewdest in the business.

Chapter 19

# When It's Time To Stop

**A**FTER returning home to Suffolk at the end of the 1982 season, I had a lot of time to think while I was recovering and I realised that the travelling to and from Halifax was starting to wear me down and a move to a club nearer to home might be a good idea. I thought that I would probably carry on at Halifax if there was no other option but I very much hoped someone else would be interested in signing me.

I did also have a few doubts about how my hand injuries would affect my riding ability. My broken arm would heal okay but I had suffered tendon damage, as well as broken bones in my hand. I decided not to ride during the close season, apart from a few outings on my son's 80cc scrambler. My hand wasn't perfect – I didn't seem able to grip as well as before – but I decided that I wouldn't let it end my career (as a few were suggesting it would).

My prayers were answered when the new promoter at King's Lynn, Martin Rogers, asked if I would sign for them on his return to the club where he had been general manager in the 70s. I jumped at the chance and, although I would miss all my friends at Halifax, I couldn't wait to start with my new team.

After leaving Ipswich the way I did, this move felt right. I would be based a lot closer to home and not get so tired due to all the driving that Halifax had required.

Another positive factor was that I would be riding at one of the tracks I had always enjoyed and generally did well at (my son Chris went on to rate Saddlebow Road as one of his best tracks, too).

I did wonder, though, what type of reception the Lynn fans would give me because, in the past, I had been given a lot of stick when I rode there as Ipswich skipper. Ipswich and King's Lynn had a rivalry that stretched back many years and all meetings between the teams were fiercely contested, with fans from both sides very passionate in their support. I had lost count of the times when abuse and various objects were aimed at me as I did a lap of honour after a race win there in Witches' colours.

Those feelings were carried over to any individual meetings held at Saddlebow Road as well. During one Pride of the East, I ending up on the deck near the third bend fence, helped by a combination of Michael Lee and Dave Jessup, King's Lynn's top two. As expected, I was the one excluded from the rerun.

That was bad enough but there I was, laying on my back in a fair bit of discomfort and looking up at a blur of animated faces glaring down at me from above the fence mouthing, 'We hope you die, Louis'. I bet some of them choked on their cornflakes when they read that I had been signed up to join the Stars!

At the age of almost 42, here was a chance for me to bring the curtain down on my riding career at a venue where I was sure I could do well. And so it proved, as I upped my final Halifax average in the two years I was at Lynn – 8.45 (from 45 official league and cup matches) in my first year, followed by 8.29 (52 matches) the following season, which was not bad for an 'old man'. In both seasons I topped the Lynn averages ahead of two former World No.2s – Gordon Kennett (1983) and Dave Jessup (1984). I was also appointed Stars 'captain, so Martin Rogers certainly showed his faith in me.

One reason for still being able to perform well at the highest level of British speedway was my switch to a new engine tuner, Reg Randall, who was conveniently based in Reepham, Norfolk. I already had a good idea of how I wanted my Weslakes set up and often worked alongside him in his workshop. It wasn't long before we had an engine that worked extremely well at King's Lynn and pretty good at other tracks too.

Reg got to know my set-ups very well and generally did just as I'd asked. Although on one occasion he tried something without telling me. He often delivered the re-tuned engines to the track and when I came in after my first heat that night I asked him if he had altered the cam timing. He replied: "I don't believe you, I only altered it by two degrees . . . how the hell did you feel that?"

I had always been very sensitive to how my bikes handled and knew instinctively that something was different, even if it was only a small 'tweak' in his eyes. From then on, Reg never changed anything on the bike without consulting me.

Don't tell Phil Hilton (current Ipswich team manager and ex-traffic policeman) but I sometimes used to do the trip from my front door to the Lynn pits in an hour. That's 70 miles, along mainly country roads, with the expected journey time usually quoted as one hour and 40 minutes.

The thing that worried me more than what Lynn fans would make of me wearing their green-and-gold was the type of reception I would get from Ipswich supporters when I turned up at Foxhall leading the 'enemy'. I didn't have long to wait – these great East Anglian rivals traditionally met, home and away, on Good Friday.

But Witches fans showed no animosity towards me at all, which was great. I must have done enough in a blue-and-white racejacket to earn their appreciation, regardless of who I was riding for.

To be fair, it all went very well for me at King's Lynn and I found their fans to be just as easy to get on with and as supportive as Halifax fans had been. The fact that I started with a maximum in a challenge meeting and continued to regularly score double figures for them probably helped my cause. I enjoyed two great years riding virtually on my doorstep and with very little stress involved. To be honest, I absolutely loved it at Saddlebow Road.

Team-wise, I already knew Kevin Jolly – another one who used to be in the King's Lynn fans' top 10 for most hated visiting riders – from my Foxhall days, and soon got to know and get on well with Richard Hellsen and Mel Taylor as well.

The 1983 season was a good one and I finished the year with a four-ride maximum as we won the Anglian Cup on aggregate – against Ipswich.

I was more than happy to accept the offer to ride for a second year at King's Lynn. Dave Jessup joined us from Wimbledon as a replacement for Gordon Kennett and we soon resumed our friendship dating back to those glorious World Team Cup days a decade earlier. He was a great little rider and a good addition to the team.

My ability to keep the big scores coming in, even at this late stage in my career, led to my qualification for the 1984 British Final and a recall to the England side for the World Team Cup qualifier at Saddlebow Road in May. New England manager Carl Glover had seen his team badly beaten 4-1 by the American around that time, so was looking to shake things up.

Bobby Schwartz was USA's captain at the time and as I went past him leaving him for dead in one race, I waved as if to say, 'thanks for letting me go by'. He took it in good part, despite calling me a cheeky so and so afterwards. I always found the Americans could take a joke and Bobby was no exception.

We finished second, just two points behind USA but qualified for the next stage by scoring seven more points than Australia. Although I finished as our joint-second highest scorer behind Simon Wigg, with eight points, I wasn't really expecting to be selected for the Inter-Continental Final round at Mariestad, Sweden on June 23. This time, although I only managed one point, we went through to the final as third qualifiers behind the Yanks and Denmark., with Sweden eliminated.

It wasn't the way I had wanted to end my long and largely illustrious England career but I can look back on many happy memories at international, as well as club, level. I wasn't too surprised to be

Still making quick starts. John Cook is alongside me in this 1984 local derby encounter at Saddlebow Road.

replaced by Peter Collins for the final at Leszno, Poland, where England – minus the injured Kenny Carter and Michael Lee, who had been banned by the SCB – trailed a distant second to the Danes.

The Danes were establishing themselves as the major force in world speedway in the mid-80s but I can reflect on some good meetings against them too. When Simon Wigg was injured in June, I received a late call-up to ride in all four home Tests against Denmark, which we won 2-1 with one meeting drawn. I scored double figures in the first match at Reading and again in the series decider at Halifax, where my 10 points turned out to be our margin of victory that afternoon.

My individual season finished well when I finished on the rostrum in the Star of Anglia at Ipswich. I almost managed to repeat my win from 1979 but Hans Nielsen scored one more point and I then lost a race-off against Chris Morton for second. Hans also took the Pride of the East trophy at my home track and I again finished third, this time behind Kelvin Tatum.

**One thing that did leave a nasty taste in my mouth was *The People* newspaper's race-fixing allegations towards the end of the 1984 season. Their main focus was that Simon Wigg had cheated during qualification for the World Final that year. It was also falsely claimed that I had been asked to throw a key race in the British semi-final at Oxford and had been paid £250 by Wigg and Malcolm Simmons for doing so. Several other riders were also implicated in their revelations but there is no need to mention them all here because, like me, most, if not all of them, were completely innocent of any wrongdoing. The Sunday tabloid then went on to describe speedway as corrupt and 'rotten to the core'.**

Although Simon and Malcolm were both found not guilty of bribery and corruption, they were found guilty of 'conduct prejudicial to the sport'. As a result the Speedway Control Board, who also imposed £1,000 fines on both riders and ordered them to pay costs, banned them from contesting the

1985 speedway World Championship.

I could only state my own case and I knew that I had done nothing wrong – as was proven at the SCB disciplinary hearing held in Belgrave Square on March 25-26, 1985, when I was totally cleared of any wrongdoing.

Every race I rode in, whether it was speedway or scrambling, I went out to win. I had never, in all my life, rolled over and let someone pass, either as a favour or for some type of reward.

I think the newspaper and its undercover reporters who interviewed Wiggy and Simmo at their homes were ignorant of many facts about speedway but the adverse publicity from a few weeks' coverage did a great deal of harm to our sport at the time. As often happens, what those reporters didn't know, they made up in order to generate lurid headlines.

A journalist came to see me for an interview about the allegations surrounding the British semi-final at Oxford. I thought it was a casual chat, as I knew I was in the clear, but unbeknown to me, he was carrying a tape recorder hidden in what he told me was a camera case. I carried on preparing my bikes while we talked, oblivious to the fact that he was gathering 'evidence' to back up his theory that I was part of a big conspiracy. This is what I related to him and what actually happened in my final race at Oxford:

*It was a wet evening and the track was very muddy when I lined up for my last race of the night. I had already qualified on 11 points and, with the deteriorating conditions, I wasn't about to stick my neck out unnecessarily.*

*The easiest thing to do if I was going to 'cheat' would have been to miss the start fractionally and then get stuck at the back in the grimy conditions. I was on the outside gate but still made the start alongside the other three riders. We went into the first bend together but I got badly filled in and struggled to clear my goggles.*

*I just couldn't see where I was going and eventually ended up pulling off my goggles in the vain hope that I could carry on. This was a bit optimistic, as my glasses then got covered in shale as well and I reluctantly accepted that I wasn't going to get anything from the race. Would I have tried harder if I needed more points to qualify? No, it simply wasn't possible to race in those conditions if you couldn't see where you were going.*

The journalist tried to suggest that I had stopped deliberately. It's true that while I was trying to clear my vision, I would have naturally slowed down, allowing the other riders to pull away from me, but there was nothing sinister in my actions. It was just a bit of self-preservation.

Surprise, surprise, the journalist twisted my words and a load of lies came out in the newspaper. I had stated very clearly that I was not approached, let alone offered any money to let other riders win. But he didn't let the truth get in the way of the story as he saw it.

Justice prevailed in the end and the SCB ruled that I had done nothing wrong. For the record, I never saw or heard of money changing hands to fix races at any meetings that I was involved in.

That particular episode was my first experience of how a journalist can change a few words and completely alter the context of an interview. It certainly wasn't going to be my last.

Back to Saddlebow Road. I may have topped the King's Lynn averages again in 1984 but I certainly wasn't thinking about calling it a day.

Martin Rogers was a top promoter and usually had a clear vision of what his team should look like. He asked me what my plans were during the 1984-85 close season and I replied that I was unsure.

He didn't show any great enthusiasm for taking the conversation much further and, when all things were considered, I couldn't say I blamed him. I wasn't getting any younger and, at 43, I guess he decided I was too much of a risk.

In my heart, I didn't want to retire but my head told me that it probably was time to call it a day.

**Back in England colours against Denmark at Wolverhampton in 1984.**

If another promoter had shown some genuine interest and it wasn't from a club based on the other side of the country, I would have considered signing up for another year but the phone didn't ring.

Hans Nielsen had always said that he would retire at 40 and I had gone nearly four years beyond that. He also said that he would hire a Rolls Royce and take his wife Suzanne out for a posh meal if he ever scored a hole in one at golf. When I heard that he had done it, I could not stop laughing and, of course, golf became a big part of Hans and his family's lives, with his daughter Daisy going on to become a professional.

I'd had a great innings and a wonderful time but now I had to accept that it was all coming to an end. Regrets? No, I had none.

I'd done all I'd set out to do and much that was beyond my wildest dreams when I hesitated about whether I was up to taking my first laps of Foxhall Stadium 15 years earlier. I'd captained my country, won gold medals and world titles, plus I'd helped win many honours for my hometown club.

Wherever I rode, my aim was very simple: to pass the chequered flag first ahead of all my opponents. The feeling when I achieved it was just as good when I was nearing retirement as it was when I was starting out.

Basically, I just loved riding speedway, no matter where it was or what condition the circuit was in.

I think it's fair to say that I was good at speedway, okay at long-track and not so good at grass-track. But I adopted the same philosophy for all three and 90 per cent of the time, I achieved what I set out to do.

My forte was getting my set-ups right. My prep. work continued at the same level right through until my final season. During the first half-an-hour or so of a journey home from an away meeting, while my mechanic drove I would get out my 'bible', as mentioned previously, and religiously keep everything up to date.

What went in was the information I've revealed before, plus what ignition I'd used and how

**Leading at Lynn from team-mate Richard Hellsen and Newcastle's Eddie Ingels and David Bargh.**

many races before I had changed gearing. Every tiny detail went into that book and before my next meeting at that track, I would study it and prepare with the confidence that I would be on the pace from the word go.

It is one reason why I have always said I never had a track that I didn't like riding. I took the approach that some may be more challenging than others but if you got your set-up right and went into the meeting with the right attitude, it was possible to win on all of them.

Starts were especially important to me, as they are with any rider. If it was slick, I would sit a bit more upright in the saddle with my arms more outstretched. If it was grippy, I'd lean further forward to take the weight off the back wheel, so that the bike would not lift out of the start.

I was always searching to see whether there was a better way of getting myself to the first corner in the lead. Once the tapes had gone up, your front wheel is ideally only an inch or two off the ground to provide maximum traction. As my bike went forward, my knees used to go down to face the track with my feet in a straight line behind, again to help with traction.

In my early days, all of this was new to me and I had to learn by trial and error. I had to teach myself and, due to the methods I used, it didn't take me too long to make progress. It is the main reason, I believe, why my career took off so quickly, from raw rookie to World Finalist in a couple of years or so.

Of course, I rode the track at Foxhall more than any other in my time in the saddle – and there was always a plan if I missed the start.

Personally, I liked the shape before the alterations were made in 2011. The long straights and tight bends offered better home track advantage and it was something that I gained immensely from.

Nowadays, yes, it provides more of a spectacle with its shorter straights and more sweeping turns but I think I was still able to generate plenty of excitement and entertainment for Ipswich supporters during my time there riding the 300-metre (328 yards) circuit.

If I was behind after the first two bends, I would ride the inside for a couple of circuits and on the third lap go outside, hopefully catching my opponent by surprise. Alternatively, I would go round the outside for a couple of laps and give the impression that I was set to do the same next time around, but would then cut back inside. It used to work more often than not and as much as I preferred to win races the easy way from the tapes, I used to get more satisfaction winning the hard way and giving better entertainment for the fans.

All the top stars came to Foxhall after we moved up into Division One in 1972 and I liked nothing better than to play cat and mouse with someone like Ivan Mauger, before swooping past him on the last bend to bring the house down. Basically, what worked for me so well at Foxhall worked at any track, whatever the size, shape or condition. I could tell after the heat was over how much more the fans had enjoyed the race when there had been plenty of passing, especially on the run-in to the line.

Fans love to see their side win, first and foremost, but it would be fair to say that a big home victory doesn't always tick all the boxes, especially if the racing is a bit processional. Speedway has all the ingredients to thrill and when a meeting contains plenty of closely contested racing, it will make an evening out more memorable for supporters, sometimes even if the result is not what they wanted.

The more experience I gained, the easier it was to 'feel' when someone was getting close enough to pose a danger. I did not have to turn my head or move, I knew when the pressure was on and I had to pull a bit more out.

On the other hand, if I found myself a long way ahead of my nearest opponent, I used to try alternative lines and different approaches to corners. Sometimes I saw people shaking their heads when I returned to the pits. "What the devil were you doing out there?" or "why did you cut back so quickly on that bend?" I would be asked.

My reply would be that nobody was pushing me, so I was doing some 'work experience'. I never knew when I might need to know how the track was 'working' and if a really tough race came along a few heats later, I would be prepared for every eventuality as it happened.

Even now, when I am out and about around Ipswich, people recognise me and come up and say: "You gave me so much pleasure at Foxhall in your riding days." How wonderful is that? Firstly, they still know who I am and, secondly, I must have entertained them and left them with some good memories from that time.

You don't get something for nothing in this life and, yes, I did put the hours and the effort in but what a pleasure it was to be doing something I loved for so long and get paid for it. I considered myself very lucky to have found a career that I enjoyed so much and clearly gave so much enjoyment to others.

One last thing before I sign off about my riding career . . .

All speedway riders need a good man in their pits. Mechanics not only help prepare and maintain the bikes but also act as travelling companions, so you all have to get on. They need to have the ability to say the right thing at the right time in the pits when the pressure is on and, in my case, know when to leave me alone.

John Bloomfield did the most travelling with me and was very quiet and unassuming; he just got on with his job and did what I asked. I trusted him 100 per cent, although I did run out of methanol at King's Lynn one night! Otherwise, he did everything to perfection from day one.

I also had other fine men in my corner at different times, including, of course, my dad, Colin Robinson, Brian 'Brassy' Goodchild and Mick McPike. They all did a great job and I was so lucky to have them working for me.

There was only one area they were not allowed to interfere in. I always set my own clutch, because I knew exactly how I wanted it to behave off the start.

With the bikes packed away and my leathers hung up for the last time, now it was on to the next stage in my life . . .

**Mick McPike, one of my regular mechanics, joins Pat, Christopher and myself in admiring these unusual prizes in 1977.**

All good things must come to an end . . . before my last BLRC at Belle Vue in October 1984.

JB, Billy and Chris Shears in a rare light-hearted moment before the sadness and misery of the 1985 season.

East Anglian Daily Times, Wednesday, April 24, 1985  Page 19

# The Australian who was an instant hit

## 'He never lost his sense of fun'

BILLY Sanders first rode for Ipswich in 1972 as a fresh-faced 16-year-old only a month out of school, *writes Mike Horne.*

The Witches had just bought West Ham's First Division licence after three years in the Second Division and contacted Sanders' parents in Sydney after hearing rave reports of his form at his local track.

His parents refused to let him come to England at first, but they relented in time for him to race in Ipswich's first senior league match against Hackney, which was watched by a record crowd.

Sanders an instant hit with the fans. His first season was marked by remarkable performances on the track and regular visits to hospital after youthful enthusiasm and inexperience landed him with injury problems.

Within two years Sanders had reached international

standard, forming a famous Witches heat leader trio with John Louis and Tony Davey.

These three riders were largely responsible for Ipswich dominating the British speedway scene in the mid 70s.

They won the British League championship for the first time in 1975 and followed it up with the League and Cup double the next season.

Sanders was already one of Australia's leading riders. He was a member of the side which pulled off one of the biggest World Team Cup shocks when they won the title at White City in 1976.

The following year Sanders reached another milestone in his career when he made his first appearance in the World Championship final, scoring six points in

Gothenburg, Sweden.

He then captured the Australian national title to emphasise his claim to be Australia's number one. He went on to win the crown five more times.

In 1979 his association with the Witches ended, if temporarily, when he moved to Birmingham to become their number one and captain.

Ipswich ran into team problems early in the season and by September Sanders was back in the fold.

By now he was a regular World finalist. He produced his best performances so far in the 1980 final, again in Sweden, when he completed a memorable night for East Anglian speedway by finishing third behind King's Lynn riders Michael Lee and Dave Jessup.

Sanders, with John Louis,

then left Ipswich in the winter of 1981 as part of a big shake-up which saw Americans Dennis Sigalos and John Cook take over as the new Foxhall favourites.

Sanders went to Hull as part of a £30,000 deal which brought the Americans to Foxhall, but he never settled with the Vikings. The following season he moved to King's Lynn, where he became a great favourite with the fans.

Although he had left the Witches he could not bring himself to leave Suffolk, which he loved almost as much as his own home in Werrington County, on the outskirts of Sydney.

He and his wife Judy bought their first English home in Hadleigh and they later moved to Trimley.

When John Cook failed to

return for the 1983 season Ipswich team manager John Berry quickly moved to re-sign Sanders from King's Lynn. He immediately struck up a tremendous partnership with Sigalos.

They became firm friends, led Ipswich to runners-up position in the British League and both qualified for the World Final in Norden, West Germany.

### Superb

This outpost of World speedway was the scene of Sanders' finest performance in the sport's top individual event.

He was deprived of the World title only by a superb display on his own track by Egon Muller, but Sanders was delighted with his runner-up position.

With Sigalos moving to

Wolverhampton at the start of the 1984 season Sanders finally took over the role which had eluded him for so long — the Ipswich captaincy.

Although the club was expected to struggle, having lost two top riders, Sanders led his side brilliantly to the British League and Knock-Out titles.

He described it as the greatest season of his career, although he flopped in the World finals at his favourite Gothenburg track when rated one of the big favourites.

He returned to Sydney last winter, vowing to take a break from speedway to spend more time with his wife and family. However he raced on, despite rumours of matrimonial difficulties, to win the Australian title again and book his place in the Overseas Final at Bradford later this year.

### Personality

He returned to this country

Billy is still fondly remembered by those who saw him rise from rookie to world class rider.

Chapter 20

# End Of An Era

**A**SK any Formula One driver or speedway rider what he will do when he retires to replace the thrill of accelerating from 0-60mph in less than a minute, or passing the chequered flag first after a battle of wits and skill with your opponent, and he will struggle to think of an answer.

You can go on to coach, manage or simply watch, which can all be very enjoyable, but will never come even close to what it feels like to take part in a motorsport. Regardless of the fact that your life is potentially at risk every time you go out on track, the euphoria you experience when you join forces with your machine and beat the very best is simply irreplaceable.

So what was I going to do now that my riding days were over? I'd reached the grand old age of 44 and it was time to look for something new. I needed something that would keep the adrenaline pumping through my veins and give me new goals to strive for.

John Berry was still at Ipswich, although he was no longer the sole promoter. A London-based businessman, Chris Shears, was now working alongside him with the intention of taking over the club completely after he had settled in.

It had been a wonderful season for the Witches in 1984, beating Reading at Smallmead to win the league and then completing the double by lifting the Knockout Cup after defeating Belle Vue in the final.

JB was straight on the telephone as soon as he knew that my riding days were over and asked me to go back to Ipswich and work for my old club. That was fine by me and as the riders prepared for the 1985 season, I was learning about track preparation, working on sponsorship and getting ready to serve my first stint as a team manager.

I had also become a partner in a garage business based in Brightlingsea, Essex, called Brightford Motors. One of the other two partners, Dave Stone, was a regular at Foxhall. We had a Ford agency and also dealt in used cars. The plan was to specialise in fleet selling to East Anglian-based companies and I attended a sales course to help prepare for my new role at the garage.

It was like being back at school but I learned a great deal about how to deal with customers – how to approach them, handle their queries and 'guide' them towards a sale. I travelled to Brightlingsea every day for a while and, yes, I sold some cars, but my heart was still in speedway and I really looked forward to my new duties at Foxhall.

It was not long before I realised that I was not so good at obtaining sponsorship as I was at riding a bike, and I have to hold my hands up and say that my track preparations trailed in behind what George Osborne did before me and Bob Ellis has achieved since.

A track curator's job is not easy and you need to be able to have a sixth sense most weeks about what the weather is going to do. Ultimately, that would lead to me leaving Ipswich for a second time but I was happy to get stuck in and learn what I could.

One day, I was driving the water tanker around the circuit and I must have lost concentration, because suddenly a number of fence panels came hurtling past the cab window. I'd strayed too close to the wooden fence and the nuts from the front wheel had got caught in some panels, pulling them out of the supports. I had to set about mending them all before I could carry on with the watering.

George Osborne did the job when I was riding and he was a true craftsman. He was so good that riders did not have to talk to him – he knew what they wanted and how to achieve it. Other clubs, in my opinion, did not have people with the same skills as George, which sometimes presented me with a less than ideal racing surface but, as I have already mentioned, all tracks were there to be ridden.

Compared to George, my skills as a track curator were about average. And when Bob Ellis took over the job, he was able to get things back up to the previous highest level again. Bob learned his own techniques as he went along and, like George, must have travelled the equivalent of round the world given the number of times he has circled the Foxhall track.

It makes you wonder sometimes where speedway would be without the Georges and the Bobs and the hundreds of others like them around the country who work on various tasks to ensure that around 30 meetings take place every week throughout the season. They are the backbone of our sport and deserve far more credit and recognition than they get.

John Berry was always going to be a hard act to follow and Chris Shears' keenness to make a name for himself in speedway meant his head was on the block. The fact that he stayed in Harrow, Middlesex to run Chalfont Coaches during the week and only travelled up to Suffolk on Thursdays was not going to sit too well with the Ipswich public, who were used to JB being based locally and spending many hours at Foxhall.

I got on well with Chris, although I realised that he had an impossible job on his hands. Nobody could match what JB had achieved and I don't think any promoter at any club has ever come even close. JB was very brave in what he did, taking gambles on local, untried riders like me to make the grade and his decisions all paid off handsomely.

He was still pulling the strings in 1985 with Chris by his side and with Billy Sanders (skipper), Jeremy Doncaster, Richard Knight, John Cook and Nigel Flatman still in the side from the previous year, we were all set up for a good campaign.

Our traditional double-header against King's Lynn on Good Friday went better than any of us had hoped for. Ipswich won both meetings and Billy scored maximums in each one, despite suffering from flu.

Billy went on to drop just two points in four League Cup matches and appeared to be in the form of his career. He also won the Golden Helmet against Chris Morton in what turned out to be his last race at Foxhall. In fact, I believe he could have won the World Championship that year based on the way he was riding in those early weeks – he was absolutely on fire.

However, unbeknown to us at the time, there was something going on in his personal life that was causing him a great deal of pain.

BILLY SANDERS
IPSWICH ADOPTED SON
1955 – 1985
REMEMBERED BY ALL
AT IPSWICH SPEEDWAY

**The bronze plaque in the Foxhall pits in honour of a Witches great.**

Other side of the fence . . . encouraging young Alan Farmer in my first season as team manager.

We were due at Wolverhampton on Monday, April 22 but Billy didn't want to ride. He asked to see JB and myself and told us that his wife Judy had stayed in Australia with their young daughter Belinda while he had travelled over to England alone with their eight-year-old son Dean. He hinted that they were having marriage problems and asked to be excused from riding that night. He said he wanted time to have another talk with Judy in the hope that she might still come over and look after Dean.

JB was of the opinion that Billy riding at Wolverhampton that night would help take the problem from his mind, or at least take his mind off it for a while. I backed him up but Billy was insistent that he did not want to ride and, eventually, we relented. We thought it was best for him to have a break, sort things out and then come back all guns blazing to continue his fantastic start to the season.

Of course, at the time, we did not know what may have already been in Billy's mind. If we had, we would never have agreed to let him miss the Wolves meeting.

The next morning, on the Tuesday, I got up and went through my usual daily preparations, half listening to the radio while I ate breakfast. When I heard the newsreader announce that "Billy Sanders, the Ipswich Witches speedway star, has been found dead in his car", my world momentarily stopped. I could not believe what I had heard and my first thought was to jump in my car and get to Foxhall Stadium, so I could ask JB what was going on.

When he confirmed the tragic news was true, I was devastated. It was one of the biggest shocks of my life. We did not speak much for quite a while, we were both completely stunned. When we did finally talk, we discussed whether we should have insisted that Billy rode at Monmore Green instead of excusing him, saying that he was suffering from tonsillitis.

We thought at the time that we were left with little option than to agree to Billy's request. But should we have been firmer, however stressed he was? I know hindsight is a wonderful thing but we felt that if we had been stronger, perhaps he might still be alive.

It transpired that Billy dropped Dean off at school and then drove to a quiet, wooded area, at

Seven Hills, Nacton, on the outskirts of Ipswich, where he parked up, connected a rubber hose to the exhaust and took his own life. A passing gamekeeper had found his body. Billy was 29.

Billy was a very likeable bloke but could be quite fiery at times. Everything was either black or white in his eyes, there were no grey areas. We did have another nickname for him in the Ipswich camp, and that was 'Billy Bugner'. This came after he thumped someone on the centregreen at Sheffield around the same time heavyweight boxer Joe Bugner was making his mark in the ring.

There was also another time at Reading when Billy was again upset by an on-track incident. On his way back to the pits, he had the other rider up against the concrete wall near to the stand and JB had to step in and calm things down. Perhaps because I was older, I was able to handle situations in a calmer fashion. If someone or something wound me up, I would use it to my advantage and channel the aggression towards winning the next time we met.

Billy was a really nice guy most of the time, we did many laps together and there was never any trouble between us. While we did all we could as team-mates to win meetings for the Witches, along with Tony Davey, all three of us desperately wanted to be the Ipswich No.1.

He did achieve No.1 status eventually and Shrimp, I'm sure, would have done so as well if he had not been so unlucky with his injuries. Of course, this friendly rivalry benefited the club while the three of us competed for that top spot. We consistently outscored many other heat leader trios in the process.

Second-half racing was big in those days and we tried our hardest to beat each other every week. The rider-of-the-night finals were fought tooth and nail, although the riding was always fair. Financially, it didn't matter who won, as we always split the prize money equally among the finalists.

JB had to identify the body, having been Billy's legal guardian when he first came over to England from Rooty Hill, Sydney, New South Wales in early 1972. I know he found it a very harrowing experience. Billy's mum Bonnie came over to attend the funeral and to look after her grandson Dean.

The coffin was draped with a Witches banner, an Australian flag and Billy's racejacket. I was among those who accompanied the cortege on foot around one lap of the Foxhall track before we left the stadium and travelled to St. Augustine's Church in Ipswich for the funeral service.

There were a phenomenal number of people outside the stadium and along the road. The service inside the packed church was fitting and very poignant. Many of Billy's Ipswich team-mates, past and present, were there, including Bruce Penhall and Dennis Sigalos.

Bruce did a reading and also read a note that Dean had written after his father's death which ended: "I love you so much. I wish you had not died." Dean went back to Australia soon after with his grandmother but how tragic was it that, in July, 1988, aged 21, he should take his own life, saying he had gone to be with his dad.

Billy will always remain in the hearts of his many Ipswich fans and there is a plaque and kangaroo painting on the wall in the Ipswich pits that is meticulously maintained to this day. The painting was done by John Cook, Mitch Shirra, John's mechanic Mike Rooney and Terry Wright. They based it on a design from a set of leathers Billy wore.

Not surprisingly, Ipswich had lost the home meeting between Billy's death and his funeral but we all picked ourselves up and reached the Knockout Cup Final, hoping to win it for the club's former Australian hero. Jeremy Doncaster and John Cook were on a 5-1 in the final heat of the second leg at Oxford that would have seen an aggregate victory for Ipswich but John inexplicably collided with his team-mate, allowing the home riders to burst through.

Initially, we were granted the rider replacement facility to cover for Billy and, after the team had settled down, we managed to start climbing the league table. At that point, several rival promotions started to complain that the R/R was giving us an unfair advantage and after a lot of to-ing and fro-ing, the BSPA told us we could no longer use it.

After all that we had been through, it was a big blow and at a time when we needed support from other clubs, we got the usual short-sighted attitude that comes from jealousy of other people's success. Dennis Sigalos came back to ride after an ankle injury in October but it was too little, too late and Witches finished fifth in the league.

A traumatic 1985 campaign came to an end with the news that JB was to leave Ipswich. I could see the events of that year had taken their toll on him and wasn't really surprised when he made his announcement. He had been at the club for 17 years and taken us from very small beginnings to multi-championship winners in that time.

JB had had enough of John Cook and speedway by the time he quit at the end of 1985.

His drive and passion had driven us upwards and brought great rewards, for both him and the club, but all good things must come to an end and, looking back, it was probably the best time for him to walk away. Ironically, he cited a poor relationship with John Cook as one of the reasons for him quitting – the same John Cook he had been so keen to bring in as a replacement when he booted me out.

It was the end of an era.

Yes, JB had done very well in his time at Ipswich but he was far from being the only winner. Where would I have been if he had not brought speedway back to the heath and encouraged my career switch? Where would the rest of the Ipswich riders have been? We had all experienced so much enjoyment and success.

And where would the Ipswich public have been? Attendances grew to around five figures during the good times and JB had always provided great entertainment for the fans to enjoy on their Thursday nights out at Foxhall Stadium.

Could Chris Shears – hclpcd by my good self – keep the momentum going?

John Cook (outside) and Kai Niemi on their way to a 5-1 at King's Lynn.

A quiet word with Jeremy Doncaster before a race at Bradford in 1986.

Chapter 21

# Moving On To Happy Hackney

**A**FTER the events of 1985, I was hoping for a smoother ride as I entered my second year as team manager at Ipswich. But it was to be another rollercoaster of a campaign.

It began with Dennis Sigalos deciding to stay in California, which posed a few challenges with the team-building, but eventually we assembled what we thought was a good septet and even the departed JB gave it his approval.

The opening challenge meetings didn't go too well but Good Friday saw a complete demolition of arch-rivals King's Lynn in our traditional double-header where the aggregate score was a whopping 101-54.

League racing proper had just started and was going okay when John Cook suddenly decided that he wasn't happy with the terms of his contract and wouldn't be turning up until it was sorted out. Withdrawing his services at this point in the season didn't endear him to anyone at the club or on the terraces.

One of the most exciting riders to watch at his peak and someone who had gone from almost unknown to a top international rider at Ipswich, 'The Cowboy' was not always the easiest person to deal with.

This left us with a big gap in the side and trying to find suitable guests was an ongoing headache. We also suffered an unusually high number of rain-offs at home, which didn't help with continuity for the riders or fans.

In the middle of all of that, I experienced the lowest point of my year when I heard the news that Kenny Carter had shot his wife and then himself. I was shocked and devastated to hear that more young lives had been ended too soon and in such a violent way. I knew Kenny was very volatile but still couldn't grasp how he had reached the point of no return. As mentioned previously, I attended the very emotional funeral to pay my last respects to my ex-team-mate.

Back at Foxhall, problems were piling up for Chris Shears and the transfer of John Cook on loan to Sheffield didn't help his cause. There was a distinct lack of suitable replacements available and I think the fans started to get impatient at what they saw as a lack of effort on our part. Opinions were voiced that Chris Shears being based in London wasn't working and 'it would never have happened in John Berry's day'.

Personally, I didn't see his absence as a problem and was happy enough doing what was necessary, including track preparation during the week and seeing him on Thursdays from lunchtimes onwards. I'm not sure if I suffered because of the frustration Chris was experiencing trying to run the club amid what seemed like constant team changes and falling attendances, but everything came to a head between us in September.

We had lost to Coventry and, according to Chris, I was totally to blame because I had provided a surface that was too slick for his liking. He decided it was time for us to part.

We had experienced plenty of rain and, looking at the track at lunchtime, it was deep and soft but not waterlogged. I thought by the time 7.30pm came around, given the good forecast, it would have dried out enough to be almost perfect. So I went off and did other things in preparation for the meeting. It turned out to be a pretty warm, autumnal afternoon and the dirt dried out faster than I had anticipated. Chris liked to see plenty of grip, which was fair enough as it normally produced better racing and therefore kept the fans happy – plus, our home riders were expecting it.

When he confronted me, I had to admit that I had made a misjudgement but, to be fair, the racing that night had been good, despite our defeat. The Bees had in their side a Czech rider, Roman Matousek, who had picked up an engine from Trevor Hedge in Norwich on his way to Foxhall and he absolutely flew, scoring a 15-point maximum. In my opinion, the main reason why we had been beaten was because this guy was simply on fire.

However, I did not feel any animosity towards Chris as I walked out of the pits for what I thought might be the last time. With so many brilliant memories of Foxhall and the Ipswich Witches, yes, it was a sad journey home and I wondered whether that wonderful link had been lost forever.

My departure did cause a big stir in the town at the time but, for my part, I just hoped Chris would be able to turn things around so that speedway would continue at Foxhall. There was still the day job at Brightford Motors and I took a complete break from speedway as the winter of 1986 turned into the spring of 1987.

I did read with interest during the winter that John Berry had been named as a potential new 'director of operations' at the BSPA. Along with many others in the sport, I thought it sounded like an excellent idea. Unfortunately, John later turned the job down after he found out during the winter conference that he didn't have the backing of all the British and National League promoters. It was such a shame, because I think he had the ability and courage to make huge improvements to how British speedway was run.

**At that time, my son Chris was making a name for himself on the youth grass-track and moto-cross scenes and I was anticipating spending much of my spare time going round the country with him. However, it did not turn out that way. Before the start of the new season, I found myself at Hackney in the position of team manager.**

I'd become friendly with businessman Dave Pavitt, whose son Lee was often riding in the same grass-track meetings as Chris. Lee was a very good exponent of the sport, along with a large number of other talented youngsters. Many of them went on to make a name for themselves in speedway, including Gary Havelock, Joe Screen, Mark Loram, Sean Wilson and, of course, Chris.

Dave was running Hackney along with Garry Muckley and Mike Western at the time and he phoned one day asking me to link up with them. I think they fancied gaining from my name and my experience. The East London-based side had been persuaded to move up to the British League and Dave, who had made his money from an office cleaning business, felt that I could play a part in getting the club re-established in the top flight.

Having a London side in the British League – which had suffered the blow of losing five tracks in the winter of 1984-85 – was seen as a positive move by the BSPA but the promised assistance from other promoters to help build a competitive HL1 Kestrels team didn't materialise. The only riders we had of a suitable standard were Simon Wigg, who was loaned from Oxford, and skipper Malcolm Simmons, who had ridden for the Kestrels at NL level the previous season.

I did the best I could with the team I had but we struggled at that level. Crowd levels started to fall and that, combined with the increased running costs in the higher league, was not a recipe for success and we finished ninth in a league of 12.

There were a few bright spots in the season, with 16-year-old first season rookie Mark Loram and Andy Galvin starting to show their potential. A stand-out meeting was our visit to Oxford, where on a surface made heavy by rain, Mark scored double figures against far more experienced riders. He was still so young but had already shown a glimpse of what he would one day achieve on the world stage. I looked forward to seeing his career develop further.

During the close season, I had to say goodbye to another close friend who was tragically killed in his own workshop. Joe Harvey was a wheelwright by trade but could basically turn his hand to

**Dave Pavitt and I are delighted to see Simon Wigg sign as Hackney's No.1, although we needed more all round strength.**

anything. Over the years, he had done various things for me, such as building a new kitchen from scratch, building a big garage/workshop and then designing some really nice metal gates for the end of my driveway (which I wish I had kept). We had become good friends and I remember going to his workshop where I was fascinated to see him make wooden wheels for the old-style carriages.

I was very upset to hear that he had died after a piece of his clothing got caught in a lathe, causing his head to repeatedly bang against it until he was unconscious. By the time he was found, it was too late to save him. They very fittingly carried Joe's coffin on its final journey in a horse-drawn carriage he had helped to rebuild.

A few weeks later, it was time to start preparing for the new season and 1988 was to prove more enjoyable and much more successful than the last.

I had expected to spend the next season in the top league again but, after a late decision not to honour a lower points limit that would have given us a much better chance of signing two decent heat leaders, Dave Pavitt and his co-promoters were left with no option but to rejoin the more cost-effective National League.

Despite all the problems of 1987, dropping down did not initially sit well with me because I had been involved in the top flight throughout my career after those initial two years at Ipswich. However, I set about putting together a young side that I knew had bags of potential. I then did my homework and decided to bring in two established riders with the right pedigree to lead the team.

Disappointingly, one decided to stay in the British League and the other opted for another National League club. So I was left to convince Dave, Garry and Mike that we had enough young assets at Hackney who would be able to do the job.

I decided to go with Andy Galvin, Paul Whittaker (returning after a loan spell at Canterbury), Alan Mogridge, Mark Loram, Gary Rolls and Barry Thomas.

Just before the first practice session, the directors decided to sign my son Chris to see what he could do at No.7. I wasn't convinced he was ready but had to go with the majority decision. It was the first steps in speedway for Chris, who went on to become known as 'Trapper Louis' that season. At just 18 and with no previous racing experience, it was a bit of a risk but it certainly paid off for him and the team.

Dave Pavitt was a very good promoter and there was always a nice atmosphere around the club. We got on really well and often travelled abroad to watch speedway together. He also had this quirky dream where he got to watch his team win a trophy, thrashing the opposition, but with him being the only spectator in the stadium. Everyone had heard the story and we often pulled his leg about it.

'Pav' had a good deal with one of our sponsors, a couple of Greek brothers who served us dinner at their Phoenix Apollo restaurant in nearby Stratford on race-day. I often went with him and I remember noticing on my first visit that there were a lot of very attractive young women in the bar, including several that looked familiar. While I was casually glancing at one of them as she waited for her drink to be served, Dave leaned towards me and said: "That's Sam Fox, the Page Three girl, in case you were wondering." I hadn't recognised her with her clothes on!

Apparently, most of the girls who went there were models but, of course, we only kept going back because the steaks were so good!

Dave did take some convincing that Hackney's 1988 side would be good enough, particularly when he realised that we had the lowest combined average of all the clubs in the league.

"How on earth can we win the league?" he asked. "Don't worry," I said. "You watch them go on the track, I am confident they will go on to become the best team in the league." My fingers were firmly crossed behind my back.

One of the most important and successful decisions I made that season was to appoint Andy Galvin as captain. He wasn't keen, by any means, as he perhaps lacked a little bit of confidence – not

Doing the double in style with Hackney in 1988. Back row: Alan Mogridge, Andy Galvin, Gary Rolls, Paul Whittaker, Mark Loram and my son Chris. Front: Little Legs, Pav, The Reverend and Garry Muckley.

'Trapper Louis' leading Middlesbrough's Martin Dixon in the 1988 NL Fours finals at Peterborough.

in his riding but in the way he could influence his team-mates.

Andy just wanted to ride as fast as he could and win as many races as possible, without having to be concerned with anything else. His professionalism was obvious when he turned up for pre-season practice with two brand new Jawa machines.

Talking effectively to other riders was something that he had to learn and, because of his laidback ways, it perhaps did not come that easy at first. But he turned out to be a tremendous leader and, in the end, I was so pleased that I stuck to my guns and convinced him to take the role.

Once he had settled into the position, the extra responsibility helped Andy and soon afterwards the team all started to look up to him as their leader, someone who was always there to help them, on and off the track.

The management team saw no changes for the season, with Garry Muckley and Mike Western continuing in their roles. Mike was a keen speedway fan who was brought up just behind the third bend at Exeter's County Ground circuit. He had answered a call from Dave Pavitt in the *Speedway Star* for some financial help at Hackney.

We also had a couple of other great characters at the club. Bryn Williams was the press officer and much more besides. He was on the centregreen for every meeting, acting almost as a joint-team manager and giving me a wise head to bounce ideas off.

The other one was far less visible but cheered us all up before any home meeting had even started. Tony Hurren, or 'Bird Brain' as he was called, wrote a column in the programme and all of us made a point of reading it before we started on our various pre-meeting activities.

Peals of laughter could be heard from all the offices as we sat reading his latest thoughts and observations. Here's a little taster:

*It's a Fact – Wimbledon riders have been banned from having sex the night before a meeting and their wives are up in arms about it. Although JL hasn't taken the same hard line at Hackney, two of the wives of our promotional tripartite have said their husbands must refrain on a Thursday night so they are fully fit and alert for their management duties on Fridays. Have a look at Pavitt, Western and Muckley tonight and the one that looks happiest is the one that did get some 'exercise' last night…*

Tony also had nicknames for all of us. I was 'Little Legs' (still used to this day), Mike was either 'The Reverend' or 'La-di-dah Western' and Dave was simply 'Pav'. His wife Jane was known as 'the delectable Jane'.

So we set off in 1988 with a good management team, an excellent skipper and a young lad at the bottom end of the side with the potential to make a big impact. And the rest of the team wasn't bad either.

Our wildest dreams came true with the Kestrels winning the league championship and the Knockout Cup, and setting a new NL record of only dropping six points during the whole campaign.

It turned out that my team building was spot-on. The riders were truly a great bunch of lads who built up a superb team spirit and wanted to win a heat as much for their team-mates and the club as for themselves. That team was the perfect blend of youth and experience, coupled with a tremendous bond.

The crowds flocked back to Waterden Road and we went on to benefit from taking out an insurance policy against winning the league.

Mark Loram topped the averages with a remarkable 9.94 (excluding bonus points) and, despite being only 17, was runner up in the National League Riders' Championship and won the British Under-21 title. I first saw him ride grass-track aged nine, and could tell then that he was born to ride. He didn't need much help, he was a natural, and if he hadn't suffered a wrist injury and a few engine failures, he would probably have topped the league averages.

Andy Galvin was not far behind on 8.92, while third was ever-present Chris Louis on 7.67. Alan Mogridge and Paul Whittaker also rode in every league meeting.

Not only did Andy set the world alight with his own performances, he also played a huge part in the early development of his regular partner Chris' career. Andy was a clever rider and he also had determination. He used to say to Chris: "You get yourself to the first corner alongside me and I'll do the rest."

They clocked up numerous 5-1s and I could see a lot of myself in Andy's attitude. He worked hard with Chris that year. Chris went on to be top scorer (13 points) on the night we clinched the league title.

Chris made his Foxhall debut in June when he guested for Wolverhampton, scoring four points, and followed that up by riding for Ipswich (in place of Gerd Riss), scoring paid eight. He was also capped for Young England.

Alan Mogridge, who ended the season with an average of 6.17, was a lovable bloke who never knew when to give up. He was a 100 per cent rider who always rode his heart out.

Paul Whittaker was next in the averages on 5.82 and he was another rider I really got on with. He once brought his souped-up sports car to the club and asked me if I wanted to try it out. I drove it cautiously out of the stadium and onto the main road. At this point, we were heading for the A12, so I decided to put my foot down a bit – the wheels immediately started to spin as it accelerated like a rocket and, before I knew what was happening, the speedo needle had passed 100mph. It was my type of car and by the time we got back, I was more than a bit jealous of Paul for owning such a monster. All great fun. And fun is what it was all about that year.

Barry Thomas averaged 5.82 and Gary Rolls 4.99, with Paul Bosley and Shawn Venables coming in for two meetings each.

Having Barry in the side gave us a rider who was unbelievable around Hackney and capable of producing a vital win just when you needed it. Gary did his job perfectly and once kept us in a meeting at Long Eaton before Andy Galvin made sure of victory in the last race.

I was enjoying my trips down the A12 to Hackney but things were about to change with trouble afoot at Ipswich and the situation ripe for a new era to begin at Foxhall Stadium.

It was great to manage the 1988 National League double winners. This was taken after Hackney had beaten London rivals Wimbledon in the KO Cup Final. Back row, left to right: Barry Thomas, Mark Loram, Chris, Paul Whittaker.
Front: Alan Mogridge, Paul Hurry (mascot), Andy Galvin, Gary Rolls.

National League promoters gather for their 1989 National League winter AGM in Tenerife. Dave Pavitt, Mike Western and myself are among them. We had decided by then that the Hackney promotion would also take control of Ipswich.

Unmasking of the mystery homecoming witch at Ipswich's 1989 opening meeting, which heralded another new era for me and the club.

Left: Proud dad moment when I joined Chris on the rostrum after he'd won the Star of Anglia. Right: Chris and I carry Mark Loram from the Coventry track after he signed-off on his National League career with victory in the 1989 NLRC.

Chapter 22

# Back At Foxhall

**W**HILE I had been enjoying an unbelievable season at Waterden Road in 1988, it had not been such a great year for Ipswich. In November, 1988, it was announced that Chris Shears had been kicked out of Foxhall.

The stadium landlords, Spedeworth, who ran stock cars at the venue, stated that he had not honoured his contract and that they had made their decision for the sake of speedway in the town. Apparently, he had failed on several counts, including work not being done to sort out problems with drainage and staging less than the contracted 30 meetings. I think the final straw came when the season finale, the 16-Lap Classic, was cancelled due to a lack of riders.

After a lot of speculation in the local press where some of the facts were perhaps a bit distorted, the headline 'Top Team Set To Take Over' appeared in mid-November. Someone had worked out that we, the Hackney promotion, were interested in taking over the club but had jumped the gun slightly. It was to be well into the New Year before everything was finally settled and we could confirm that we were taking over at Ipswich and that we would be running in the National League, as rivals to the Kestrels.

The first person to telephone me with congratulations when he heard the news was . . . John Berry. He said he had always hoped I would return to run the club and, despite a few detours, it had now happened. Little did I know that John was in the process of planning a new life; in July that year, he and his new wife Linda emigrated to Australia.

The man who played a leading part in making everything happen was the late John Earrey, who was employed by Spedeworth as their stadium manager. He always looked after the interests of his employers but, at the same time, John was determined not to see Ipswich Witches suffer. He felt the speedway club and their fans deserved to be looked after much better than they had been since John Berry's departure.

John Earrey had previously been a high profile figure during meetings at Foxhall in my riding days. He was the centregreen announcer and kept the fans entertained in a way that I have not seen done since. The fans in the home straight grandstand used to throw Mars bars at him because he happened to mention one day that he liked them. I'm sure he collected enough at some meetings to feed us all for a week!

His joke-telling always had the crowd in stitches and he was very good at getting them behind the team, with his Witches' war-cry ('give us a W . . . '). Of course, his sign off catchphrase, 'As long as we know', is still fondly remembered by many today.

We managed to attract a major sponsorship deal with the late Dave Hunting, of Hunting Hire, whose company name appeared on the team race-jackets, which was a first for us. With me moving back to Suffolk, we knew it would make business sense to bring my son Chris and fellow up-and-coming youngster Mark Loram with us from Hackney.

Alan Mogridge also made the transfer from East London and was appointed skipper. Dean Standing, 19, was signed from Eastbourne with two Australians, Craig Hyde and Steve Widt, coming over to fill the reserve berths. Local youngster Robbie Fuller completed the side.

Chris and Mark had spent time riding in South Africa while Dean had spent the winter in New Zealand, so at least three of our team were race-fit going into the 1989 campaign. Our first home meeting was rained off, so we finally got started on Good Friday in front of a (very welcome) 3,000 crowd. The afternoon started with a mystery rider, dressed as a witch, completing a lap of the circuit. He looked like an old hand, albeit a bit rusty. When the mask came off, yours truly was revealed. Did I hear someone say: "Put the mask back on!"?

We won that first meeting, which was the first leg of a Knockout Cup tie, with an impressive 60-36 scoreline over Middlesbrough and went on to win the second leg as well. However, Wimbledon prevented us from progressing any further, beating us in the second round.

Unfortunately, I had a bit of a falling out with Dave Hunting over a misunderstanding about a local lad, Jonathan Cooper, signing for the club. He had tried out for us and I did expect him to join properly at some point but the boy went off and signed for Peterborough, which is when Dave got upset. It all got blown out of proportion in the press but we soon got over it and I remained on friendly terms with Dave until his sudden death last year (2014).

We did have a few team changes that season. Craig and Steve injured themselves when they collided riding in a junior challenge at Hackney and we replaced them with Pete Chapman and Warren Mowatt. Kevin Teager then replaced Warren after only a few meetings. Ipswich went on to finish a respectable fourth (out of 18) in the NL.

Chris and Mark Loram both enjoyed individual successes that year. In July, Chris won the Star of Anglia Trophy at Foxhall, exactly 10 years after I won the first staging of the meeting. It was another 'proud dad moment' when he was presented with his trophy.

Mark won the National League Riders' Championship in early September and, along with Chris, qualified for the World Under-21 Final in Lonigo, where Dean Standing went through as a reserve. Chris finished second in Italy after a race-off against the Dane Gert Handberg, with Mark coming fifth after a pointless first outing. Dean scored five points.

As a club, we were very proud to have three of our riders performing at that level and it proved

I've seen plenty of cups in my time as Ipswich rider and promoter but none quite as big as those revealed to me on the centregreen at Foxhall in 1990. But sshhh, don't tell Frank Ebdon!

that the youngsters we brought on at Ipswich were some of the best.

Not long after that, the news broke that Mark was moving to King's Lynn in 1990, which was inevitable really. He had wanted to move back up into the British League in '89 but Dave had persuaded him to spend another season in the second tier with Ipswich.

It was a natural progression for a rider with Mark's potential and I already had ideas about some possible replacements I could bring in. To his credit, Mark continued to give 100 per cent to Ipswich until the end of the season, finishing runner-up in the 16-Lap Classic behind his old Hackney skipper Andy Galvin.

An off-track incident that left co-promoter Mike Western fuming was caused by referee Frank Ebdon fining him £50 for bringing the sport into disrepute. His 'crime' was to receive a strip-o-gram on the centregreen during the interval. Apparently, Mr. Ebdon wasn't impressed that he had to wait for the young lady to take her clothes off and finish her show before he could restart the meeting. What a party pooper!

Mike's response was that he believed the fine was in retaliation for an earlier meeting when he had reported Frank for starting a race while the grading tractor was still out on the track. He also pointed out that I had received a similar strip-o-gram a few weeks earlier without being penalised for it.

It was just as well I didn't get fined, as I was traumatised enough by the strip-o-gram itself! I'm not sure if the same person booked both of them or not, but Mike received a very attractive, slim young lady dressed as a policewoman, whereas mine came in, shall we say, a 'plus' size. I became concerned that I was expected to pick her up after she had stripped down to her red undies but that wasn't going to happen without the help of a forklift. I'm only little and if I had fallen down the front of her bra, only my feet would have been visible!

Mike Western and I were both surprised and pleased to be named 'Promoters of the Year' and the club also received a 'Best Prepared Track' award at the end of the season.

Posing for the traditional pre-season team shot with our new sponsors for 1990. The riders are (standing, left to right): Robbie Fuller, Craig Hyde, Billy Lellman, Alan Mogridge. Front: Dean Standing, Chris, Shane Parker, David Norris.

As a sign of how obviously happy Spedeworth were about how we were running speedway at their stadium, they offered us a two-year lease in October. The down side was it came with a significant increase in the rent payable, so we had no option but to increase admission prices for the 1990 season. They appeared to have forgotten about the large sum of money we had invested in the new drainage system, which was as much a benefit to them as it was to us.

We started the new decade with new team sponsors, Connells Building Supplies, and several new team members. We had brought over Shane Parker and Billy Lellman from Australia and signed another emerging young talent in David Norris from Eastbourne. Craig Hyde, Dean Standing, Moggo and Chris completed the team.

Billy rode well initially but things then took a turn for the worse. I took a call one night at home from the police who had found Billy wandering around Ipswich, not knowing where he was. I picked him up and took him back to his digs. A few nights later, the same thing happened again.

It was obvious that Billy was having problems and, after seeing a doctor, he was detained in a psychiatric hospital in Ipswich, not that far from the stadium. I believe it was eventually diagnosed as depression that had been brought on by the death of his father two years earlier.

Most days, I went to visit him and we used to chat – nearly always about the same thing: how his father had pushed him into riding. His mother came over to take him home and it was great to hear later that after taking the correct medication, he was back to full health again and happy with himself.

In fact, he rang me up after a few months and asked if he could come back and ride for Ipswich again. But having already replaced him, I had to turn him down gently.

His fellow Aussie Shane Parker fitted in well and you could see that he had potential. He came over with his own tagline – 'flat out and lovin' it' – and he was a great entertainer out on the track, quickly becoming a firm fans' favourite. Parker had admired the late Billy Sanders' approach to the sport and told us that he wanted to follow in his tyre tracks at Ipswich, with the aim of achieving at least as much as his idol.

It was a team of energetic youngsters that year, with Chris finishing up as the No.1 with an average of 10-plus per meeting. He could only manage runner-up in the NLRC but more than made up for any disappointment by winning the World Under-21 title in Lvov, USSR. Several of us travelled out to support him and it was an incredibly proud moment for me when he was standing on the top of the rostrum while they played the British national anthem.

Being a former moto-cross rider helped Chris on a circuit where a heavy shower had left puddles laying on the inside line. I told him that good starts were very important and to then ride a sensible line for the rest of the race. He carried out my advice to the letter and reaped the rewards, finishing on 14 points.

However, I think Chris could have done without the Russian way of parading the new champion – they produced one of the largest horses I have ever seen. I could look underneath it without bending and Chris really didn't want to get on. But he had no choice because the soldier who was leading the animal helped him up onto its back and led a terrified Chris out to the presentation area.

More fatherly pride came when Chris was named Young Rider of the Year by the *Speedway Star,* in recognition of his World Under-21 title and rapid progress that year. All of this led to rumours that he may leave Ipswich to move up to the top league.

The whole Ipswich team experienced some international challenges that year. First, we entertained a team from Russia that we beat 66-30, before travelling to Rzeszow and Tarnow in Poland to race two meetings. Although we lost both matches, we enjoyed good hospitality.

I had hoped for better but we finished third in the National League that year, one place higher than 1989.

In 1991, the National League and the British League were amalgamated, with four teams (Ipswich, Berwick, Poole and Wimbledon) moving up to the British League. There were plans for promotion and relegation between the two leagues to allow movement. I wasn't convinced that it was a good idea, because the administration side of the National League was so well run, merging it with the top layer could make it more complicated and time-consuming for clubs.

Meetings would now be run over 15 heats, with the final race for nominated riders. Heat 2 would be a reserves' race and all seven riders would have four programmed rides. Teams would receive a bonus point if they won on aggregate after home and away league meetings.

There was good news and bad on the team front. We retained Chris, Shane Parker and Dave Norris, who had already indicated they were ready for the top flight, but lost Alan Mogridge and Dean Standing, who both preferred to stay in the NL. The first new rider we went for was a local youngster, 16-year-old Ben Howe, who looked to have a lot of potential in the sport.

Dave Pavitt and I were mulling over a few ideas on how to fill the rest of the team in the speedway office at Foxhall Stadium one day because we needed to bring in at least one more quality rider to boost our chances of doing well in our first year of top flight racing.

"Was there anybody in Lvov who would be worth taking on?" he asked. I immediately thought of the young Swede, Tony Rickardsson, who had finished third on 10 points. I told Dave how he had caught my eye by overcoming a number of obstacles, changing his bikes and doing all he could to get the best out of himself in the difficult, rough conditions. When he had missed starts, he went through the field in some style and I felt he had what it took to become a top rider.

I had obviously convinced Dave because the next thing he said was: "Go and get him now."

"What, now?" I stammered. Dave was adamant and I was pleased, if a little shell-shocked, to be setting out the next day for Stockholm.

It was arranged that I would meet Tony at the airport, where I had booked a return flight that would bring me back to London on the same plane. We chatted and I was introduced to his dad Stig, who had unknowingly helped shape my style in my scrambling days. I had adopted his way of standing longer after I had watched him ride in meetings at Shrubland Park, near Ipswich. I soon agreed a deal with Tony and was on my way back home.

Czech rider Zdenek 'Sam' Tesar, who had been a senior world finalist in 1990, and Frenchman Phillipe Berge completed the team. The only thing left was to choose the new skipper and Chris got the nod.

It was to be the beginning of a long, successful association between Tony and the Witches, which would see him lead us to great heights in later years. As we all know, during that time, he developed into one of the best speedway riders in the world, eventually winning the World Championship a record-equalling six times.

And I would like to think I helped him reach the dizzy heights he achieved. At the 1991 Ipswich press day, he came up to me and asked for some advice. "I'm happy with my riding, but not with my starts. Can you help me, please?"

If anybody has had their life shaped in half-an-hour, then the next 30 minutes may well have done so for Tony. As you know, as a rider, I went to great lengths to ensure that I was getting to the first corner ahead as often as I could and I still had diagrams and drawings from the time I spent working on my starts.

I advised Tony on how to position his arms, how to straighten his back, where to sit on the bike and to drive his knees towards the ground, trailing his feet when the tapes went up. It didn't take long for Tony to master these new techniques and he was soon flying from the tapes. I watched him throughout his career and he was still using them right up to the end.

Chris also benefited from my advice in his early years and, even though my racing days ended in

1984, I could still see myself in action on the track when Tony and Chris were riding.

Sam Tesar had a different starting problem in that his starts weren't really legal. Referees eventually got wise to what he was up to and put a stop to it. Watching from the pits, we could all see that his back wheel was already moving when the tapes went up, giving him a huge advantage.

It's tricky to explain but he would push his right foot in front of his foot rest and lock it with the additional assistance of his other foot arched in front of the left side 'pin'. He would have his throttle going, but without any weight bearing down on his seat. When the tapes went up, he would drop himself onto his seat and, with the back wheel already spinning, he would be off like a shot. Good if you can get away with it!

Ben Howe had natural talent but his starting technique also needed work and, to me, his equipment did not always look as though it was quite up to standard. Hopefully, these things would improve as he watched other riders and became more professional.

None of the team we assembled for the step-up had any top flight experience, yet we were able to compete on an equal footing and finished a creditable sixth in the table. We may not have won the league but some silverware came our way when Shane, Chris, Tony and David won the Fours Championship at Peterborough, finishing seven points ahead of second-placed Cradley Heath. On the individual front, Tony Rickardsson finished an impressive second to Jan O.Pedersen in the World Final at Gothenburg, while Chris finished third in the British Final.

We had re-established ourselves in the top flight and the terraces at Foxhall were starting to buzz with excitement again. We were now set to push on and bring success back to Ipswich.

I was back out on a bike briefly for Jeremy Doncaster's testimonial at Reading in August, where I beat Peter Collins in a match-race. We were neck-and-neck for three-and-a-half laps, with him always slightly in front, but going down the back straight for the last time, I had to go in really hard around the last two bends to just beat him over the line. That felt good!

Another very proud day . . . Mike Western and I in Russia with Chris moments after he won the World Under-21 title.

**Back in the silverware as 1991 Four Team champions at Peterborough.**

A new name appeared on our sponsors' list in 1991 – Tim Woodward, a farmer from Old Newton, who had only started watching the sport during the previous season. He was already hooked and was very keen to help out by sponsoring several of the riders. Without people like Tim, many riders would struggle to get started and I know his sponsorship made a big difference to the lads he helped during that season and for many years to come.

Tony Rickardsson, one of Ipswich's greatest-ever signings, with club sponsor Tim Woodward.

Chapter 23

# Battle For Survival

**B**Y now, I had settled down to my new career as a promoter and enjoyed working alongside Dave and Mike. The icing on the cake was that I was doing it at my hometown club. My main job was team-building and, although it could be very stressful at the start of the season, I really enjoyed helping new riders settle in and mentoring anyone in the team who needed advice on their riding technique, bike set-up, etc. Some needed more perseverance than others, while others got it right almost straight away.

This is something I continue to be involved with today and I still get the same sense of satisfaction when I see someone take my advice and go on to fulfil their potential.

During the 1991-92 close season, I had been involved in several training schools. One was for 20-plus young Polish riders at Mildenhall that came about through Chris riding for Wroclaw. They arrived by ferry at Dover and took a bit longer than expected to reach Suffolk. After joining the M25, they missed their turning and, instead of taking the next junction, did a complete circuit of the motorway before finally turning up the A12!

They were a bit shocked when they saw the small, tight West Row track but over a couple of days we got most of them up to a reasonable standard and they all seemed to enjoy themselves. In fact, we staged a small meeting on the last day with Chris acting as the referee. I also got asked to run a school at Brokstedt in Germany and when I arrived, my old 'roomie' from New Zealand, Egon Muller, was there, so we had a good catch up and did the training together.

Anyone who knows me will confirm, without hesitation, that paperwork is not my thing, which is why I left as much of that as possible to Dave and Mike. In fact, by now Mike was on the BSPA management committee, so who better to deal with all the admin. work they required from each club? I did have to attend some of the general council meetings and the AGM and, although I found them hard work, I had to accept they were a necessary part of (hopefully) working with other clubs to improve the sport.

We had managed to keep most of the 1991 team and decided to look further afield for new talent. As he was also riding in Poland, Chris recommended a number of riders. His No.1 choice was Miroslaw Kowalik but he was unable to commit to a full season in the UK, so we signed Jacek Rempala who had impressed on a previous visit to Foxhall in our NL days.

We also had a good reserve side, the Sorcerer's Apprentices, which, at that time, rode in a separate league intended to bring on young British riders. Brian Messenger looked after these lads and riders such as Lawrence Hare and Savalas Clouting started to demonstrate their potential. Ben Howe also benefited from riding in this league, on top of his senior team appearances.

Believe it or not, I came very close to riding in the World Pairs again in June! I had travelled out to Norden in Germany with Chris and when we arrived people were starting to panic, as the ACU paperwork hadn't arrived. Just before the meeting was due to start, a fax came through giving permission for Gary Havelock, Paul Thorp and *John* Louis to take part. Just as I was wondering if I could borrow Chris' leathers, Eric Boocock, the England team manager, said that he would prefer it if Chris took part. The team went on to win the semi-final in some style.

Just a few days later, Chris and I had donned top hats and were standing in the garden of Buckingham Palace eating cucumber sandwiches and sipping cups of tea. We had been invited to attend a Garden Party to honour World Champions – I think Jeremy Doncaster was there as well.

I had been successful in the World Pairs and multiple World Team Cups, while Chris had won the World Under-21 title.

This time, I didn't get to speak to The Queen when she arrived on the lawn but it was still a big honour for us, and I could see that everybody else there felt the same. Chris and I were happy to nod our regards as Her Majesty moved past us but for boxing star Chris Eubank, who was standing close by, that was simply not good enough. He was out of his corner like a shot. We watched as he quickly walked further down the line and wriggled his way through to the front again, only to be missed for a second time, much to our amusement. He had probably spent hours choosing his outfit as well!

After a slow start, Jacek Rempala began to show signs of the talent we knew he had but then he missed a few meetings because he had to return to Poland for rescheduled meetings over there. It did give Sal Clouting a chance to step up and gain some more experience in the main team but Dave Pavitt, in particular, was not impressed with the lack of commitment from Jacek. A short while later, we brought in another Swede, Tony Olsson, to replace Jacek and he did a good job for us.

Our young reserve team did exceptionally well that year, winning both the Reserve League Championship and the Reserve KO Cup. Little did we know that this would be the last time these trophies would be used.

At the end of the '92 season, I was voted Promoter of the Year, although I'm not entirely sure why because we finished only seventh in the table.

**Another year, another rule change – 1993 saw the introduction of an 18-heat format with eight-man teams. It caused the demise of the reserves' league, as there would be no time to fit in their races at the end of a meeting. However, two of the juniors would be given team places in the senior side – in our case, Savalas Clouting and Shaun Tacey.**

When we took over at Ipswich, we gave ourselves four years to produce a championship-winning

The *Executive Committee of the Central Council of Physical Recreation*
*requests the pleasure of the company of*

Mr John Charles Louis

*at a Garden Party at Buckingham Palace*
*by gracious permission and in the presence of*
*The Queen and The Duke of Edinburgh*
*on Thursday, 9th July, 1992 from 4 to 6 p.m.*

*Lounge Suit*

**Another proud occasion in my life and a second appearance before The Queen.**

side. Up to this point, we had made good progress but were hoping that 1993 would see bigger strides towards lifting some silverware.

Chris, Sam Tesar and Tony Rickardsson were signed up and Ben Howe was promoted to the senior team. With David Norris opting to sign for Eastbourne, we were dealt a blow when Shane Parker picked up a bad foot injury in Australia, sidelining him for five months.

After a couple of false starts, we brought in Mitch Shirra on loan from Swindon. He was a committed and likeable character who always had good equipment. He served us well for two seasons but there were times when he was unable to control his temper. I remember one meeting when he was so incensed by the referee's decision that he stormed up to the control room, barged in and voiced his opinion in no uncertain terms. Allegedly, he also bit the referee's ear but whether that was true or not, I don't know. Things were certainly never dull when Mitch was around.

It took us a while to gain a work permit for a second Pole, Miroslaw Kowalik, but, like Rempala, his stay was curtailed as he also failed to deliver what was needed. We were several months into the season and not making the progress we wanted.

In July, at the tender age of 52, I became a grandfather for the first time when my daughter Joanne and her partner Mark Loram had a son, Rhys. With Chris and his wife Julie expecting their first in a few months' time, and my two-year-old daughter Maria (with second wife Magda), there were suddenly a lot of very small people joining the Louis household. To this day, I still wince when I hear, 'Hello Grandad'. My reply is always: "Can you just call me John or JL . . . 'Grandad' makes me feel SO old', but they just do it even more!

We also lost another good friend that year. Paul Osborne ('Oz'), one of our loyal mechanics, was tragically killed in a road accident. He had always been a great help to all the riders, travelling many miles driving them to meetings, and would be sorely missed. A remembrance plaque hangs on the pits wall in his memory, near to the one for Billy Sanders.

My proudest moment that year had to be in August, when I saw Chris on the podium at the World Final in Pocking, Germany. I firmly believe he could have finished higher than the third place he achieved but it was still a fantastic result and he was only 24. Apparently, we were the first father and son to appear in a World Final and, of course, Chris had matched my own third place finish of 1975, so another matching milestone for the family scrapbooks.

Around that time, and despite significant competition, we signed Leigh Lanham on his 16th birthday. Leigh had enjoyed a lot of success riding grass-track but he had decided to follow in his dad's tyre tracks and take up speedway. Mike Lanham, of course, had been a team-mate of mine back in the 70s and it was great to see his son sign for the club.

From the very start, Leigh was an out-and-out professional with first class machinery and a preparation that was second to none, something he has continued to the current day. Totally dedicated and a very good team man, Leigh is a much better gater than his dad and that ability has won him many races over the years.

With Leigh coming into the team for the injured Shaun Tacey, and Shane Parker returning from injury in August, we finally started to see some good results, climbing off the bottom to finish eighth in the league.

**It was a real body blow to the club when Tony Rickardsson announced he would not be returning to the UK for the 1994 season. His reasoning was that he would have a much better chance of making an impact on the world scene by limiting his club commitments to his native Swedish League, along with Poland and Denmark. He would still be riding in 50 meetings a season but, with the continental leagues always running on a set day of the week, Tony was able to plan his schedule much easier.**

Shane Parker was sidelined for months in 1993 with a foot injury he suffered in his native Australia.

It was a blow when Tony Rickardsson decided to opt out of British league racing in 1994 but he made it pay by winning the first of his six individual world titles.

Leigh Lanham followed in his dad's tyre tracks at Ipswich but he was a better starter than my former team-mate.

MP Jamie Cann, his wife Rosie, my son Chris and Bradford's 1992 World Champion Gary Havelock. Jamie was a big help in raising awareness for the 'Save Our Speedway' campaign.

The BSPA AGM was held in Cyprus that year and, when I returned, I had a new job – joint-England team manager with James Easter, who was then co-promoter at Peterborough. We replaced Eric Boocock and Colin Pratt, who had taken over from John Berry, so Suffolk was set to have a big influence over the national team again.

The 1994 season started with yet another team/meeting format change – this time, we went back to seven riders and 16-heat meetings. We decided to appoint Brian Messenger as the 'official' team manager – he had gained a lot of experience during his many years in charge of the reserve team, which we didn't want to lose. I still held a team manager's licence and we both attended all meetings. Two heads are better than one, as they say, and we had some great times travelling to away meetings together. We both enjoyed driving 'on the edge' when conditions allowed, although I think Brian's common sense chip cut in a lot earlier than mine!

I now had a bit of spare time to oversee track preparation, which we knew would be key after the introduction of dirt deflectors. Plus, our track curator George Osborne was forced to retire after suffering a heart attack while preparing the track for our press and practice session. He had done such a brilliant job for 21 years and would be an extremely hard act to follow.

Our riders were very fortunate on the sponsorship front, with retired farmer Tim Woodward sponsoring six of them that season. Tim was a small man with a big heart and a huge speedway fan. His involvement didn't stop with his backing of the riders – he also arranged the use of graders, rippers and harrows at the track. Sometimes, if conditions allowed, we let him grade the track between heats, much to his great delight.

He had previously provided a large workshop for Tony Rickardsson in one of his many outbuildings where his engine tuner Carl Blomfeldt could work on his bikes. Savalas Clouting also gained tremendously from Tim's generosity from early on in his career. Tim so wanted Sal to do well that the lad was provided with virtually anything that he needed – and asked for.

Tim's help, along with the Anglia Weekly Bingo scheme, went a long way to keeping us in Division One. Our commercial manager, Keith Rodwell, ran the bingo scheme and he had built it up to having 17-18 rounds all round Ipswich. It was a very good fund-raiser for the club for at least three or four years and we were very grateful to Keith for all his efforts on the sponsorship front.

As expected, it proved very difficult to replace Tony Rickardsson, so we breathed a temporary sigh of relief when he agreed to do six weeks for us before the Swedish racing got started. Just before his time was up, Jeremy Doncaster returned to the side, which proved a popular move. As opposed to the one that saw us drop Leigh Lanham for the Austrian Franz Leitner, who came highly recommended but didn't live up to expectations, so we quickly re-instated Leigh.

Another visiting favourite bowed out that season when Coventry's Hans Nielsen decided to retire from British speedway after 18 years. On his last night at Foxhall, he said that it had been one of his favourite tracks and that Witches' fans had always been great. I had certainly always enjoyed riding against him (especially when I won) and could understand our fans admiring him for some of the performances he had put in.

Led by skipper Chris, the team had a good second half to the season and finished a creditable sixth. He also did well on an international front, helping England win a three-match Test series against Sweden (the second one was held at Foxhall), which greatly pleased the new England team managers, James Easter and myself.

Our youngsters were still progressing well, with Ben Howe finishing runner-up in the British Under-21 Final, while Tony Rickardsson's decision to miss British racing certainly worked for him as he won the last of the 'one-off' World Finals, at Vojens, to take his first World Championship.

Another change happened that year which caused quite a stir within the sport but for all the wrong reasons – the introduction of dirt deflectors. They were intended to do three things: keep more shale on the track and help prevent slick surfaces; stop following riders from being covered in shale to the point that they couldn't see; and prevent spectators from being covered in flying shale.

In many riders' opinion, the first model had a big design flaw in that it affected how the bikes steered, especially in a full broadside when going round a corner. It had a flat surface that acted in the same way that jet skis work, in that the shale coming off the tyre would hit the deflector in such a way, and with such force, that it affected the direction the bike took.

By May that year, the Speedway Riders' Association, of which Chris was vice-president, were calling for a strike if their concerns about rider safety were not listened to and, at that point, the SCB stepped in, agreeing to hold a meeting. When it took place a few weeks later, experienced riders such as Hans Nielsen and Sam Ermolenko stood up and spoke of their problems caused by dirt deflectors. The decision was taken to suspend their use to avoid compromising rider safety and allow further tests to be done. The next meeting at Foxhall saw a dirt deflector throwing contest as the riders celebrated their 'victory'.

Chris' engine tuner, Richard Arbon, got involved in designing an alternative dirt deflector and I know that advice was sought from experts at Reading University that backed up our theory about the basic shape being wrong. I believe that I suggested basing the shape on the attachment that had been added to the rear mudguard of a Honda 50, which directed water from the tyre back on to the road – it looked a bit like a duck beak.

He produced about 12-14 prototypes for testing – I'm not sure when or where it may have taken place but I do know that some riders did get to try them and agreed they were much better. Richard, for whatever reason, didn't take the project any further but it was noticed that when an updated version of the original model was re-introduced, it contained several elements there were very similar to his design. The most important thing is that this time they worked as they should, and are still used today.

Attendance levels were still falling nationwide and it was a huge bonus for us when Tim Woodward agreed to sponsor the club and we became the Woodward's Witches.

**It was announced that for 1995, the first and second divisions would merge – this was something I had campaigned for, so I was more than happy. We were planning to field a team of local riders, if possible, with Mitch Shirra no longer being available after he had received a 12-month ban. It was a shame, as it effectively ended his career which, despite his fiery nature, he didn't deserve.**

Chris was the first to sign on, followed by Jeremy and newest Ipswich asset Scott Nicholls. Leigh Lanham, Savalas Clouting, Ben Howe and Emmerson Fairweather completed the septet. At last, a team full of English riders and, apart from Ben, who was based near Gatwick, they were all local as well. Hopefully, the fans would get behind them as they had in JB's era.

Scott, alongside Leigh, had already given supporters a glimpse of his potential when doing laps round Foxhall after meetings had finished when he was still too young to become a team member. I believe he had enough natural talent to have been crowned World Champion but, unfortunately, he never managed to achieve what many thought he could at that level.

Early on, we were going really well and things were looking very good for the team as we topped the league. In April, Ben Howe was crowned British Under-21 champion with Savalas Clouting third. They both qualified for the World Under-21 semi-finals, along with Leigh Lanham.

As so often happens in this sport, injuries to riders then put a spanner in the works. Ben broke his collar-bone in three places at the end of June, sidelining him for two months, and Scott was out for a few weeks after he suffered severe concussion while riding for the England Under-23 team.

We recovered our form when these two returned but there was too much ground to make up and we finished sixth for the second year running, albeit in a much bigger league. Ben finished sixth in the World Under-21 Final soon after his return from injury, scoring a very impressive 12 points. One wonders what he could have done if fully fit.

Chris enjoyed a good year. He was close to topping the league averages on 10.52, was part of the England team that took silver in the World Team Cup and rounded off his year by winning our season finale, the 16-Lap Classic, for the second time.

He also won the first heat of the first new format GP rounds at Wroclaw in Poland and went on to finish third overall that night. As England co-team manager, I got to attend most of the GP rounds with Chris and it was great, both in my official capacity and as a father, to watch him progress that year. I was very impressed by his professionalism, his preparation for each event was meticulous and he presented himself very well. This was a theme that he carried throughout his career, remaining the ultimate professional. It was certainly something that I had tried to do myself when riding. It was always my mantra: 'if something is worth doing, it is worth doing to the best of your ability'.

**The winter of 1995-96 was to prove a very difficult one and the very future of Ipswich Speedway was put in doubt. After we had both realised the club wasn't making enough for both of us to continue at Ipswich, Dave Pavitt took the decision to move to Oxford. Mike Western had a full-time job restoring old manuscripts for the British Museum in London but speedway was the main source of income for Dave and myself.**

Dave was also the type who needed a new challenge every so often. He had successfully taken on Hackney and then Ipswich before Oxford and eventually the Isle of Wight, bringing sensible and skilful management to every club. Dave certainly didn't leave on bad terms with either of us and I still catch up with him once a year to talk about old times.

When we discovered that our stadium landlords were to significantly increase our rent, Mike and I realised that, combined with the trading loss from 1995, we had a big problem on our hands. We had various meetings with Spedeworth but they were adamant there was no room for reducing the increase. One solution for us would have been to hold more meetings but that would never have been allowed by the local district council who, to this day, control how many times the stadium is used each year.

Early in the New Year, stories started circulating in the local press and around the town that I was looking for a buyer and/or we were considering a move to Mildenhall. Most of it wasn't entirely accurate but if such stories helped to raise awareness of the problems we were having, then who was I to dispute them? I think there was another front page 'exclusive' suggesting we were all going to move to Oxford with Dave Pavitt but, again, it was all just speculation.

The Ipswich MP at the time was the late Jamie Cann, who rang me out of the blue one day asking to arrange a meeting. He had read about the problems we were having in the *Ipswich Evening Star* and, having been to a few meetings along with his charming wife Rosie, he wanted to do all he could to help the club.

We met at the Garland public house in Rushmere, near Ipswich, and Jamie explained that he felt the Witches and I had helped spread the name of Ipswich all round the world and he was not prepared to let us just disappear. He ended by saying that he was going to give us his solid support and so the 'Save Our Speedway' campaign was launched with a target set at £15,000.

A public meeting was held soon afterwards at Ransomes Sports Club in Sidegate Avenue, Ipswich and the response was unbelievable. I think there were about 400 people there, filling every available space. Jamie gave a very passionate speech about how everyone in the town needed to get behind the club and help as much as they could. I also got up and explained what we would use the money for and emphasised that we would do everything we could to keep speedway in the town.

Fans in Suffolk have always been very supportive and are generally passionate about their speedway but we were still surprised and extremely grateful when £6,000 was pledged straight away, with more to come in the following days. We couldn't believe how many people got involved and the riders did their bit by getting out and about to spread the word and hopefully collect some donations along the way.

Things really started moving very quickly after that. Collections were made in the town centre with Jamie Cann, Jeremy Doncaster and the Witches Winner girls standing at The Cornhill, while Ipswich Town FC got involved by allowing us to make a collection at their home game against Birmingham City game that weekend.

The *Evening Star* gave us great coverage throughout the campaign and regularly interviewed people from the club, past and present, who were all backing the appeal, including JB from his home Down Under.

One of the people involved in the music presentation during meetings, Mike Ashby, worked at a local radio station, SGR, and he helped get them involved in our plight. Keith Rodwell, our commercial manager, then met with them and Mike and the outcome was that SGR agreed to become team sponsors.

Combined with collections and other fund-raising, it meant our initial minimum target of £15,000 was passed in less than two weeks. The *East Anglian Daily Times* soon carried the news, along with local radio stations, that the Witches were going to continue. Mightily relieved, and with a huge worry removed, Mike Western and I were left with the 'simple' task of assembling a team.

We were fortunate to retain six of the riders from '95, with Kevin Teager replacing Emmerson Fairweather, enabling us to continue with a local team. Chris and Jeremy Doncaster then showed great loyalty by volunteering to have their pay frozen to help the club.

As we had hoped, the publicity surrounding the club's financial plight raised our profile locally and we enjoyed better attendances that year, which boded well for the future. We had worked hard to improve our meeting presentation with Dave Richardson, the Ipswich Town announcer, taking over on the centregreen (John Earrey had stepped down in '95 to concentrate on his Spedeworth role), Mike Western took over race results and sponsors SGR installed new music equipment. We also introduced rider theme tunes, competitions with prizes and 5-1 boards for fans to hold up during meetings.

The year 1996 saw lay-down engines allowed in league racing with Chris, especially, a big fan as he believed they were much more powerful than the traditional upright model. He had been using one successfully in the GP series during the previous season but knew that it may take time to find the right set-up for the tight Foxhall circuit, although he soon got it dialled in at some of the bigger away tracks.

Another change that didn't go down so well was the attempt to introduce solid block tyres for the GP rounds. Race Director Ole Olsen believed the tyres would increase riders' skill levels but, having tried them at our press and practice, Chris and Jeremy Doncaster thought they were dangerous. Many other GP riders shared their opinion and delayed signing their contracts until the governing body agreed to delay their introduction.

They wanted to bring them in for the last three GP rounds but, after several top riders tested them and stated they still believed them to be unsafe, the plan was shelved. I was more than happy to hear that because, after listening to Chris and witnessing how the tyres performed, I agreed they were not a good idea.

Just when we thought it was safe, the authorities switched their attention to the World Team Cup Final in Germany, insisting the solid block tyres be used in that. It led to the event looking second-rate because many star names boycotted it, including most of the English riders and two top Danes.

As England team manager, I fully supported the riders' action but it left me with only 'juniors' to fill the team places and, not surprisingly, we only finished in sixth place.

The solid block tyre issue, plus the previous year's dirt deflector fiasco, did not help the sport's reputation. While we all accept that new developments will continue to emerge and, in some cases, will improve the sport, they have to be fully tested before they become compulsory. If not, the bad publicity that results from things going wrong with seemingly untried changes works against all of us.

On the home front, our young riders did us proud again. Savalas Clouting won the British Under-21 title, with Scott Nicholls finishing second and Leigh Lanham fifth. We finished eighth in the league, which was disappointing as we were unbeaten at home, but our away form often left a lot to be desired and that's where the points were lost.

Chris was runner-up in the British Final and the ELRC, captained England in a successful Test series against Australia and qualified for the next year's Grand Prix series. He also got plenty of second looks for another reason when he added a new sponsor to his bike covers. One of ex-Witch Mitch Shirra's pit crew was now running a sex shop in Antwerp, Belgium, so Chris had 'Madame Sarre, Erotika Shopping' emblazoned across his bike! I got to visit the shop with Chris when we were en route to a German meeting but we didn't try or buy anything. Honest!

Another quick mention of the 'Save Our Speedway', or SOS fund as it is now known. It has mainly been run through the Ipswich Speedway Supporters' Club and everyone involved has worked very hard to keep money flowing into the fund. It still provides invaluable support to the club today. We are very grateful for all their efforts and for all the fans who have contributed to the fund-raising – without this type of ongoing support, Ipswich and several other clubs may not have survived this far.

**After two years of running one big league, another change for 1997 was confirmed at the promoters' AGM. There would now be three leagues – Elite, Premier and Conference – and it was back to six-man teams. It was also confirmed that I would stay on as England team manager and Chris was granted a testimonial (already? Surely he'd not been riding that long!). He also announced another unusual new sponsor – filmmaker Brian Griffin under the Griffin Racing banner.**

We decided to ask our fans what they wanted after their heroic efforts to save the club and they voted strongly to stay at the top level. Team-wise, we opted to keep Chris, Jeremy, Ben and Scott, joined by new signings Steve Johnston and Toni Svab.

Steve was a typical Aussie extrovert and always up for a laugh, so great for team spirit, while always willing to help out if he possibly could. Toni, although much quieter, was to evolve into a key member of the side, although it didn't happen overnight.

Chris had his testimonial in July and the weather gods were very kind to him, providing ideal conditions for his special day. A healthy crowd was treated to a good afternoon's racing, with the added spice of the northern v southern feud theme, plus all the extras that were laid on. The North v South thing came about after Chris took a team to Gary Havelock's testimonial with the idea that Gary would return the favour and the scores from both meetings would be combined. The rivalry was great for the advertising, with the South winning on this occasion but the North taking the aggregate victory by four points.

Two of the highlights for me were Paul Bickers roaring up a ramp on his bike and jumping the starting tapes in exactly the same way his dad Dave had done at my testimonial. Just like his father, Paul damaged the wheel rims on his bike due to a heavy landing after reaching such a great height. The other was when Mark Loram and Shane Parker stripped down and did several laps in their jockstraps, with Shane being voted 'best bum' – reminiscent of Siggy, John Cook and Michael Lee in the early 80s but no fines this time around!

I was really pleased that Chris had such a great day. He had been a loyal servant to the Witches despite offers to move away but, like me, he preferred to ride for his hometown club and would continue to do so for some time to come.

By mid-season, it was apparent the team were not going to achieve anything much better than the previous season and something needed to be done to improve our fortunes. Around this time, Tony Rickardsson made it known that he would like to ride in England again and that he wanted to come back to Foxhall.

That left us with a dilemma – who would we drop to bring him in? We couldn't turn down the opportunity of taking back our asset and the world's top performer at the time. I laid awake for several nights sweating over what to do. And then I made a phone call that I would never forget.

In the end, I plumped for what I thought was best for the club and the supporters. It was purely down to a numbers game and one rider had an average that, if he was dropped, meant we could bring Tony in. Ben Howe was the man to make way. He hadn't performed badly for the club, which made it even harder to drop him, but it had to be done.

I felt terrible for him and found it hard to get the words out on the phone but, at the end of the day, the club has to come first and sometimes difficult decisions have to be made. In this case, it was definitely the right one. Tony's inclusion in the side turned our fortunes around, although perhaps not as fast as some fans wanted.

We reached the play-offs for the newly-introduced Craven Shield and were pleased to hear we were drawn against local rivals King's Lynn. Before reaching this point, however, I had yet another run-in with my 'favourite' referee Frank Ebdon. One of our last meetings before the play-off was at Wimborne Road against Poole, where Frank constantly calling the pits telephone for one silly reason after another spoilt the whole meeting. An exclusion for Tony Rickardsson in one heat had

The 1997 Witches. Left to right: Jeremy Doncaster, Savalas Clouting, Toni Svab, Chris, team manager Brian Messenger, Steve Johnston, Scott Nicholls.

a big effect on the outcome and many people went into print afterwards (including me) saying they couldn't believe what they had just witnessed. Many of them suggested that perhaps Mr. Ebdon needed to go to Specsavers.

We beat King's Lynn by 10 points at Foxhall but, disappointingly, they went on to win by 12 at Saddlebow Road. That was a big blow as Chris and Tony Rickardsson gave their all in the second leg but unfortunately, for whatever reason, the other four just didn't deliver. I remember Scott had bike problems in both legs, which is not what you need from a rider who should have scored freely. No rider ever goes out to under-perform (at least, I hope they don't) but to lose by just two points in a tie we should have won was a bitter pill to swallow for the whole management team.

There was a lot of nonsense in the press afterwards, accusing the club of not wanting Scott for the next season. I think some of it came from a comment about improving his professionalism after too many engine failures in a short period of time. I guess he was still very young and not mature enough to just take it on the chin and perhaps consider there may be something in his set-up that needed further investment to take him up to the level that everyone thought he was capable of.

Tony and Chris narrowly missed out in the ELRC, finishing second and third respectively behind World Champion Greg Hancock, but there was more Ipswich success in the British Under-21 Championship when asset Leigh Lanham took the title.

Witches fans had their first glimpse of Tomasz Gollob when the Polish superstar rode in our end-of-season 16-Lap Classic event. He had wanted to ride in England for some time and was keen to clean up his image after the much-publicised 'punch up' with Craig Boyce in the first British GP at Hackney in 1995. My Polish-born wife Magda was aware of it and arranged the booking on behalf of Ipswich.

Tomasz lived up to all the pre-meeting hype and scored a very impressive 14 points in the qualifying round to reach the 16-Lap Final. However, it all fell apart, literally, when the extra fuel attachments required for the marathon race came adrift and he had to pull up. Testimonial man Chris won the 16-Lapper final and also lifted the trophy, which gave him a good end to his year.

We didn't know it at the time but Tomasz's arrival on the scene was to spark one of the biggest years ever experienced by a British speedway club.

It was a privilege to see two of the sport's greats, Tomasz Gollob and Tony Rickardsson, combining their special talent for the Witches' cause in 1998. Below: What a year, what a team! The all-conquering 1998 Witches (left to right): Toni Svab, Tomasz Gollob, Chris, Tony Rickardsson, Savalas Clouting, Scott Nicholls.

Chapter 24

# Simply The Best

**I**T was the year that beat all others, when Ipswich Witches tracked what many hailed as the 'Team of the Century', with all major titles going to Foxhall.

But before all that happened, we had to rebuild the team and make a few changes behind-the-scenes. There was no-one more pleased than me to welcome back Tim Woodward as joint-team sponsor with SCR Radio. He had left at the end of '95 under a bit of a cloud after an argument with John Earrey but that was all water under the bridge when Tim returned as keen as ever to get behind his beloved Witches.

We had started our team-building in the previous October by re-signing Tony Rickardsson and then had to wait until after the BSPA AGM in November to confirm that Tomasz Gollob would be a Witch in 1998.

Several British clubs had been attempting to sign world No.3 Tomasz for some time but he had resisted their advances. Our situation was helped because a Polish TV station was in the throes of negotiating a deal to transmit Elite League meetings. It was felt that with Tomasz riding over here, it would go a long way to making it a more attractive proposition.

After riding in the 16-Lap Classic and meeting up with us, Tomasz had already decided that Ipswich was where he wanted to be. I think the main reason for his decision was that by joining us, he would have a Polish-speaking co-promoter to deal with in Magna because, at that time, his English was a bit limited, to say the least.

Chris was named as the third heat leader and the team was starting to shape up nicely. The final three riders were soon confirmed as Scott Nicholls, Toni Svab and Savalas Clouting. We all felt very positive that this time we had got the makings of a team to go places – but little did we know just how far they would go.

We had to appoint a new team manager after Brian Messenger had decided to step down because he could no longer commit to all the time taken up by travelling to away meetings. But he wasn't lost to the club; we gave him the job of trainer/coach as he enjoyed working with the young up-and-coming riders.

It was suggested that I take over the role as I had finished my stint as England team manager, which I was happy to do, but I also asked Mike Smillie to 'double up' with me. He had already been at the club for a long time, working behind-the-scenes, and was very good at keeping up with all the riders' statistics, which you needed to be on top of when building teams, choosing guests, etc.

We also had a new presentation team that year, with Kevin Long stepping up to the mike on the centregreen and Bryan Knights taking over the role of announcing the official results. Everyone seemed to like the new look with Kevin quickly building up a rapport with both fans and riders. He perhaps said a bit too much, though, when Shane Parker visited with King's Lynn and he received the first, but certainly not the last, soaking from our former Aussie. Shane 'played up' after being excluded for not making the two-minute time allowance and Kevin, who had kept the fans informed of what he'd been was up to in the pits, was rewarded with a bucket of icy cold water over his lovely cream jacket! We had already witnessed some of Shane's antics on a previous visit, when he hijacked the tractor after King's Lynn accused us of preparing the track differently on the gates for the visiting team – as if!

Our fans' first glimpse of Tomasz that year was actually in a pair of football shorts – no, he hadn't changed his mind and switched to Ipswich Town! Another event organised by Chris' testimonial committee was a football match, which took place at the beginning of March. Tomasz liked his football and was a good player in his youth, to the point that he had to decide at one point as to which sport to concentrate on. Luckily for speedway, he made the right choice.

His ball skills were evident in the match and he appeared to really enjoy himself. Tomasz had an equally famous advisor, Zbigniew Boniek, who is perhaps the best-known Polish footballer of all-time. He was born in Bydgoszcz and had a keen interest in speedway, watching Tomasz ride there whenever he could. 'Zibby' came over to Ipswich with Tomasz when time allowed, so we all got to know him quite well. I seem to remember he helped calm Tomasz down one night at Eastbourne when things got a bit lively in the pits area (as they often did at Arlington) but the details escape me.

The stage was set and the cast assembled, but would the show be a success?

It didn't take long for a taste of what was to come when we welcomed arch-rivals King's Lynn to Foxhall for our season opener, the first leg of a KO Cup tie. There was a bit of extra spice in that Piotr Protasiewicz, one of Tomasz's team-mates from Bydgoszcz, had signed for the Norfolk side, so they would be very keen to outdo each other.

A resounding 60-30 victory followed, much to the delight of the Foxhall faithful, with Tony and Chris on paid maximums. Tomasz scored 12 points and was only beaten once by an opponent – and it wasn't Piotr, who scored only five.

With the return leg rained-off, we then faced Poole in another KOC tie at Foxhall and they were sent home on the wrong end of a 56-33 scoreline. This time around, the 1995 GP protagonists Craig Boyce and Tomasz managed to avoid any 'handbags' during or after racing – mainly because Craig was half a lap behind! Tomasz: 15 points. Craig: four.

Eastbourne were our next victims at Foxhall, although they put up a bit more resistance. The real test came when we went down to Arlington for the return fixture and won there. It was only the second time in three years that the Sussex side had been beaten at home and the first time Ipswich had won there since I took over in 1989. It guaranteed our place in the KOC semi-finals.

The wins just kept on coming after that and we set a new club record of 19 consecutive matches unbeaten. The terraces were now buzzing on a Thursday night and the conversation switched from 'are we going to win?' to 'how many will we win by?' Although a massive home win is nowhere near as exciting as a meeting decided in the last heat, there was still plenty of good entertainment, despite our dominance, with Foxhall fans surely going home happy after every meeting that year.

But, like all successful speedway teams, the best of the action was often to be seen in away meetings where our riders were put more to the test. Some of our hosts didn't take too kindly to our victories and I remember one visit to Arlington ended with us being threatened with a £100 fine if we didn't clear up the ticker tape that our fans had thrown everywhere to celebrate our win. What a load of sour pusses!

On the other hand, a few recognised that our strength could be a crowd-pleaser. We had some epic away tussles at Coventry with Colin Pratt, the Bees' team manager, admitting that our two visits that season had drawn bigger attendances than the British Final.

It was an away meeting at Belle Vue that finally ended our unbeaten run but, in our defence, Chris was missing through tonsillitis and Scott was on international duty. With our usual line-up, we probably would have won but it was only a slight hiccup in our season and it barely registered, with our next trip resulting in a 64-26 demolition of Poole.

The KOC semi-final saw us drawn against Eastbourne (again) and our win at Arlington in the first leg led to the headline 'We Surrender' appearing in the press. Eagles promoter Jon Cook was not a happy bunny losing to us for the third time that year and was quoted as saying that we were too good for the British League and that we should be in the Polish League. He went on to say there was no point in holding the second leg and that he would be trying to get it changed to a league fixture.

He either changed his mind or the BSPA turned down his request, because they did turn up for the second leg and, yes, we did beat them again (54-33), with Tomasz scoring his first 18-point maximum. Oh, to be a fly on the wall in JC's car on the way home and his misery didn't end there as we went back to Arlington and beat them for a fourth time.

Many fans would automatically assume that such a year would be very lucrative for the club but, despite the attendances being generally much improved, they were still not up to a level where they covered the huge riders' wage bill that comes with such a successful team. When, like us, the only money raised comes through the turnstiles, even a top year trophy-wise doesn't necessarily put a smile on your bank manager's face.

The success enjoyed on the track helped to build a terrific team spirit, with the riders all supporting and encouraging each other. The team we had built that year certainly had the X factor, perhaps the like of which we may never see again.

Mike Smillie's hardest job as joint team manager was deciding who would go into Heat 15. It used to worry him and he came to me and asked what he should do as he didn't want Tony, Tomasz or Chris to be left frustrated after a meeting. I told him to buy a notebook and to keep a record of who had been nominated each meeting, so that all three would end up at the completion of the season with an equal number of extra rides. In other words, unless the final race was critical when current form came into the equation, it was a case of Mike sharing out the extra rides equally.

The SGR Woodwards Witches were simply unstoppable and went on to win the treble – Elite League championship, Knockout Cup and Craven Shield. We had three riders who were among the best five in the world with Tony winning the world crown (his first GP title), Tomasz third and Chris fifth.

Chris was captain again, not only of the Witches but also of the England team, putting paid to the rumours that he was only picked previously because his dad was the national team manager. Dave Jessup, who had replaced me, shared my view that he was the best man for the job.

Chris realised another of his personal goals in 1998 – he finally won the British Championship, again following in my tyre tracks with a 15-point maximum. Perhaps the brilliant season he was having with the team boosted his confidence to the next level and was the added extra he needed to win the trophy. Whatever the reason, I was there to share in his success and it was another great moment when he stood on that rostrum. I can never quite make up my mind if I got more pleasure from my own achievements or from witnessing my son's.

Tomasz was an enormous entertainer and at every meeting he rode for us in nearly three seasons, he turned in a display of immaculate riding. He used to hurtle round the outside of the Foxhall track, at times getting within inches of the fence, yet always having perfect control. He was a joy to deal with and, when fit, he made every meeting and always had immaculate machinery.

As well as being a very good rider, he is also a first class mechanic and engine tuner. I often helped him if he had engine problems while over here, although my role only extended to holding or cleaning things for him while he did all the technical stuff. I can see him during a home meeting changing the cam timing on his bike, which is something usually only done in a workshop with special tools. Not Tomasz, he simply tipped up the bike with the front wheel against the pit wall and, while a couple of people held it steady, did the necessary. He then promptly went out to win the next race.

Tony Rickardsson was voted Rider of the Year and what a season he had. As well as the trophies he helped to win with Ipswich, he won his second world title and the ELRC for good measure. He was another great bloke to deal with, always a joy to watch on track. In one meeting at Wimborne Road, I was struck by the very different set-ups used by him and Tomasz. They were both winning races easily but the rpm of their engines were worlds apart. Tony's engine would rev so high that it screamed when it went past, whereas Tomasz's engines would appear to be just ticking over but would be pulling just as hard and producing the same speed.

There was one point that year when Tony wasn't going flat out and his horsepower was greatly reduced. We did something a bit different to celebrate his world title by transporting around the Foxhall stock car track in a horse-drawn carriage, which made quite a sight.

The other three riders all played their part as well and I believe they all benefited hugely from riding with such experienced and talented riders as Chris, Tomasz and Tony – it gave them all something to aspire to. Scott, Savalas and Toni regularly outscored their opposite numbers and there was also a rivalry between them as to who would finish top of their trio at the end of the year. Toni had already started the season as Argentinian Champion and Scott won the British Under-21 crown. He may not have picked up any individual honours but Savalas had gained much more consistency than shown previously and this was something that definitely helped the team as well.

It was just two years since we had been on the brink of closing up and here we were, top of the pile. What a great way to reward our faithful fans for their generosity and support during the Save Our Speedway campaign – we had given them a season they would surely never forget.

One memory I have from the end-of-season celebrations was when we managed to persuade a very reluctant Tim Woodward to present the KO Cup to the team. His sponsorship had been such a help to the club and individual riders that we wanted him to share the limelight. He told me he had never achieved anything before but that this season had been magical and had brought the proudest moments of his life.

Tim went on to publish a personal message in the local paper thanking the fans, riders and management for making it such a great year. He explained he loved speedway, not only for the thrills on the track but also for the fact that the sport was filled with regular people who were happy to talk to the fans without the need for acting like a prima donna, as so often happened in other sports.

I've been asked many times which team was best to be a part of – the Witches side that won the double in 1976, which I rode in, or the 1998 version that I promoted. It's another difficult one to answer as they happened in two very different eras. It was a brilliant experience leading the '76 team on the track and, at the time, you think you can't possibly feel the same euphoria again. But it was equally brilliant building a team and seeing it achieve everything you had hoped for – and then some – in '98. Both were such huge high points in my career, so I think I will have to call it a draw!

A bit prematurely, we were given a reception in the Town Hall in mid-October where the Mayor presented us with a trophy to commemorate our season's achievements. All six riders took their bikes and were introduced to the huge crowd by Kevin Long. Unable to resist the temptation, Tony then thrilled them all by doing several 'donuts', leaving behind circles of black tyre marks. It was to be a few more weeks before we added the Craven Shield to our haul after we beat Coventry at Brandon, after the season was officially extended into early November.

All good things must come to an end, as they say, but we certainly enjoyed several weeks celebrating our successes first. Inevitably, we were brought down to earth after the BSPA AGM, which brought about the return of seven-man sides and a new 40-point team-building limit. Predictably, fellow promoters, still smarting no doubt from the loophole that enabled us to bring in Tomasz on a 'deflated' average, had combined to ensure our super-team was broken up.

There was no point in arguing, so we took it on the chin, as most clubs must after they have had a successful season. Obviously, we would have to lose one of our top riders and many discussions would be required before we all decided on which one. One thing was certain – in the fans' eyes, we would be wrong, whoever we chose to let go.

It wasn't going to be an easy decision as we all had our favourites. Mike's wife Aja was Swedish and he had a close affinity with Tony; Magda, being Polish; would equally favour Tomasz; and I would obviously want to keep Chris in the team. However, before we sat down to talk about it, I switched on the local evening news to hear that Mike Western was moving to King's Lynn . . . and taking Tony with him!

Unbeknown to me, this had started during the AGM but, despite us travelling home together, Mike had never mentioned it. The rest of us were a bit shocked to say the least but, as the deal was already done, we had to move on and build our 1999 team without Tony.

Tomasz had already made it clear that he was keen to stay at Ipswich, so was happy to sign a new contract. Chris followed suit but there were even rumours about him going to Saddlebow Road after it was announced that his sponsor Brian Griffin was moving there as co-promoter. However, he wasn't tempted and that meant he lost an important sponsor.

The other rider who left us for a loan spell at Poole was Scott Nicholls – it was no real surprise as he had wanted to leave for a couple of years. With Savalas and Toni retained, we added Ben Howe, Brent Woodifield and Jason Bunyan to the line-up.

We also added a new team sponsor to our list that year, the *Ipswich Evening Star,* who would provide us with invaluable support for several years to come. Both home and away, they gave us two full pages of coverage for every meeting – plus spacious meeting previews.

Unfortunately, Ben Howe again failed to live up to our expectations and when we were presented with the chance of signing Tomas Topinka from King's Lynn, we dropped Ben for the second time. It was a shame as he was a nice lad with obvious talent, and also very brave at times, but there was just something missing that prevented him reaching his full potential. If he could have dedicated himself more to developing his techniques, I think he would have gone a lot further than he did.

Talking of our rivals from Norfolk, they came up with a plan to humiliate us on a visit that year but it all ended in tears – and they weren't ours! Brian Griffin's theatrical background gave him the idea of building effigies of witches on the centregreen with the plan being to set one alight every time the home side scored a 5-1. It would have been a great publicity stunt but only two went up in flames, much to the amusement of our travelling fans. Strangely, the Lynn fans didn't see the funny side. The team went on to finish a creditable fifth that year.

The new millennium saw Chris Louis figure in his 12th consecutive year as an Ipswich rider and we had a strong enough side to finish third in the Elite League. Tomasz signed on for his third season and was joined by Toni, Savalas and Jason. Slovenian Matej Ferjan was a new recruit, along with popular local rider Lawrence Hare. Mid-season, we needed to strengthen up with Savalas being the man to go when we recalled Jeremy Doncaster. It was another difficult decision but sentiment is rarely allowed any room at such times and most fans were very pleased to have Jem back as a Witch.

We endured several injuries to key riders, losing Tomasz at a crucial time when he was involved in a serious road accident in Poland. It effectively ended his season and, unknown to any of us at the time, his UK career as well.

Chris was riding for Polish club Pila at the time and he happened to mention a young rider he often partnered as being someone we ought to consider bringing over. Jarek Hampel made his UK debut in October but not until I had checked his passport for his date of birth. When he first turned up on my doorstep, I couldn't believe I was looking at a 16-year-old because he looked more like 12!

Chris was convinced that Jarek had the talent to go all the way and his starting was certainly very fast. Passing appeared to be a bit more challenging for him but he was still young and would hopefully develop that part of his riding as his career progressed.

Louis junior went one better than his old man during the 2000 season by winning the British Championship for a second time. He thoroughly deserved it and it was a big achievement as it was so much harder back then to win at this level with more riders of a similar standard to compete against.

James Easter and me in the Vojens pits with Chris and Mark Loram after the 1994 individual World Final.

Chapter 25

# Managing England

**I**WAS appointed joint-England team manager with James Easter at the 1993 BSPA AGM. To be honest, I was a bit hesitant about accepting it at first because running Ipswich was a full-time job on its own. However, after a discussion with James, in which he emphasised that we would split the role equally, so it wouldn't cause too much extra work for either of us, I agreed to take the job.

I was also struck by what a big honour it is to be considered good enough to run your national team.

James had been a familiar figure around the speedway scene for many years, not only as boss of Ipswich-based Travel Plus Tours, but also for his spell as co-promoter (with Peter Oakes) at Peterborough and, before that, in his role as team manager of Australia and the USA.

I did have a slight concern that I would be in the firing line concerning the selection (or not) of Chris, who was one of England's top riders at the time. But I had already gone through that at club level, so I was prepared for what may be thrown at me by supporters, other riders and possibly the press.

Selecting a team wasn't very difficult at that time – it more or less picked itself. As well as Chris, we also had Gary Havelock and Mark Loram, who all got on really well together because they came into speedway via the same schoolboy grass-track route. Then there was Martin Dugard, Dean Barker, Joe Screen, David Norris and Ben Howe starting to show potential for inclusion in the national squad.

The only time team selection became a bit tricky was in the pairs meetings. From 1994, the FIM did away with the World Pairs and decided to merge it with the World Team Cup, although it was still essentially a pairs event – two main riders, plus one reserve who could be used as a 'tactical sub' at any stage of the meeting. With Havvy, Mark and Chris all in form, someone was going to be disappointed to be named at reserve. There was little to choose between the three of them, making it difficult to know who to pick.

As Mark was by now living with my daughter Joanne and had ridden for me at Hackney and Ipswich in the first three years of his speedway career, he was virtually part of my family.

Gary had ridden brilliantly at Wroclaw in a rain-interrupted meeting to win the 1992 world title. This showed how good a rider he was and I was fortunate to have three so accomplished stars to call on.

Any 'comeback' from Gary was perfectly understood by me. I could see how he may have looked at some of my decisions, as I had anticipated when I was reluctant to take the job in the first place. Although there was no real malice shown, I could sense an underlying tension at times. I have feelings like every other human and I used to worry constantly about how I could keep everybody happy.

But, hand on heart, I chose who I thought would do the best job in that particular heat or meeting, and I always thought I was doing what was best for the team and the country. In fact, checking the record books some 20 years later, I see that we actually made Chris reserve for the '94 WTC final at Brockstedt, where we finished tied at the bottom with hosts Germany. Chris scored four points from two rides, Gary scored three (a win) from four outings, while Mark got nine from his six

All smiles in the England camp after we'd just beaten Sweden in the 1994 Test at Foxhall. Along with myself are (left to right): Chris, Paul Hurry, Gary Havelock, Dean Barker, James Easter, Mark Loram. Kneeling: David Norris, Ben Howe, Martin Dugard. We won that series against the Swedes but tougher challenges lay ahead.

programmed rides.

All three rode their hearts out for their country. I recall one occasion when Gary came in after a poor ride and said to me: 'Put Chris back in'.

My partnership with James proved to be shortlived because, before our first year was up, I received a phone call from him one day telling me that I was on my own. Apparently, he had a disagreement with the BSPA, although I never did find out what it was about. Effectively he had handled all the dealings with the BSPA office as I wasn't keen on that type of work while I concentrated on team selection and rider motivation, etc. I think he may have tried to change too many things too quickly and also felt restricted by the regulations that govern the running of the sport.

Initially I was horrified at the thought of being left in sole charge. Thankfully, Graham Reeve, a top referee at the time who went on to manage the Speedway Control Bureau, stepped up and helped me enormously over the next two years or so. He had a vast knowledge of the rulebook, which I sometimes struggled with, and it was great to have someone else I could bounce ideas off. We got on very well and had so many laughs as we travelled Europe trying to win honours for England. Before big meetings, we would often have a nightcap in the hotel and discuss how to get the best out of the riders the following day.

Graham was a great one for using local transport and loved jumping on buses and trams in European cities. I was quite happy to go along with it, although once off the bus I struggled to keep up with him. He had a tendency to walk very fast and my little legs were stretched to their limit keeping up. We must have looked an odd couple, with him striding along and me almost sprinting to keep pace.

Some time during my three-year reign, it was announced that riders on international duty would be paid more in line with their club deals. That was something I was in full support of because, with the

European scene being much more active than in my day, riders were often left with difficult choices when international and club fixtures clashed. Hopefully, this change would see riders less likely to cry off from riding for England because they could get paid better elsewhere.

Our best result in the World Team Cup during my involvement was finishing runners-up to Denmark in the 1995 final at Bydgoszcz, Poland and we also enjoyed success against the USA and Australia in Test series. Looking back, in the main I did enjoy team management at that level and, of course, it gave me more opportunities to share in Chris' international career.

I can't recall the details of why I resigned as England manager at the end of 1996. I think I was feeling pretty demoralised after picking what I thought was a good team for the World Team Cup that year and then have the authorities insist on the use of the block tyre which effectively ended England's chances before a wheel had turned. All of our top riders refused to ride, which left me with a team made up of juniors and we finished sixth. I probably thought that I could do without that type of outside interference.

On a different subject, and one that people are always asking me about, the annual BSPA conferences that have such a bearing on the running of the sport in the following 12 months. I am not able to voice my opinions about the many rule changes that seem to happen every year, or indeed anything else that is discussed, because I still hold a promoter's licence, so am bound by BSPA protocol.

I will, however, relate a couple of humorous incidents that I can remember while away on a couple of AGMs. The first one was abroad and the weather was very pleasant, so after our morning session we all decided to go outside to stretch our legs. There was a walkway through a park with grassed banks on either side and some people decided to sit along the top to enjoy the view. Unfortunately, one of them was providing a view of his own without realising it!

One of the promoters was wearing baggy shorts and in those days there was no inner lining. He must have forgotten to put his pants on, because when a few of us glanced up to wave a greeting, we saw a lot more than we had ever seen of him before. His 'meat and two veg' were on full display as he lounged on the grass with his legs apart. We all laughed and then proceeded to tell everyone else to look out for him and give him a wave too. He must have wondered why his popularity had soared during the lunch hour and I never did find out if he realised what had caused it!

Another experience that provided a lot of laughs came at my expense during an AGM held near Bournemouth. After a hard day around the conference table, Jim Lynch suggested that we all go out for a drink in the evening. I wasn't too keen but went along anyway. He took us to a nightclub that had two of the biggest bouncers I have ever seen on the door. Once inside, I noticed a few young ladies wrapping themselves around some poles (metal ones, that is, not the Gollob variety!) and performing various routines, some of which made my eyes water.

We all sat down and were enjoying the show when I noticed one of the young ladies approaching our group. To my surprise, she stooped in front of me, wiggled around a bit while lowering her ample chest towards my face, before turning and lowering her scantily clad bottom onto my lap. She then proceeded to move around, very slowly. I had no idea what was going on (honest!) and didn't know where to put my hands. I looked up to see Jim almost hysterical with laughter and realised I had been set up. I'm not sure how long it lasted – probably only a few minutes – but it was very enjoyable and I didn't have to pay. Thank goodness there were no smartphones and Facebook in those days, or the expression on my face would no doubt have gone viral within minutes!

I'm not sure if I ever repaid the compliment but they never stopped reminding me about it throughout that AGM.

Action from two internationals who proved popular at Foxhall. Above: Danish star Hans Andersen joined us in 2004. Below: Former World Champion Mark Loram rejoined us in 2006 but his career was ended in the first home match of the following season. Inset: Blast from the past . . . Bert Edwards, one of the 50s heroes I used to cheer from the Foxhall terraces as a kid, was moved to tears at our 50th anniversary meeting in 2001.

Chapter 26

# Premier Bound

THE 2001 season dawned with me alone at the helm after Magda had decided to give up her promoter's licence. It was a new experience because, in the past, I had always had someone else to share the role with.

We were celebrating our Golden Jubilee that season – 50 years since the first speedway meeting was held at Foxhall – but the year got off to the worst possible start with the sudden and untimely death of Tim Woodward. The generous help of the Old Newton-based farmer had not only helped the club enormously but also benefited riders like Tony Rickardsson and Savalas Clouting.

There was a huge turn-out for his funeral at the village church, with the Witches well represented as we said goodbye to a man who had played such an important part in the club's fortunes in the last few years. They even had to erect a marquee outside to accommodate all the people who couldn't fit into the church. We were all going to miss the small figure that had become such a big part of our speedway family at Foxhall and decided to keep his name in the Witches title that year as a mark of respect for all he had done. We also renamed our hospitality room the 'Tim Woodward Lounge'.

Chris began his 13th season with the club while Jeremy Doncaster, who had reached a remarkable 500 Ipswich appearances the previous season, was also in the team. With Scott Nicholls back after two years at Poole, there was a local flavour to the side again. Jarek Hampel started his first full season with the club and the remaining places were filled by Australian Craig Boyce, Savalas Clouting and Jason Bunyan.

A special Golden Jubilee meeting was held on Saturday, June 16, featuring a clash between two Select sides under the captaincy of Chris and Mark Loram. The many fans who attended didn't really come for the racing – they simply wanted a chance to see all their favourites from years gone by as they were paraded around the track and hear them being interviewed throughout the meeting, reliving memories from their time at the club.

My lasting memory is seeing 50s Ipswich legend Bert Edwards in tears as he took over the throttle of a JAP machine that Bob Jennings was warming up in the pits. It was obvious that Bert had loved his time riding at Foxhall. He just couldn't believe that he was still remembered so long after his Witches days were over.

Derek Hewitt and Rod Laudrum, who had ridden in the first-ever Ipswich meeting at Rayleigh in 1951, were there, along with Sid Clark, Charlie Frenzel, Tich Read, Ken Last and more recent stars like Ron Bagley, Ted Howgego, Clive Noy, Mick Hines and Trevor Jones.

Tony Davey and I had a match-race but it didn't go to plan. I had man flu and had to pull up after three laps – the fact he was winning had nothing to do with it! Despite the bunged up chest, I did enjoy being back on a bike but definitely lacked the race fitness to make a real go of it.

Our season started really well with signs that we could challenge for the title but injuries were soon to put us off course again, leading to a fifth place finish. The first meeting after the Golden Jubilee saw Scott Nicholls sidelined with a nasty shoulder injury, which put him out of action for several weeks. Worse was to come the next day when Chris suffered a serious head injury while riding for Pila in Poland. It was a freak accident in that the pole used to support the start tapes wasn't removed by the start marshal after the tapes had gone up – one of the other riders clipped it and it flew up, hitting Chris on the head and knocking him out.

My first thoughts were to fly out to be with him along with his wife Julie but Magda suggested she would be better at dealing with the Polish medical staff. I reluctantly agreed to stay behind to look after our young daughter Maria while they travelled to Czestochowa, where he was in intensive care with a swollen brain. It was a very harrowing time for all of us but after several weeks he was fit enough to return home, where I'm very glad to say he made a slow, but full, recovery.

The 2002 season saw Chris suffer more problems, this time a severe back injury sustained while riding in Sweden during April, which was to lead to a very long break from racing. From this point on, he would be restricting his speedway to just riding for Ipswich as his wife and daughters had been traumatised by two serious accidents in two years and had initially wanted him to give up completely.

The same month saw local rider Lawrence Hare badly injured in a crash while riding for Exeter at Newport. A broken vertebrae in his neck caused paralysis and he will be in a wheelchair for the rest of his life. Having started in the sport after being introduced to it by Chris, he rode for and captained the successful Witches reserve team for two years from 1991 before moving to Rye House when that level ceased to have a separate league. He went on to be a big fans' favourite at Edinburgh and Exeter.

It would have been great to use more of our young riders in our own main team but we could only fit in a couple at most, which meant the unlucky ones had to move to other clubs to progress. Oh, to have the same problem now!

Being sidelined through injury did give Chris the opportunity to plan something that he had wanted to do for a very long time – hold a moto-cross meeting at Foxhall. It took place in September with over 400 lorryloads of dirt shipped into the stadium to make a course that covered parts of the stock car and speedway tracks, as well as the centregreen. It was a huge success, attracting a crowd of several thousand with Carl Nunn, a local rider from Mildenhall, being the star of the show. Unfortunately, the time and cost involved in the preparation and removal of the dirt afterwards prevented it being repeated, which is a shame.

It was the end of an era when young Swede Kim Jansson replaced club stalwart Jeremy Doncaster at the end of August. The Witches reached the Craven Shield Final, where we were runners-up to Poole and ahead of Coventry in a three-club shoot-out. Apart from that, there is not much to report with a seventh place finish in the league.

The following season, in 2003, was a bad year all round. In February, I lost my brother Tony at the age of 60 to a heart attack. He was in hospital recovering from surgery on his lungs and appeared to be on the mend when it happened. To be honest, I think the damage was done when he was working with asbestos – Health and Safety wasn't as rigorously enforced as it is now. I remember Tony telling me they wore no masks. Although he had moved away, he had always followed my riding career and we had met up regularly for family celebrations, etc.

Witches finished rock bottom of the table that year, 12 points behind Belle Vue. Scott Nicholls was still averaging over nine points a meeting and we had Canadian-Pole Krzysztof Slabon in the side for a second season but it was a very frustrating campaign, leading us to briefly consider dropping down to the Premier League.

We decided to stay in the top flight, with 2004 being much more enjoyable and successful. Finishing third in the league, we also reached the KO Cup Final where we lost on aggregate to a strong Poole outfit. Chris was finally back in the team after his back injury and did well to average over eight points a meeting. We also added two more Scandinavians to our ranks, this time from Denmark – Hans Andersen and Jesper B. Monberg.

We were involved in an unforgettable televised league play-off semi-final against Wolverhampton. Ipswich fans groaned when Scott Nicholls left the track after a fall when he should have remounted to score a point, which would have won us the tie. We were shouting to him from the other side of the fence (the pits being behind the first bend where he was) but he had already switched off and was on his way back. The meeting finally ended 45-45 with Mikael Max beating Hans in a close run-off to decide who would reach the final.

Hans did an excellent job for us for two years – he was very easy to deal with, contract-wise, and always professionally turned out. He won his first GP while he was with us and I remember how proud he was parading it in front of the Foxhall fans. I know he went on to win a least a couple more and, of course, enjoyed World Team Cup success with Denmark.

We also had another promising British youngster in the team that year and I liked what I saw of Danny King from an early stage in his career. When a planned move to another club fell through and it looked as though he was going to be without a ride, I juggled our team around to fit him in. It would have been wrong at that stage of his career not to be riding full-time.

While he was with us, we gave him as much help and encouragement as we could and I think he has always appreciated that. He was certainly more than happy to return to Foxhall in 2015, despite overtures from a host of Premier League clubs.

Scott had a very successful testimonial during 2004, so there were more than a few eyebrows raised when it was announced that he would not be riding for Ipswich the following year. After being unable to agree a new deal with him for 2005, I agreed to allow him to talk to other clubs and he reached an agreement with Coventry. The way that the move was handled was far from ideal, so when they offered to buy his contract, I accepted straight away.

For the record, and contrary to popular belief, the proceeds didn't go towards a brand new Mercedes, exotic holidays or a new des-res for yours truly. It simply went into the bank and helped keep the club afloat through some difficult times. Anyone who thinks that around £35,000 goes a long way when you are running a speedway club is a bit out of touch with reality, to say the least.

In 2005, we went back to Poland to recruit riders with the experienced Piotr 'Pepe' Protasiewicz and the up-and-coming Robert Miskowiak joining the club in place of Scott and Jesper. Pepe turned into a good signing, although he had a tendency to tire towards the end of a season, while Robert's career really grew with us and he stayed a Witch until Ipswich dropped out of the top flight in 2011.

The next year, I took sole control of the club after Magda and I split up. Mike Smillie stepped in at this point and took over the paperwork side of things – he was so much better than me with figures, etc, and by now things were starting to get computerised. The word technophobe was created for me – I just don't get anything 'clever' like e-mails. Even today, my phone is one that just makes calls and receives texts – anything else is completely out of my comfort zone. Mike, however, is fully up to speed and can handle all of that, so I left it in his capable hands.

Mark Loram rejoined the side, much to the delight of his many Ipswich fans. He had lived in the area since he moved up to join Ipswich from Hackney in 1989 and was still regarded as a local, with his reputation enhanced by his world title win in 2000.

Another important milestone for me that year, and something that was greeted with much delight by my daughter Maria, was that I gave up smoking. I had dabbled a bit in my early years – watch a film from the 50s and not only would the hero of the story be smoking but the leading ladies as well. It was regarded as the norm, a social accessory and not something that damaged your health. I then gave up when I was scrambling and never smoked in all the time I was riding speedway but the habit then crept back about a year after I hung up my leathers.

After puffing away for a couple of decades, I decided it was time to stop. By then, the health hazards around smoking were well known and I had also developed a chest problem, probably caused by all the dust and dirt I had inhaled while roaring around scramble circuits. We only had a scarf to protect us in those days.

Initially, I couldn't kick the habit, despite trying patches and other supposedly helpful aids. Then, one day, I arrived home on a mission. There were six fags left in the packet, so I sat down and smoked them all one after the other – they weren't going to be discarded after paying good money for them. Once I had finished, the empty packet went into the bin along with my lighter.

It was one of the hardest battles I have had in my life but, to this day, I have not touched another cigarette, and I'm so pleased. One of the best decisions any government made was to ban cigarettes in restaurants and pubs and it is such a shame to see youngsters still smoking these days, knowing the damage to their health.

One thing I wasn't best pleased about was that I lost my driving licence that year after being stopped on my way home from the stadium on a Thursday night. I did have one drink in the bar before I left Foxhall and then called in at my local – a short drive from my house – to see a sponsor He already had a drink waiting for me and I drank that while we were talking. I left shortly afterwards and took the right turn that would lead me back to the estate where I live, less than a five-minute drive.

Flashing blue lights then appeared in my rear view mirror and I was waved down. What followed was bizarre to say the least. I felt like I had been transported to an American cop show on TV. I was invited to get out of my car and then asked to blow into the breathalyser kit – with my chest problems, I wasn't able to blow hard enough, so they couldn't get a reading. One of the officers then explained that I would have to go to the local station, where they would redo the test. At no point did I get stroppy with them, so I was a bit taken aback when I was turned round, pushed hard up against the police car and had my arms pulled backwards in such a way I thought my shoulders were going to come adrift. This was followed by handcuffs being clamped on my wrists so hard, they were bruised for a couple of weeks.

The officer doing all this was obviously enjoying himself while his colleague watched from a distance and appeared slightly awkward about how the other one was behaving. When we got to

**Lawrence Hare (left) and Kim Jansson (with me in 2015) both saw their careers cut short and their lives changed forever after serious crashes.**

the police station, I explained about my limited lung function but they managed to do another test, which showed I was just slightly over the limit. I paid the ultimate price and lost my licence for 12 months, with my face taking centre stage on the front page of the local papers. A few weeks later, a senior police officer was arrested after driving up and down pavements and found to be well over the limit. That story was buried on about page 10 of the same paper and no picture, which says it all really.

For the next 12 months, I went back to two wheels, cycling everywhere I could and getting lifts if the distance was too far by bike. I accepted my punishment and was obviously pleased when I regained my licence. Looking back, I think I was harshly dealt with. Perhaps being well known locally went against me but that still doesn't explain why I was treated like someone who was a danger to society when I was pulled over.

German Tobi Kroner also joined us in 2006 and looked to have bags of potential. He lodged with Mark Loram and his style did sometimes remind you of a young Mark. Always smiling, Tobi fitted into the team quickly but he didn't quite appear to have the killer instinct that is required in some races to achieve the victory and appeared to take a long time to recover his confidence after quite small injuries. He was probably too nice to be a top rider and I mean that in the best possible way.

Mark and Chris had some memorable races in that season and I remember one when they were up against Todd Wiltshire. The three of them all had great respect for each other and put on a brilliant show for the fans with the lead constantly changing – I can't remember who won but I think it was one of our two. Mark readily agreed to return for the next year and spent a lot of time training over the winter months to improve his fitness.

Heartbreak followed for him and our fans when, on the opening lap of the first heat of the 2007 season against Reading, Mark badly broke his thigh in an horrendous crash along the back straight at Foxhall. It was a huge loss to speedway because, after several attempts to regain a level of fitness that would enable him to ride again, Mark announced his retirement. Thankfully, after such an awful injury, he's stlll able to walk and enjoy a full life. Mark's injury took all the wind out of our sails before we had even started that year but the following season we managed fourth in the league.

We had a new team manager, Pete Simmons, in 2008 as Mike took more of a backstage role. On the down side, Chris injured his arm quite badly towards the end of April and missed the rest of the campaign, which again hampered our attempts to mount a serious challenge for honours. We did manage to sign Rory Schlein mid-season and he rode well for us but couldn't quite match Chris' expertise of the Foxhall circuit.

We also had bad news from Sweden in August, when Kim Jansson suffered a bad crash and was left paralysed after breaking his back. Although he was no longer a Witch, Kim still had a special place in many Ipswich fans' hearts and everyone was shattered to hear the news.

Once we had all recovered from the shock, a fund was set up and several events were held to get things moving with team manager Pete Simmons heavily involved. His company Sano had sponsored Kim for most of his time at Ipswich and they had become very close friends. A cricket match and a golf day were both well attended and I know that Kim was very grateful for the money raised. The cricket matches continued for several years and the golf day is still held annually as far as I know.

Jarek Hampel had returned that year, alongside a new Pole, Piotr Swiderski. Piotr started at reserve and finished second in the Ipswich averages behind Jarek. The language barrier wasn't a problem. Both spoke enough English to get by and Piotr quickly became known for his sense of humour (quite unusual for a Pole).

I think everyone remembers him being interviewed by Kevin Long after he had scored a paid maximum at Poole while suffering with a leg injury. For some reason, the interview for the meeting

DVD (by ReRun) was done at Foxhall the following night, with Kevin having to remind Piotr that he was 'still at Poole'. Piotr went on to explain, while trying to keep a straight face and failing, that his k-nee injury was quite bad and that he had been quite ill while at Poole, to which Kevin replied: "You mean you were ill earlier tonight and what was that you injured? It's called a knee, the k is silent." More giggles from Piotr as he practiced a silent k, which didn't quite happen!

At one point in that season, we had a very good run of form and reached second in the table but slipped back down to fourth before the end of the season.

The following year, the ladies (or so I am told) were very pleased to welcome young Australian Kozza Smith to the team and we added another new Pole, Dawid Stachyra. Completely opposite personalities, they both proved to be good signings and I remember spending a lot of time with Kozza to develop the lines he took around the track. He didn't get the hang of it right away but a couple of years later, he came back and won the Star of Anglia. He made a point of thanking me afterwards for my help when he was in the team, which was very nice of him. We had started the year with Jarek at No.1 but he decided part way through the season that he wanted to concentrate on his Polish riding, so we brought back Scott to replace him, which appeared to please most Ipswich fans.

Chris finally announced his retirement in 2010 as he moved towards a promoter's role alongside me. At this point, he took over the running of the club with me finally able to 'retire', although I would still hold a licence, as there is a requirement for two promoters at every track. Chris obviously wanted to stamp his own mark on the club and his first move was to alter the shape of our track, as he wanted to see better and safer racing. I must admit, I had mixed feelings initially, I thought it might take some of the home track advantage away.

It was quite a costly exercise but, as ever, our faithful fans supported us. Based on an idea from an old programme, a Shale Sponsorship Scheme was set up with the track being divided into 200 plots at £25 each. As well as that, we held an event at a local social club called 'An Evening With John Louis', where I was interviewed by Kevin Long, in between several DVDs of racing from my era, including the British Final in '75. I demonstrated that I could still fit into my orange 'Tiger' leathers without the use of a shoehorn or any lubricating fluid! Altogether, an impressive £7,500 was raised for which the club was very grateful.

I measured out the new track dimensions and we went two metres in at the apex of both bends and one metre in along the straights. It brought us up to FIM requirements and now that I am used to the new shape, I think it has improved the entertainment value of the racing but I also believe I was right about the home track advantage being reduced.

Would I have fared any differently if I had ridden the current track? No, I prided myself on riding all tracks well. It's a case of how much you want to ride speedway, and how much you want to win, rather than whether it's a small track or a big one.

Robert Miskowiak could be frustrating but he proved a consistent middle order scorer for us – who can forget his spectacular crash at Oxford which club photographer Steve Waller captured so brilliantly with the Pole upside down, somersaulting over the fence before landing on the greyhound track. He picked himself up, won the rerun and completed the meeting before returning to Ipswich in the early hours. He went straight to A&E, where he had a hole in his leg patched up. It was typical of many Poles, who will always choose to carry on riding unless they have actually broken a bone.

Danny King had also rejoined the team along with young up-and-coming Swede Linus Sundstrom. On paper, we looked to have a competitive side but, for some reason, they didn't gel together or achieve anything like what we had hoped for, finishing with the wooden spoon.

We were getting into a precarious financial situation with our poor league form having a lot to do with it, and the time was ripe for a change. After much soul searching, we announced a drop down to the Premier League – leaving the top flight after two decades. One of our biggest supporters for dropping down at the BSPA was King's Lynn – they were already talking of renewing the fierce rivalry between our two clubs that had raged when both Chris and I rode. Looking back, I'm not sure how sincere this support was because, almost immediately after it was confirmed we could join the Premier League, King's Lynn were shouting about joining the Elite League. The incentive they received no doubt helped their decision.

Our intention when we started the 2011 campaign was to re-group and get back to the top flight of British speedway as soon as it was feasibly possible. The move did provide closer racing than we had experienced at Foxhall for some time, with riders at that level more evenly matched. With the help of the new track shape, away riders could now dial in more quickly and there seemed to be more overtaking.

Sackers Recycling came in as new team sponsors and we captured some silverware that year by winning the Premier League Fours, plus we also finished third in the table. By dropping down to the second tier, we had to rebuild the team from scratch with younger riders such as Lasse Bjerre, Taylor Poole and Jerran Hart joining the ranks alongside the more experienced Kevin Doolan and Morten Risager.

In 2012, we got through to the KO Cup Final, where we lost to Newcastle, and finished seventh in the league. On the up side, it saw the introduction of two exciting, young Australian riders in Rohan Tungate and Cameron Heeps.

Rohan is a natural motorcyclist who Chris was keen to have in the side from the first time he saw him. He has the ability to go places, although his progress has slowed a bit of late. John Berry recommended Cameron to us after seeing him ride as a schoolboy in Perth – Chris wasted no time in securing his signature. Cameron made lightning early progress but in the last 12 months has also levelled off. Hopefully, this is only a temporary loss of form.

It was fitting that a link with JB should continue in the year that the former Witches promoter died unexpectedly of a heart attack while watching his other passion of cricket at home on TV. We were all very saddened to hear the news and held a memorial meeting for him later that year. I've said much about JB, some good, some not so good, but without doubt he was responsible for bringing speedway back from the dead in Ipswich and providing high levels of entertainment and success throughout the years he was in charge.

Seasons 2013 and 2014 saw the Witches enjoy very good league campaigns but lose momentum just as the play-offs arrived, which is very frustrating for all concerned. We reached the finals of the League Cup and the KO Cup during that time as well but the silverware still eluded us. In 2015, Danny King and Rohan Tungate did us proud by winning the PL Pairs championship at Somerset in July.

**During my time as promoter, I have given board and lodgings to a host of foreign riders, mostly staying over for only a short period of time. It comes with the territory when you have people who jet in for a meeting and then head off home the next day or to another country to race. Most organise their accommodation in advance but when they don't, or can't, my spare room is made available.**

Tomasz Gollob used to want to travel home whenever he could but, if we had two meetings in quick succession, he would stay over. He was a very good natured and considerate guest and fitted in well with the family. He liked nothing more on free nights than to don a pair of slippers and sit with us in the lounge to chill out. Although when the mood took him, he also liked to go ten-pin bowling, go-karting or swimming at a local pool. Whatever he did, he was good at, especially the go-karting.

I'm not sure how it came about but we had a group of Polish fruit-pickers turn up in a mini-bus one Thursday night after travelling about 20 miles from where they all worked. They also had a priest on board and they all assembled in my back garden after the meeting, where Tomasz talked to them about his life in speedway over here. I could see in their faces that it meant such a lot to them being with a big celebrity from their own country and I think Tomasz enjoyed it as well.

These days, Ryanair fly daily flights out of nearby Stansted to most Polish cities but in the 90s Tomasz had to go to Heathrow to catch his flights. Nine times out of 10, it was me who drove him to and from the main London terminal that is at least two hours away on a good day. His outward flights were at 7.00am, which meant a four o'clock departure from my house, with Tomasz reclining the passenger seat down as far as it would go with a pillow and blanket for the journey.

The car heating had to be turned up full as well and it wasn't long before he was asleep. After a while, I began to sweat, so I would slowly move my hand to the control and turn it down. A few minutes would pass and then, with his eyes still closed, out would come Tomasz's hand ever so slowly to turn it back up again – and this continued all the way to Heathrow. When we reached the airport, Tomasz would ask me to park up so that he could sleep a little longer before making a last-minute dash to check-in but I told him every time that it was best if he continued his snoozing in the airport, as I was keen to get back on the road. The journey home was much cooler and, with a following wind, I would be back asleep by 8.00am.

Jarek Hampel was also good fun to have around and he would stay more often and for longer periods. He would also mix in with family life easily and was extremely polite and easy to get on with, plus his English was better. Apparently, he learned a lot from singing our pop songs and was always keen for us to help him improve. I'm pleased to see that he has continued to improve since leaving us and enjoyed success both in the GPs and the World Team Cup.

Kim Jansson was the other rider to stay at Louis Towers and he was another fun-loving lad who was a pleasure to get to know. Being a Swede, his English was better than mine and after meetings we used to sit down in the kitchen and re-live each of his races.

We talked about the right lines to take and how to get the maximum return from every ride. He was happy to chat for hours. But however hard I tried, I could not get across the need to concentrate fully for 60 seconds. Kim could ride three circuits as though he was a World Champion and then, on the last lap, he would wander off and go round the boards, sometimes coming to grief. I could put a sixpence down on the track and ride over it all four laps but Kim would slowly drift wider and wider with each passing lap.

I remember he had real problems when riding at Lakeside, where the turns are tight and tricky. He just couldn't get his head around the track there at all and was already expecting a zero return before he was halfway there.

Alan Mogridge had exactly the same problem and, in his case, I walked him round the track on his own while I explained the best lines and how to go into the corners. It meant changing his usual style but Alan gave it a go and got about seven points that night. Several of us tried the same approach with Kim but his head still told him that he couldn't ride the track and so he never did.

Despite siffering that life-changing crash in Sweden and being confined to a wheelchair, Kim is still the same fun-loving, rounded person and a credit to himself and his family. He has been back to college and is continuing to make a success of his life, which is great to see. I try to catch up with him when he comes over for the golf day, as he usually pays a visit to Foxhall at the same time – that's if I can get through the crowd of fans who want to speak to him.

With Chris joining me on the other side of the fence, 2011 brought a new era of Premier League racing to Ipswich.
You can see from this shot of me celebrating with Nico Covatti and Gino Manzares, I'm just as excited by
Danny King's first heat victory from a 15-metre handicap as they are.

Just like old times . . . on parade with all the other former riders at our 60th anniversary meeting in 2011.

**Young Chris has his eye on a fast start against the 'Old Man' while (above) Ron Bagley does a none too impressive Paul Johnson impression. But as this later picture (below) shows, Chris was soon dialled in at Foxhall.**

Chapter 27

# Like Father, Like Son

**I**CONSIDER **myself to have been very lucky the way my life has panned out. Not only did I enjoy a wonderful career doing what I loved, and achieving many successes on the way, but my son Chris has followed virtually the same path, which means I have been able to re-live all the excitement and enjoyment again.**

In some ways, he has achieved more than me, as I did not start out in speedway until I was 28 and therefore had no involvement in the under-21 scene.

Like every father, I'm proud of all my children. Daughter Joanne, with her horses and family and how she has battled so bravely through the loss of her eldest son Rhys. My youngest daughter Maria, with her boundless energy, who has already shown enough to confirm to me that she has the ability to achieve her dream of becoming an actress if the right breaks come along. I'll talk more about Joanne, Rhys and Maria in the next chapter.

Obviously, Chris and I have spent a lot more time together. Having narrowly missed out on the World Under-21 title in 1989 after a run-off with Gert Handberg in Lonigo, Italy, he went on to win the title 12 months later in Lvov, Ukraine. Later, he matched my third place finish in a World Final, won the British Championship twice, captained his country and his hometown club, won titles with Ipswich and then followed me into promoting the Witches.

It has been uncanny really how our career achievements are so similar. Chris would have won the Elite League Riders' Championship as well if he had not suffered a machine problem on the last lap at Bradford, gifting Sam Ermolenko the title.

I bought him a 50cc bike when he was four-years-old but it was really just something for him to have fun on. He soon got the hang of which way to turn the throttle to go faster or slow down while riding around our back garden. I remember that one of his friends wanted to have a go, so I talked him through the same things and off he went down the garden. As he approached the end, I realised he had forgotten how to stop and ran after him, shouting instructions. Too late! He careered through a couple of shrubs and only came to a halt when he hit the back fence. Luckily, he was okay but I decided that only Chris would play on his bike after that.

As he became more confident, we took the bike up to the stadium and I built little ramps for him to jump over. We had great fun riding round the track, me on my Bultaco trials bike and Chris trying his hardest to keep up with me. He started grass-track around the age of eight and went on to be a good little rider. A few years later, he started moto-cross – many of his friends had taken it up and he was good at that too.

For most of Chris' teenage years, I didn't think about him becoming a speedway rider. He seemed more than happy just doing his moto-cross and speedway was never discussed. I have never been a pushy parent – I had seen several examples of what happens when you push a child too hard on the grass-track circuit – and I preferred that Chris made up his own mind as to which direction he wanted to take.

Returning home one day, I was a bit surprised when I went into my garage and found one of my bikes, plus toolbox and bike stand, had gone. I had an inkling of where they might be, so I decided to wait for Chris to come home. Sure enough, when he returned, it transpired that he had been to Hackney and taken part in the open speedway practice sessions that were held weekly there in those days. It was a time when significant numbers of boys wanted to try the sport and the east London club were keen to let them have an opportunity. These sessions proved very popular and it's a shame that nowadays you would struggle to fill a monthly practice session.

I was secretly pleased that Chris was showing an interest in speedway but decided not to show it to him. After he told me where he had been, I simply said: "I'm glad you enjoyed yourself. If the bike is dirty, please clean it before you put it away."

It was soon obvious that Chris was interested as he carried on travelling down the A12 with pal Dick Partridge to have further laps around Hackney. This was in late 1987 and early 1988, and it was not long before I was slipping down to Waterden Road myself to watch his practice sessions.

It did not take a trained eye to see that Chris was a natural, who had watched others in action and taken it all on-board. He did not require too much tuition and, remarkably, his starting techniques were almost identical to mine. From then on, his career path was decided and if he wanted any help, I was happy to assist. But he climbed the ladder rapidly without too much outside interference, starting by making a name for himself as a free-scoring reserve when Hackney won all before them in 1988.

Just before he began riding for Hackney, Chris did something I'm not sure I would have attempted when he accompanied Dick on the Paris to Dakar rally and nearly got lost in the desert. They came across another competitor who had broken his leg, so Chris agreed to ride his bike while the injured rider went in the 4x4 with Dick. Somehow, they got separated and Chris was left on his own with no sign of life anywhere. He had the sense to go to the highest point around and scan the horizon. Finally, he picked up something that looked like dust being thrown up by a vehicle, so he headed in that direction. His hunch paid off when he caught up with Dick and stuck to him like glue from then on to the finishing point.

The following season, he moved to Ipswich when I took over at Foxhall with Dave Pavitt and Mike Western and he has stayed loyal to his local club ever since. There were occasional rumours over the years that Chris might move on but, to be honest, he never showed any real interest in doing so.

Chris gradually became more involved in the off-track affairs at Ipswich and joined me as co-promoter in 2010. Since then, he has effectively been running the club, allowing me to take more and more of a back seat, and he has done very well. In fact, he has kept the Witches going in what are difficult times for the whole sport.

Speedway meetings are costly to run with rent, riders' payments and meeting day expenses to cover week-in, week-out, and with the attendance figures country-wide appearing to drop every year, it is difficult. I'd love Chris to have a season like I enjoyed as a promoter in 1998, when Ipswich won the treble, but those teams only come along once in a decade or so.

He made the decision to drop down to the Premier League in 2011, which I backed fully. I'm happy to stick my neck out and say that the racing is closer and more exciting to watch than in the Elite League. We have won a couple of trophies at this level and hopefully more will come, but picking a winning team is very hard.

At the beginning of 2015, experts were predicting that Ipswich would win the league and, to be honest, on paper, I thought we had a good chance. However, injuries and a few riders not progressing as well as we had expected has prevented us achieving what we had hoped for. This same problem is faced every year by many teams and it won't get better in the short-term. I'm glad in a way that I am no longer running the business. I am too old for all the worry that goes with it nowadays.

**Now that I have spare time to pursue other interests, you may be surprised to hear that three or four times a week you will find me donning my dancing shoes and heading off for a three-to-four hour work-out at one of several venues around Suffolk and Essex. I have taken**

Ceroc is fun and energetic and I hope to have more than a few laps on the dance circuit left in me.

**up Ceroc, which is a form of modern jive, and it brings back memories of my dancing that I so enjoyed as a teenager.**

It took a while for the lessons to sink in but after five years I have reached a reasonable standard and can now go to freestyle events, knowing that I can dance with most people without making a prat of myself.

I even go to a holiday camp on the east coast once a year for three days where we have a mixture of workshops, dance sessions and entertainment in the evenings, which I thoroughly enjoy.

It was Dennis Maskey who introduced me to Ceroc. I have known him since the company he worked for, Connells Building Supplies, sponsored the Witches in the early 90s. We bumped into each other at a local pub where he was performing and I took to the dance floor. He told me about the dance lessons he went to and suggested I give it a look. I duly turned up and have been hooked ever since.

It is quite energetic and has helped me stay fit at an age when many take to their armchairs with a pipe and slippers. Kevin Jolly's wife Jill supplies me with something that helps keep my energy levels up – she works for James White, a local drinks company who produce 'Beet It', organic beetroot shots. She suggested I give them a try when Kevin and I were talking once about not being as fit as we once were and I mentioned that I was tired after my first few dance lessons. I'm not sure if it's all down to them but my staying power has definitely increased and I do notice a difference if I go for a couple of weeks without taking them. They help with my dancing as well!

The main thing is that I'm still challenging myself, which is something I've been doing all my life and don't plan on giving up any time soon. Unfortunately, I'm a bit too old to put my name down for *Strictly,* which is a shame as being partnered with Kristina Rihanoff would definitely make my eyes sparkle.

Hopefully, I can stay fit and be around for a few more years, working beside Chris at Foxhall. He is doing a great job and doesn't really need any help from me anymore but I still enjoy being involved and get just as excited now with a win as in the previous 46 years of my association with Ipswich Witches.

I was lucky enough to have inherited natural motorcycling skills from my father Jack and I'm so happy that I made the most of that talent. Everything about my life – home, work, college, riding, promoting – has been wonderful. I've enjoyed a fantastic innings.

Some say you have to be mad to be a speedway rider. Oh no, I'm just mad that it's all coming to an end . . .

Chris and I on the day we were invited to Buckingham Palace in 1992.

Chapter 28
# Family Affair

THOSE closest to me, and some who are no longer as close, have all played a part in my life, a life I can look back on with so much satisfaction and happiness.

My family life has been a bit eventful, to say the least, but regardless of what has happened, I have no bad feelings towards anybody. Yes, there has been some pain along the way but that's nothing unusual and, despite a few episodes that I prefer not to dwell on, I have no regrets as my immediate family have always supported me 100 per cent.

My parents shaped the early part of my life. Jack spent countless hours ensuring that when I set out on my career, my machinery was spot on and the best it could possibly be. He taught me so much and it means more to me than anything that in a sport he loved – speedway – I was able to make him so proud.

Vera was the calm centre of the family in the early days and provided us all with the values that we would take forward in adulthood. She gave us all an upbringing that pointed us in the right direction to make the best of ourselves. She lived well into her 80s and was a regular spectator at Foxhall until her health prevented it. As I have already acknowledged, the collection of press cuttings she left me has provided the basis for this book and I never knew she was doing it.

My brother Tony, who was an expert cycle speedway rider in his early days, was always there with wise words, praise and encouragement, even after he relocated to Derby to work as foreman at a power station after moving from the Sizewell site in Suffolk. Like me, he was fortunate to travel the world as part of his job, working in Canada, South Africa and Anglesey. He and his wife Jill had two lovely daughters, Suzanne and Jane. In 2003, he died prematurely from the effects of asbestos poisoning and I remember him once describing the stuff falling like snow when they were stripping out a redundant building. This was before the dangerous side effects were commonly known.

My sister Pat moved to Manchester for several years with her husband Dave Wilkins, who worked as an accountant for a shipping company after initially starting his career with the Inland Revenue in Ipswich. While they lived there, I would often stay over when riding at Belle Vue and they came to watch the meetings when they could. They are now back living in Suffolk while their only daughter Jenni currently lives in the USA. Although now retired, Dave has been doing the books for Ipswich Speedway, alongside Mike Smillie, for about 10 years.

Dave and I have been long-time friends and he was best man when I married Pat at Great Bentley church, Essex. Dave arranged for a guard of honour as we left the church with exhaust pipes being held aloft to salute the happy couple. Not one to arrange things too efficiently off the track, I had to rush into Ipswich at the last minute to buy some suitable wedding shoes. In my haste, I forgot to remove the price tag from the soles, which amused the congregation in the church when I knelt down during the ceremony in front of the vicar.

Our first home was a bungalow in a small village outside Ipswich called Debenham. We later moved to a semi-detached house in Ipswich when we needed extra bedrooms. As my career took off, Pat and I were able to purchase Ashton House, a property where we installed a swimming pool and did extensive work, inside and out. It was located in Bramford, another village on the outskirts of Ipswich. A good friend of mine that I have already mentioned, Joe Harvey, did most of the work for us, while I 'managed' various projects over a 12-month period.

It was all very lavish, with real studded leather on one wall in the dining room, although, to be honest, it would not have been to everybody's taste. I was a tad concerned when we put the house up for sale. I needn't have worried, though. A South African, who was the main engineer during the building of the Orwell Bridge in Ipswich, came in and looked at just three rooms. He was inside for about five minutes without even going upstairs but he must have liked what he saw because a few days later he put in an offer and it all went through from there.

We moved to a large converted cottage at the end of a quiet lane a few miles away. Three small cottages had been converted into one and there was a big double garage that was ideal to act as my workshop.

We were beside a large sandpit and there was quite a steep drop down into the pit nearby the cottage. The manager of the site was happy for me to use it in return for keeping others, who were perhaps not so respectful, off his property.

It was here that I gave Chris an introduction to how much fun you can have on a scrambling bike. He was about nine or 10 at the time and I used to sit him down on the petrol tank in front of me and take him through a course that I had arranged for myself.

It was not any old machine either, but a powerful 360cc CZ that had plenty of power. I was not long enough in the leg to get astride the bike, so I had to set things up by a bank so I could put myself in a position to kick-start the bike into action. Once on the move, we dropped down the bank and set off around the pit at a fair old speed.

Chris used to take control of the throttle sometimes when sitting in front of me, and also go round on his own for a bit. It was quite a funny sight as his feet were about a foot away from the footrests but even then he showed good control and didn't do anything silly. When he was ready to stop, he had the sense to slow down enough so I could catch the bike and let him get off.

We would then wind the throttle up so that we could get back up the steep incline – and home.

My eldest daughter Joanne brings a much different kind of horsepower to the family through her love of horses.

To give you an idea of the height we scaled, it was approximately the same as a two-storey house.

Chris, of course, has an older sister Joanne who has barely had a mention so far. She has always had a love of horses and, as she grew up, she had several different ones and took part in gymkhanas which I used to attend whenever possible. She is much more at home on the beasts than I ever was and has a talent for being able to break in difficult horses for other people – it's almost like she knows what they are thinking.

This was to be our last family house before Pat and I split up soon afterwards and went our separate ways. Both children stayed with their mum until Chris reached his 16th birthday, when he arrived on my doorstep and moved in with me. Chris often used to cycle over to my house and occasionally I would pass him in my car – when I saw him, I slowed down until he was alongside me and he then grabbed the car door handle on the passenger side. We continued home like that, with him coasting along beside the car.

As many of you already know, Pat later married Jeremy Doncaster and they had a son Jens. They are all part of the wider Louis family and there is no awkwardness when we all meet up for family celebrations. Jem, in fact, took over as the main machine examiner at Foxhall when Fred Cotton retired a few years back, so we are in close contact throughout the season.

It was on the trip to Ukraine to see Chris win the 1990 World U21 title that I met my second wife Magda. Local travel agent James Easter arranged the trip and we flew from Heathrow via Frankfurt to Krakow in Poland. The speedway club in Rzeszow, where we were going to spend the first night, had been asked by James to provide an interpreter. Magda met us at Krakow airport and helped our party cope with the Russian border crossing and then throughout our time in Ukraine.

I kept in touch with her, making regular visits to Poland, and by the time she came over to live in England, we had a daughter, Maria. We were married at Stowmarket Registry Office with Magda's parents, Maria and Mikel, coming over for the ceremony.

Maria grew up speaking fluent English and Polish and, as a family, we spent holidays in Rzeszow on a regular basis. Magda regularly wrote articles on the British scene for a top Polish speedway magazine and she became increasingly involved with Ipswich Witches, becoming a co-promoter for a while after Dave Pavitt left.

We had some great times in the cul-de-sac where we lived in Kesgrave, which is only a few minutes away from Foxhall, with regular parties that we all took turns in to play host. Our next-door neighbours were Ipswich Town footballer Paul Mason, his wife Andrea and their three young children and we got on really well with them. It was nice to socialise with people who were not connected with speedway, although they all helped us celebrate the successes of 1998 – I think the whole town knew about that, even if they weren't a speedway fan. That's all in the past now because many of our 'party crowd' have moved out, to be replaced in the main by people who can just about nod 'Good Morning' but not a lot else.

From an early age, Maria liked putting on a show, first in the house with friends and then, as she grew up, I was her regular chauffeur as she joined various amateur drama groups and appeared in shows at local theatres around our area. In her teens, she was one of the four start girls we had at Foxhall, along with her friends Alexandra and Sophie Cantwell and Lauren Johan, with Maria planning their routines.

Magda and I split up while Maria was in her mid-teens and she lived with us both equally, although she finished her schooling here in Kesgrave. She then went on to attend a top London drama school and, since gaining her degree, has made a number of television appearances, including a BBC series *The Doctors* and *People Just Do Nothing* as well as working in Harrods and Harvey Nichols. She now lives permanently in London and is currently working for a marketing company while she waits for her big opportunity to come knocking.

One incident I must include here happened when I was well into my 60s and I had access to a mini-motorbike – known as a 'monkey bike'. I took a break from getting things ready at Foxhall for our traditional Good Friday afternoon meeting to take a ride in the woods around the stadium.

It was great fun but I got too carried away for my own good. Deciding to do a few laps of the track for old time's sake, I rode back into the stadium. I managed the first circuit okay but the second time around, with me rather stupidly trying to replicate my heyday, I turned the bike into a slide and tipped over.

I banged my head hard on the ground and was knocked unconscious. I came round a bit in the ambulance after a 999 call had been made but they whisked me off to Addenbrooke's in Cambridge, where they kept me in for four days doing tests. To be honest, they were never going to find too much evidence of intelligence and I was allowed home, thankfully none the worse for wear.

But if ever there was a lesson to be learnt, this was it – always wear a crash helmet, folks.

I was very lucky on that occasion but tragedy was to strike the family in 2011. My daughter Joanne had a son Rhys with Mark Loram. A lovely, well-liked lad, I used to watch him ride moto-cross behind Mildenhall Speedway stadium and he was a quick and clever young rider. I believe he had natural talent on a bike and could have gone on to a career in moto-cross or speedway if he had wanted.

He had a brush with death at the age of just three when he fell into a pond in the family garden. He was saved on that occasion by the family dog Henka barking furiously to raise the alarm and Joanne was able to pull him out in time. The dog was awarded a medal, only to sadly lose his own life shortly afterwards.

Fifteen years later, on a November evening, Rhys was walking in a country lane near his home on the way to pick up his car from his dad's garage when he was struck on the head by the wing mirror of a passing van and was killed almost instantly. The news hit us all very hard – he was barely 18 and had so much to live for.

The church at Coddenham was absolutely packed for Rhys' funeral and it was a very poignant service, with all his school friends wearing casual gear at the request of his mum. He was obviously a very popular lad and his friends were clearly heartbroken. It's impossible to get over such a tragedy and Joanne naturally still spends time doing things in her son's memory.

We all deal with grief in different ways and I make a point of saying goodbye to loved ones in the Chapel of Rest. I did the same for my dad, my mum and my brother, as well as Rhys. I ask for a few minutes to be left alone and I then relive all the good times we shared. After which, I end with a kiss on the forehead – it's my way of saying goodbye for the last time.

Joanne also has another son, Haydn, with ex-partner Andrew, who was greatly affected by the loss of his big brother. He is another really nice boy who is probably already taller than me and will, I'm sure, do his mum proud, whatever career path he decides to follow.

Along with Haydn, I have two other wonderful grandchildren in Hannah and Freya, who are the daughters of Chris and his wife Julie. Hannah and her partner Morten Risager live together in Loughborough, where she is studying for a degree at the local university. Freya has a big interest in photography and media work; she has produced videos of Ipswich home meetings and shows a great talent in that direction.

**Yes, I have been very fortunate to have such a loyal and supportive family but I also have to mention my other 'speedway' family – the dedicated bunch that have helped and supported me during both my riding and promoting careers.**

I'm sure many clubs up and down the country have come to rely on dedicated volunteers giving up their time to help wherever they can. Some perform manual work that has to be done before and after

Rhys Loram, my daughter Joanne's eldest son, demonstrating his moto-cross skills and (inset) pictured just eight months before he was tragically killed in 2011.

Daughter Joanne and her youngest son Haydn.

With my youngest daughter Maria on her 18th birthday.

Still playing around on two wheels, this time with Paul Hughes

every meeting, regardless of the weather, while others work constantly behind-the-scenes to ensure all the paperwork, advertising and general running of the club is kept up-to-date.

At Foxhall, there have been so many who have played their part over the years, from team managers down to turnstile operators. The list is too long to mention everybody but they will all be forever in my gratitude. I apologise now if I don't remember you all.

When I was riding, my main support (apart from Dad) came from my mechanics and they were all great at their job. I can't remember any of them letting me down, apart from the odd hiccup with fuel. **Brian 'Brassy' Goodchild** and **Colin Robinson** were with me in the early days and the mainstay later on was **John Bloomfield,** who accompanied me on many a trip abroad but we could never share a room because his snoring kept me awake! **Mick McPike,** based in Birmingham, also helped out whenever I was riding in the Midlands. A big thank you must go to all of them for doing what was needed to keep my bikes and me ready for action.

On to promoting, where I really discovered the myriad of roles and skills that are required to keep a club running smoothly. As a rider, I had always been aware of the many people milling around at Foxhall, and indeed the other tracks I visited, but I don't think I ever appreciated what they all did to advertise the fixtures, sign up sponsors, get the stadium ready and ensure the meetings ran on time and within the rules, etc. In fact, on occasions, I thought that some of them were a pain in the a*** because they wouldn't let me take the lap of honour I wanted, tried to change my starting position or just generally told me what I couldn't do!

In no particular order, I am hugely indebted to the following staff who have stood by me through thick and thin since I started promoting at Foxhall (and some of them were there when I was riding as well). You are all brilliant and I honestly believe that I have the best group of people out of all speedway clubs in the UK. A very big thank you to all.

The work of the track curator is a huge undertaking and, of course, the weather plays such a part in how well it goes every week. At Foxhall, we also have the added problems associated with running so soon after large stock car events, with all the debris that can be left behind afterwards. **Bob Ellis** is our current man and has been for many years – I reckon he has done the most laps around Foxhall of anybody.

Bob can be found at the stadium virtually seven days a week, come hail or shine. If you can't find him on the track, he is bound to be busy repairing fence panels, dealing with leaks in the changing rooms or something that we all do every 30 minutes on race-day – checking the weather forecast. Bob keeps close tabs on the weather as conditions play such an important part in how a track will ride. His preparation depends on both short and long-term weather prospects and what he does is down to how he expects conditions to pan out.

If he expects rain on race-day, he will tyre-pack beforehand so that the rain runs off or, if dry weather prevails, then his water bowser is constantly on the go all day. It's a very physical job and one that requires a thick skin as well – if the track is not deemed to be perfect on race-day, fans and riders can be quick to point their finger at the preparation, which is extremely unfair but human nature I guess. It really is a job where you will never please all of the people all of the time.

Bob's wife **Chris** is also a long-standing member of staff. In the past, she used to keep the offices and changing rooms clean and did all the teas and coffees for staff during the interval but has reduced her hours since becoming a grandmother. She still sells the programmes at every home meeting and organises an annual three-day trip to the Cardiff GP with Kevin Long, which is always over-subscribed. Another thing she is very well known for is her delicious fruitcakes that appear before a meeting and often provided for the fence gang when they assemble on Monday mornings.

His title is now general manager but he has also been team manager (including the glorious 1998 season) and programme editor. **Mike Smillie** is very quiet and unassuming but he has done a great job in all his roles since he first started helping out in 1989. He currently does the accounts with my brother-in-law **Dave Wilkins.**

Another long-term stalwart is **Brian Messenger,** who preceded Mike as team manager and resumed the role on a temporary basis in the latter half of 2014. He was also team manager of our reserve team back in the 90s before they were done away with. Brian has a motorcycling background and can turn his hand to any job that might need doing in the pits area. His official title currently is training instructor but he also steps in when the clerk of the course or pits marshal is unavailable. Brian's wife **Norma** acts as receptionist on race-nights and telephones the result through at the end of the meeting.

**Pete Simmons** did well during his time as team manager, before former policeman **Phil Hilton** took on the role in 2015. He is also a centregreen photographer of many years. Phil, in his previous life, did on occasions have reason to pull alongside me when I was cruising down the A12 towards London to indicate that perhaps my foot needed to come off the throttle a small bit. He now has the opposite problem – trying to get some of the boys to open up their throttle and look as if they have something stronger than a lawnmower engine in their bikes!

Someone who was definitely around in my riding days was **Keith Barton,** our current clerk of the course. I don't think he remembers this but once, after a good win, I was preparing for a lap of honour when he stood in front of me, waving his arms indicating that I should get off the track. I decided to play up and just carried on towards him at a sensible pace, picking him up on my handlebars and carrying him a few yards down the track. I suspect his language was unrepeatable but I thought it was quite funny. Keith's role can be a pressurised position if passions run high, which they often do, but he is very good at keeping everyone under control.

Pits marshal **Richard Amott** is another key man who will be found with a clipboard in one hand and walkie talkie in the other, keeping everybody in the right place at the right time. He does a similar job at Mildenhall, so he must enjoy it – another 'veteran', I can remember him shouting to hurry me up with the two-minute siren already sounded.

**Shane Silburn** is meeting co-ordinator – his job is to kccp the evening moving smoothly in another role that most supporters are unaware of. And the man with his finger on the button should not be forgotten. **John Bennett** is incident recorder at Foxhall and has clocked thousands of races over many years by pressing his stopwatch when the tapes go up and again when the race winner crosses the line. In fact, he probably clocked me breaking the Foxhall track record the 14 or so times I did it between 1970 and 1979. John also has to report every accident and incident in detail, and his work has to be spot on as it can be used for insurance purposes.

Every rider knows that **Jeremy Doncaster** will be checking his bike to ensure all is legal before a meeting in his role as machine examiner. Back in the 70s, **Fred Cotton** occupied that role and continued to do so until he retired just a few years ago. He was, of course, a manager at Dave Bickers' shop where I worked before I turned professional.

Some of the most important – and vital – staff on duty are the medical team that comprises of a paramedic, backed up by the wonderful St. John's Ambulance volunteers. Their faces have changed over the years with **Jason Gillingham** currently the chief paramedic at Foxhall. His treatment of numerous riders has earned many plaudits, with his cheery paramedic's skills evident by his call-up to take his place on the centregreen for recent GPs at the Millennium Stadium, Cardiff. He was also on hand when Lewis Kerr was seriously injured at Peterborough during the PL Fours in 2015.

Things are so different nowadays to when I was riding. I can remember coming off at Foxhall and after a quick once over, I was literally dragged off by my ankle so the racing could restart. A great deal more care is taken today and we all have to be patient sometimes while the medical team do their checks.

We have always had very competent start marshals, first with **Ray Chinnery** and the flamboyant **Paul Johnson** in JB's day. **John Fitch** followed and is still 'first reserve' if our current man, **Peter Ingram,** is unavailable. Such is their professionalism that Peter and John were invited to officiate at the British GP in Cardiff last year (2014), when they did their usual expert job.

If you need advice on how to reach any tracks abroad, you could do worse than speak to **Richard 'Strawb' Scales,** who can be found on the pit gate with his daughter **Julie.** 'Strawb' is so nicknamed because of his liking for strawberry ice cream, which he eats on his numerous journeys, covering thousands of miles, driving Ipswich riders all over Europe for meetings.

Once he's been somewhere, he can find it again without the aid of any maps or sat nav, regardless of distance travelled. He can set off from Calais and turn up at the required destination perhaps 12 hours later with his passenger having enjoyed a sleep most of the way, relaxed in the knowledge that they won't get lost.

While we are on the subject of people travelling long distances to meetings, I must mention a long-time fan who has followed the Witches since I was riding and has probably clocked up more miles than anyone else. In the early days, he got about purely by hitchhiking, including places as far flung as Russia and Italy. At the last count, **'Noddy' Fordham** had attended 5,355 Ipswich home meetings, 1,301 away meetings and travelled a mind-boggling 1,660,750 miles – now that is a man passionate about his speedway!

Racing takes up around 20 minutes of the time a spectator spends in the stadium during a meeting, so it is vital to keep supporters entertained for the remaining 90-ish minutes. **John Earrey** was a truly great presenter who had a big following in his day and Ipswich is now very lucky to have **Kevin Long** filling that role. **Chris Ellis** recommended him after he had been given rave reviews from fans travelling on coach trips to away meetings – Kevin had taken to the mike helping to pass the time with quizzes, sweepstakes, etc.

Kevin's pristine cream jacket is easily spotted on the centregreen during a meeting and he is ably assisted by my former co-promoter **Mike Western** announcing the official results and times. If Kevin is away, we can usually call on speedway enthusiast and BBC Radio Suffolk presenter Stephen 'Foz' Foster to take over the mike.

Someone else who has been on the team since 1989 is **Julie Last,** our excellent advertising manager. She also now assists Chris' wife **Julie Harrison-Louis** with corporate hospitality duties (i.e., handing out beers to the meeting sponsors). My daughter Joanne has also been roped in to look after the team sponsors in a newer lounge that has become available following stadium improvements.

Lower profile in the catering team, but equally important, is **Pat Webb** who has tea and coffee ready and waiting for all the track and pit staff during the interval. She also helps with any buffets the Supporters' Club put on at their social events. Which leads me on to the group of volunteers that, since the days of Jamie Cann and the setting up of the SOS fund, still work hard to keep the money flowing in with various fund-raising activities.

The Supporters' Club committee has seen many faces come and go but they have all given up a lot of time and brought different skills to the various events they have been involved in. Currently, they run a monthly quiz, a Meet the Riders event just before our first meeting and an End-of-Season Party in late October. They also run events for the Junior Witches, such as an Easter Egg Hunt on Good Friday and a mascot scheme that allows one lucky youngster every week to toss the coin with the two captains and have their photo taken. All of these added together require a lot of organising and takes up a considerable amount of time throughout the year. The current team consists of **Cheryl O'Keefe, Mark Styles, Mandy Bell** and **Suzanne Cosgrove.**

When Dave Pavitt and I first came to promote at Foxhall, we introduced the Witches Winner girls who sold raffle tickets at the turnstiles and around the stadium for a cash prize and a selection of other prizes. A mother and daughter team were very active from the start and, incredibly, they are still selling tickets today and hardly look a day older. **Margaret** and **Heather Lay** must have worn out a few pairs of shoes walking the terraces over the years but they always have a big smile for everybody and I can still get a cuddle with Margaret (she has a very accommodating chest). They have been joined by **Emma Punchard** and **Cheryl O'Keefe** in recent years.

Another lady who spends hours working for the club behind-the-scenes is **Sue Stevens,** our press officer. Not only does Sue keep our website up-to-date and issue all club press releases, she also

My two granddaughters, Hannah (with Chris' former mechanic Nigel Wells) and Freya (with me at a Halloween-themed night at Foxhall).

looks after the Mildenhall website and, in her spare time, helps prepare questions for the Supporters' Club quizzes.

This year, she has taken on another small job – helping me get this book written! I suspect I may be responsible for her literally falling asleep across her laptop after reading through yet more press cuttings or proof reading another chapter. She knows how grateful I am for all her help and I've told her to add a thank you card to her shopping list next week. I am so rubbish at picking things like that.

When speedway died at Foxhall in the 60s, a hard surface stock car track was built where the shale used to be. John Berry brought speedway back to Suffolk in 1969 and he created a new speedway track inside the former circuit. Before and after most home meetings, a fence has to be erected and dismantled between the two tracks consisting of wooden panels and airbags in front of them around the four corners.

This takes several hours and I am at Foxhall around 8.30am on Mondays if there has been a weekend stock car meeting. One by one, the 'fence gang' turn up and we set about our tasks hoping that we don't have too many hold-ups along the way. Bob Ellis will already be out on track starting his preparation work and after a couple of tea breaks to sustain us, the fence is back up and we can head home praying for a dry Thursday. A big hand for the fence gang: **Bob Jennings, Barry Young, Dale Coulson, Bruce Wade** and **Reg Harrison.**

There is also a larger gang that dismantles the fence immediately after the end of racing on Thursdays. Some of the above are included in that as well – sorry, but I don't have names for you all.

**Lewis Hood** manages the turnstiles, along with all his staff; **Gordon** is on security; and we have a bunch of guys who man the car park every week. Most of them have put in many years of service.

Our official photographer **Steve Waller** takes some of the best speedway pictures around. **Phil Hilton** also did a great job during the 20-plus years he was on the centregreen, providing photos for the track shop and club website. **Jeff Higgott** also deserves a mention for also regularly supplying photos for the club website and for this book.

Ensuring that fans have plenty to read and a scorecard to fill in at every home meeting are our long-term programme editors **Peter** and **Roger Thorpe.** Theirs is another job that requires many hours of hard work and, in their case, to tight deadlines.

JL with Sue Stevens and one of the many scrapbooks that provided so much research material for the book.

Another name from the past I have to mention is **Keith Rodwell** who was commercial manager for the club over a number of years, setting up a successful bingo scheme that saw a collection of sellers going to people's homes around Ipswich and beyond and bringing in much-needed income. Keith also sponsored Chris for a while and played a big part on his testimonial committee.

As I said at the start, please accept my apologies if I haven't mentioned your name. I really appreciate what every volunteer has done over the years and thank you all again.

## Major Individual & Club Achievements

**RIDER**

**1970** British League Division Two Knockout Cup Winner (Ipswich)

**1971** British League Division Two Riders' Championship Winner

British League Division Two Knockout Cup Winner (Ipswich)

**1972** World Team Cup Winner (Great Britain)

**1973** Daily Mirror International Tournament Series Winner (England)

**1974** World Team Cup Winner (England)

**1975** World Championship Bronze Medal Winner

World Team Cup Winner (England)

British Championship Winner

British League Division One Winner (Ipswich)

**1976** World Pairs Champion (England – with Malcolm Simmons)

British League Division One Winner (Ipswich)

British League Division One Knockout Cup Winner (Ipswich)

British League Pairs Winner (Ipswich – with Billy Sanders)

**1977** British League Pairs Winner (Ipswich – with Billy Sanders)

**1978** British League Division One Knockout Cup Winner (Ipswich)

**1979** British League Riders' Championship Winner

**TEAM MANAGER & PROMOTER**

**1988** National League Winner (Hackney)

National League Knockout Cup Winner (Hackney)

**1991** Four Team Championship Winner (Ipswich)

**1998** Division One Winner (Ipswich)

Division One Knockout Cup Winner (Ipswich)

Division One Craven Shield Winner (Ipswich)

## Season-By-Season British League Averages

| Year | Team | Div | M | R | P | BP | TP | AVE | FM | PM | TM |
|------|------|-----|---|---|---|----|----|-----|----|----|----|
| 1970 | Ipswich | Two | 35 | 156 | 325 | 16 | 341 | 8.74 | 7 | 1 | 8 |
| 1970 | Newport | One | 6 | 30 | 57 | 3 | 60 | 8.00 | 1 | 0 | 1 |
| 1970 | West Ham | One | 1 | 4 | 8 | 0 | 8 | 8.00 | 0 | 0 | 0 |
| **1971** | **Ipswich** | **Two** | **38** | **162** | **452** | **6** | **458** | **11.31** | **21** | **4** | **25** |
| 1971 | Oxford | One | 1 | 5 | 7 | 0 | 7 | 5.60 | 0 | 0 | 0 |
| 1971 | Wembley | One | 1 | 4 | 6 | 0 | 6 | 6.00 | 0 | 0 | 0 |
| 1972 | Ipswich | One | 36 | 158 | 358 | 13 | 371 | 9.39 | 5 | 1 | 6 |
| 1973 | Ipswich | One | 36 | 155 | 373 | 17 | 390 | 10.06 | 5 | 5 | 10 |
| 1974 | Ipswich | One | 40 | 172 | 448 | 16 | 464 | 10.79 | 10 | 3 | 13 |
| 1975 | Ipswich | One | 36 | 152 | 398 | 4 | 402 | 10.58 | 16 | 1 | 17 |
| **1976** | **Ipswich** | **One** | **35** | **144** | **389** | **10** | **399** | **11.08** | **12** | **6** | **18** |
| 1977 | Ipswich | One | 37 | 157 | 361 | 12 | 373 | 9.50 | 6 | 1 | 7 |
| 1978 | Ipswich | One | 44 | 183 | 389 | 24 | 413 | 9.03 | 6 | 3 | 9 |
| 1979 | Ipswich | One | 36 | 169 | 383 | 11 | 394 | 9.33 | 1 | 2 | 3 |
| 1980 | Ipswich | One | 35 | 160 | 335 | 17 | 352 | 8.80 | 2 | 4 | 6 |
| 1981 | Halifax | One | 45 | 222 | 418 | 16 | 434 | 7.82 | 2 | 1 | 3 |
| 1982 | Halifax | One | 42 | 176 | 315 | 16 | 331 | 7.52 | 0 | 0 | 0 |
| 1983 | King's Lynn | One | 45 | 187 | 371 | 24 | 395 | 8.45 | 6 | 0 | 6 |
| 1984 | King's Lynn | One | 52 | 222 | 433 | 27 | 460 | 8.29 | 5 | 2 | 7 |

**Headings key:**

**M** = Meetings, **R** = Rides, **P** = Points, **BP** = Bonus points, **TP** = Total points, **AVE** = Average,
**FM** = Full maximums, **PM** = Paid maximums, **TM** = Total maximums

## British Championship
## Coventry, July 30, 1975

| | | | | | | | | | |
|---|---|---|---|---|---|---|---|---|---|
| 1 | Gordon Kennett | Oxford | 2 | 1 | 2 | 1 | 0 | 6 |
| 2 | David Jessup | Leicester | 0 | 0 | 2 | 2 | 2 | 6 |
| 3 | Martin Ashby | Swindon | 3 | 3 | 1 | 3 | 1 | 11 |
| 4 | Doug Wyer | Sheffield | 1 | 1 | 2 | 1 | 0 | 5 |
| 5 | Dave Morton | Hackney | 0 | 0 | 1 | 0 | 2 | 3 |
| **6** | **John Louis** | **Ipswich** | **3** | **3** | **3** | **3** | **3** | **15** |
| 7 | Jim McMillan | Hull | 1 | 1 | 0 | 2 | 1 | 5 |
| 8 | Peter Collins | Belle Vue | 2 | 2 | 3 | 3 | 3 | 13 |
| 9 | Malcolm Simmons | Poole | 3 | 3 | 2 | 2 | 3 | 13 |
| 10 | Chris Pusey | Halifax | 1 | 2 | 3 | 2 | 2 | 10 |
| 11 | Tony Davey | Ipswich | 2 | 2 | 1 | 1 | 3 | 9 |
| 12 | Ray Wilson | Leicester | Fx | 3 | 3 | 3 | 2 | 11 |
| 13 | Bob Kilby | Swindon | 2 | 2 | 1 | 0 | 0 | 5 |
| 14 | Chris Morton | Belle Vue | 3 | 1 | 0 | 0 | 1 | 5 |
| 15 | Carl Glover | Sheffield | 0 | 0 | 0 | 0 | 1 | 1 |
| 16 | Alan Wilkinson | Belle Vue | 1 | 0 | 0 | 1 | 0 | 2 |

**Fastest time:**
Heat 2 - **John Louis** - 63.6 (equalled track record)

## British League Riders' Championship
## Belle Vue, October 24, 1979

| | | | | | | | | | |
|---|---|---|---|---|---|---|---|---|---|
| 1 | Gordon Kennett | Eastbourne | 10.43 | 1 | 0 | 0 | 0 | 0 | 1 |
| 2 | Phil Crump | Swindon | 10.30 | 0 | 3 | 3 | 3 | 0 | 9 |
| 3 | Hans Nielsen | Wolverhampton | 10.35 | 2 | 2 | 1 | 2 | 2 | 9 |
| 4 | Michael Lee | King's Lynn | 10.46 | 3 | 3 | 2 | 1 | 3 | 12 |
| 5 | John Davis | Reading | 10.15 | 0 | 1 | 2 | 0 | 1 | 4 |
| 6 | Ivan Mauger | Hull | 10.54 | 1 | EF | 2 | 0 | 3 | 6 |
| **7** | **John Louis** | **Ipswich** | **9.04** | **2** | **3** | **3** | **3** | **3** | **14** |
| 8 | Malcolm Simmons | Poole | 9.11 | 3 | 0 | 0 | 1 | 1 | 5 |
| 9 | Peter Collins | Belle Vue | 10.04 | 2 | 3 | 2 | 3 | 1 | 11 |
| 10 | Larry Ross | Wimbledon | | 3 | 2 | 1 | 1 | 3 | 10 |
| 11 | Andy Grahame | Birmingham | 8.70 | 0 | 0 | 1 | 0 | 0 | 1 |
| 12 | Ian Cartwright | Halifax | 9.38 | 1 | 1 | 1 | 2 | 0 | 5 |
| 13 | Ole Olsen | Coventry | 9.91 | 2 | 2 | 0 | 2 | 1 | 7 |
| 14 | Scott Autrey | Exeter | 11.14 | 1 | 1 | 3 | 1 | 2 | 8 |
| 15 | John Titman | Leicester | 8.91 | 0 | 1 | 0 | 2 | 2 | 5 |
| 16 | Bruce Penhall | Cradley Heath | 9.91 | 3 | 2 | 3 | 3 | 2 | 13 |

## World Final Record

| Heat | 1st | 2nd | 3rd | 4th | Pts |
|------|-----|-----|-----|-----|-----|
| 4 | Lofqvist | Persson | **Louis** | Olsen | 1 |
| 6 | Mauger | **Louis** | Kalmykov | E Boocock | 2 |
| 11 | **Louis** | Trofimov | Va Gordeev | Waloszek | 3 |
| 13 | Pavlov | **Louis** | N Boocock | Chlynovski | 2 |
| 20 | **Louis** | Michanek | McMillan | Kuzmin | 3 |

Year: **1972**   Points: **11**   Position: **4th**   Venue: **Wembley, England**

| Heat | 1st | 2nd | 3rd | 4th | Pts |
|------|-----|-----|-----|-----|-----|
| 4 | Sjosten | Collins | **Louis** | Plech | 1 |
| 8 | **Louis** | Lofqvist | B Jansson | Lovaas | 3 |
| 9 | Mauger | Chlynovski | Plech | **Louis** | 0 |
| 15 | Michanek | **Louis** | Betts | Jancarz (R) | 2 |
| 18 | **Louis** | Johansson | Krasnov | Jancarz (R) | 3 |

Year: **1974**   Points: **9**   Position: **4th**   Venue: **Ullevi, Gothenburg**

| Heat | 1st | 2nd | 3rd | 4th | Pts |
|------|-----|-----|-----|-----|-----|
| 3 | Collins | **Louis** | Plech | Glucklich | 2 |
| 6 | Olsen | **Louis** | Mauger | Rembas | 2 |
| 12 | **Louis** | Va Gordeev | Wilson | Cieslak | 3 |
| 15 | Michanek | **Louis** | Simmons | Persson | 2 |
| 17 | **Louis** | Crump | Trofimov | T Jansson | 3 |
| 21 | **Louis** | Mauger | Run-off for third place | | |

Year: **1975**   Points: **12**   Position: **3rd**   Venue: **Wembley, England**

| Heat | 1st | 2nd | 3rd | 4th | Pts |
|------|-----|-----|-----|-----|-----|
| 2 | Mauger | **Louis** | Jancarz | Va Gordeev | 2 |
| 7 | Collins | Simmons | **Louis** | Rembas | 1 |
| 12 | Wyer | Crump | **Louis** | Cieslak | 1 |
| 13 | **Louis** | Muller | Stancl | Vl Gordeev | 3 |
| 18 | Plech | **Louis** | Morton | Autrey | 2 |

Year: **1976**   Points: **9**   Position: **6th**   Venue: **Katowice, Poland**

Finals: **4,** 1st place: **7,** 2nd place: **8,** 3rd place: **4,** 4th place: **1,** Average: **10.25 pts**

## World Team Cup Final Record

| Year | Venue | Date | Round | POS | PTS |
|------|-------|------|-------|-----|-----|
| 1972 | Olching, Germany | 24th Sept | Final | 1st | 9 |
| 1974 | Ipswich, England | 11th August | Semi-final | 1st | 12 |
| 1974 | Katowice, Poland | 15th Sept | Final | 1st | 12 |
| 1975 | Reading, England | 14th July | Semi-final | 1st | 10 |
| 1975 | Norden, Germany | 21st Sept | Final | 1st | 8 |
| 1976 | Ipswich, England | 30th May | Semi-final | 2nd | 8 |

**Headings key:**
**POS** = Team finishing position, **PTS** = Points scored by John

--------------------------------------------------------------------

## International Caps

**British League Division 1:** Great Britain = 4, Rest Of The World = 6, England = 52

**British League Division 2:** England = 27

--------------------------------------------------------------------

## Foxhall Heath Track Records

| 11th June 1970 | 70.8 |
|----------------|------|
| 25th June 1970 | 70.2 |
| 1st April 1971 | 69.2 |
| 29th April 1971 | 69.0 |
| 17th June 1971 | 67.2 |
| 5th August 1971 | 66.6 |
| 8th June 1972 | 65.4 |
| 17th August 1972 | 64.8 |
| 20th April 1973 | 64.6 |
| 17th May 1973 | 64.4 |
| 5th June 1975 | 62.6 |
| 23rd August 1975 | 62.0 |
| 28th June 1979 | 61.0 |
| 17th July 1979 | 60.8 |

# Tributes

**I'M sure I've had more run-ins with John than most people. Over 32 years covering his exploits with Ipswich Witches for the *East Anglian Daily Times* and *Evening Star,* we often crossed swords.**

Several times John came to me after a quote that I had seized on because of its newsworthiness had put him in hot water with perhaps over-sensitive authorities.

Knowing full well what he had said in his admirably open attitude to life, I still took it on the chin and did not argue when John – after a word – indicated that he had been 'misquoted'.

And I was happy to do so, because the closer you get to the man the more likeable he becomes. Not that he is unlikeable at all, as thousands of adoring fans during his brilliant riding career testify.

But there is a side that fans do not have the chance to see – a kind, generous, considerate man to go with his undoubted talent for riding a motorcycle.

His caring and loving upbringing did much to form the man that he became.

And has anybody served the town of Ipswich better? His exploits have played a big part in the rural East Anglian outpost becoming known around the world.

Along with perhaps former Ipswich Town FC managers Sir Alf Ramsey and Sir Bobby Robson, his sporting prowess has helped put Ipswich on the map more than anyone.

One incident possibly sums John up. He was driving through a forest area in Germany with his then wife Magda, Mike Western and myself on our way by road and ferry from Ipswich to Vetlanta, Sweden to watch Chris Louis ride in a World Championship semi-final.

The petrol gauge was on red and there was no sign of any housing, let alone a petrol station.

But that didn't worry John. The positive attitude that saw him reach the top on a 500cc machine with no brakes shone through as he shrugged away our fears and continued with foot flat down on the floor.

He didn't deal in danger. He loved the thrill of the uncertain. And sure enough, we later took on petrol with no alarms.

Not a man to be beaten.
*ELVIN KING*

**Elvin King joins JL in celebration of Witches' 1998 treble-winning season.**

**I FIRST saw John race in the second half at Ipswich way back in 1969. He had everything a speedway rider needed and more. Determination and limitless ability backed up, we soon found out, with a terrific personality. What's more, he was local!**

John's presence as a rider brought us so many accolades, along with championships. There was a glowing team spirit and regular thrilling second half finals between John, Billy Sanders and Tony Davey.

As a promoter, John has helped keep Ipswich Speedway alive and vibrant.

Maybe the best memory I have, and it brings a lump to my throat recalling it, was the 1972 World Final. My wife and I travelled to Wembley on one of the supporters' coaches and from the off, all the way along the A12, car after car overtook us displaying the Ipswich Witch and of course Tiger's scarves and flags. One car that went past had a message in the window. 'My Son John Louis'.

Perhaps Tiger didn't win the title but he certainly won a whole host of English hearts that day.
*DAVE FEAKES*
*Co-author of Ipswich Speedway: the First 50 Years.*

**BORN and bred in Ipswich, John has been an admirable ambassador for speedway and the town.**

Few have served the town as well as John and over the years his contributions to Ipswich Witches brought pleasure to thousands.

John spread the name of Ipswich to the speedway community around the world.
*BEN GUMMER*
*MP (Conservative) for Ipswich*

**SPEEDWAY in East Anglia in the 70s was a veritable hot-bed of teams, supporters, star names and genuine rivalry.**

Well to the fore among those 'star names', there was arguably none bigger than John Louis. A late beginner, initially claimed by John Berry to be just 24, and in fairness to the ex-scrambler, he looked far, far younger than his years.

Ipswich had enjoyed a quiet but reasonably supported first year back but the sudden, and it was mercurial, rise of 'The Tiger' galvanised the Foxhall faithful, as they flooded onto the heath in their thousands.

During those heady days of the 1970-80 era JL achieved superstar status in Suffolk and across Europe. He was bigger than any Ipswich Town footballer (in the days of seasoned internationals and a team in Europe) and was always in demand to open fetes, stores, carnivals. And to my knowledge, never turned down a single request.

There were literally hundreds of cars throughout Suffolk with John Louis stickers adorning their front windscreens.

But with his natural modesty and humour, never in all those heady years did he forget his friends, mates and colleagues.

I know of no-one in or out of the sport who resents his fame, popularity and achievements.

JL has always been good company, never full of his own importance. Despite his fame he never acted 'big-time'.

Thanks, JL, you have given me huge enjoyment, lots of laughs, some sad times, but, above all, good company.

We have known each other for 40-odd years and it has been one of life's pleasures to count him as a good friend.
*JAMES EASTER*
*Travel Plus Tours*

**MY family and John's lived close together at Rushmere, so I have known John and his family for many years. We were at Copleston Boys' secondary school  together, although John was two years older. However, his younger brother, the late**

Tony Louis, was in the same form as myself. They were both very good at school sports events.

I regularly called in at Jack and Vera's home in Renfrew Road, where John had his workshop.

On a personal note, many years ago JL sold me his blue Ford Corsair. His former team-mate Clive Noy worked on it to make it roadworthy but, I have to say, it wasn't one of my best buys! I do, though, wish I had kept it – it would be a collectors' item now.

I was involved with Ipswich Speedway Supporters' Club from the 60s. Together with the late Jill Cotton and the Bickers Coach Hire Company of Coddenham, we arranged transportation for fans to many away venues, the highlight being the 1975 trip to Wembley to see JL finish on the rostrum. Not only did we require every available coach in Suffolk from other coach operators, we also hired a train which went direct to Wembley Hill Station.

*JOHN BOOTH*

JOHN was a legend when all of us young fellas were growing up on the junior grass-track seen around East Anglia.

Before some of us, including his son Chris, moved on to speedway, John was always giving advice were he could. As a local rider made good, he was someone most of us looked up to.

And he is still an influence at Ipswich Speedway today, offering invaluable advice to youngsters.

*ANDY NIGHTINGALE*

I REMEMBER his first laps at Foxhall riding an old JAP.

Wearing a green moto-cross top, little did we know that within a short period of time he would take the Second Division Riders' Championship at Hackney and be riding at reserve for Newport in the top flight. It was an extraordinary rise to fame.

*BARRY SCOWEN*

WHEN John started out riding at reserve for Ipswich I soon became a fan of the Tiger.

I remember as a boy of 12, in 1971, he came to visit me in hospital. When he was about to leave he asked: 'When would you like me to come and see you again?'

I replied: 'When the Witches are in the First Division'.

A few days later he returned with team manager Ron Bagley to tell me: 'Yes, we are now in Division One!'

That kind gesture meant a lot to me at the time.

*JULIAN MOORE*

JOHN was an amazing rider in the 70s. I met him several times as we travelled all over watching him in the Golden Helmet and for the Witches when he was virtually unbeatable. He was excellent with the supporters, always had time for a chat and to talk about his bikes.

I loved his Tiger leathers and I remember him giving a pair to second string rider Dick Partridge to use, to help Dick save money. It was weird seeing Dick riding in John's leathers, although the amber-and-black tiger stripes were removed.

John Louis was the reason I got into speedway. He was exciting to watch and I remember the pop hit *I'm A Tiger* playing over the PA after he had won, with John Earrey whipping up the crowd.

When John was testing a new Weslake or trying out new set-ups ahead of a big meeting, he would do a few practice laps after the Foxhall meeting had officially ended. I'm not exaggerating when I tell you several hundred spectators would stay behind and watch him long after the meeting had finished.

*PHIL BULLARD*

AS a teenager supporting Exeter in the 70s, naturally enough, Ivan Mauger was my hero, followed very closely by John Louis.

Two reasons: firstly, he was a cracking, entertaining rider. Secondly, at the time, to a spectacle-wearing kid like myself, seeing a sporting hero wearing glasses as he raced showed that having less than perfect eyesight didn't have to hold you back. Many a time I looked at the poster of JL on my wall and thought that.

I also never forgot that he ALWAYS signed autographs, unlike some of the other stars of the time.

In my role as Mildenhall press officer in 2011-12, I often watched the action at West Row in the hugely entertaining company of my boyhood hero. When I told him about the poster on my wall, such is the modesty of JL he seemed both embarrassed and flattered at the same time.

That is typical of a man who is a true speedway great, someone I am proud to know and who will always be one of my sporting heroes.

*DAVID GOLLEY*
*ITV News and former Mildenhall Speedway press officer*

GLASGOW is the farthest track in the UK from Ipswich, so how did I become a Tiger Louis fan?

Our cycle speedway team had a blank Saturday in April, 1970, so we decided to head down to Berwick. The gloom of a dismal misty night was lit up by a small figure in Tiger sleeves.

Ipswich were pipped for the league points but not before John had lowered the colours of the leading Bandits. He made it to the ROTN final but looped at the gate, probably unaware that the Shielfield home straight had quite a slope.

I've no doubt he learned from that . . . and went on learning, as he was back in Berwick riding for Young England against Young Sweden just three months later. I saw him ride in the first three Tests of that series and was by now a confirmed Tiger fan.

The next year he came to Hampden and scored five points in the prestigious Scottish Open. I was there cheering him on and my Berwick friends weren't best impressed when I bought a Louis rosette! Glasgow fans venerate the 1972 World Final at Wembley, because it was the only time a Glasgow Tiger made it to the big night – Jim McMillan being a reserve. However, Ipswich's 'Tiger' was not only there, but finished joint-fourth. If he'd had easier early rides he may well have made the rostrum.

When he beat Ivan Mauger in a run-off for third place in the 1975 World Final, I watched saw from the top of the Wembley terracing before dashing off to get the tube back to Euston, followed by the night train home to Glasgow. Sadly, I never did see him on the rostrum.

His Tiger leathers (mark II?), made by Kett with the red, white and blue stripes down his left leg and around his right thigh, were the most iconic ever in my view.

*DOUG NICOLSON*

I MIGHT just be the only person, certainly one of few, who saw John Louis' undertake his first and last rides on speedway.

In the intervening years we had plenty of contact as I plied my journalistic, managerial and promoting activities.

In 1969, around the middling stages of their comeback season under the John Berry/Joe Thurley banner, Ipswich Witches followers began to be aware of the 28-year-old track artist formerly known as a scrambles and moto-cross rider.

Even Messrs Berry and Thurley couldn't quite believe their luck when the next couple of seasons unfolded, propelling their 'Tiger' creation from virtual novice to the most in-demand rider in the land.

He was front and centre in all the thrilling progress the Witches made in those heady years.

As if dominating the lower tier and suggesting tantalising possibilities at a higher level was not enough, the Louis phenomenon was central to Ipswich's ascent to the top flight in 1972, and their later emergence as one of the finest homegrown team and club acts in the history of the sport.

All of that is embedded in the history books and speedway folklore, a monument to its architects, and the influence of JL as standard bearer, No.1 and captain.

World Team Cups and World Pairs gongs notwithstanding, arguably his finest hour was the World Final at Wembley in '72, when thousands of true believers decamped by coach, car and train to festoon the old stadium with blue-and-white, to raise the rafters with their raucous Suffolk welcome – not to forget the famed Foxhall Heath bugler's call to arms.

There's the old adage 'nobody remembers who came second' but, in fact, this final probably is best remembered for the guy who sparkled on debut with 11 points . . . if not the Briggo crash which has garnered 50,000 YouTube hits (and counting).

This was some effort for a rider, who despite his birth certificate,

was far and away the least experienced top-flight competitor on the night of the nights, yet appeared thoroughly at home in such august surroundings.

It capped off a hectic few weeks during which I worked with John on a slim volume of his life story and anecdotes to that point titled *Tiger* (cover image left), which sold several thousand copies in the run-up to Wembley.

Ultimately, John was invaluable to Ipswich, as a performer of shining temperament, team ethic, stellar consistency and winning desire, a remarkable ambassador and icon. Not irreplaceable, though.

John Berry, who built his dream factory on emotion and engagement, was unsentimental enough to move on his man when he perceived his use-by date to be looming, justifying his actions by proclaiming the need to refresh – and how Dennis Sigalos and John Cook repaid him while JL ruefully continued to ply his trade at Halifax for seasons 1981 and 1982.

Although he bore the snub like a man, it definitely scarred John.

By the end of his second year at The Shay, he made no attempt to disguise the fact he didn't enjoy the weekly long-distance commute and was seriously minded to give speedway away.

He was, after all, 41, still accomplished and feisty, but probably lacking the missionary motivation so evident during his Ipswich days.

The chance to return to East Anglia, as captain of King's Lynn helping front a complete makeover at Saddlebow Road, reignited the light in his eye.

Eric Boothroyd of Halifax accepted this was a move bound to happen, apologised for the fact he was asking for a nominal transfer fee and a deal was done with a minimum of fuss. For 1983 and 1984, the one-time 'enemy' endeared himself to Stars fans with regular reprises of his golden days, rarely failing to come up with the goods.

Above all, John was courteous, helpful, worth every penny of an eminently fair deal, professional on and off track, one of the very best signings I ever made.

From a personal angle, I have always believed it's a wonderful thing to be able to choose the timing and manner of your exit.

So many sportsmen, not just speedway riders, and so many administrators, including some speedway promoters whose names spring to mind, unwisely lingered longer than their legacy demanded.

So when John told me at the end of '84 that he had decided to call it a day, I congratulated and supported him. In many senses, the moment was precisely right.

He had demonstrated that he possessed more durable powers than Ipswich had suspected, and provided an object lesson in putting together a highly satisfactory second coming. Not coincidentally, King's Lynn were a respectable sixth in a 16-strong league (best of 'the rest' after all the big-name, big-money clubs) which, results-wise, was the peak of my five years as Stars promoter.

And although during the winter days John had those inevitable second thoughts which accompany almost every retirement, I didn't take him up on an offer to have one last crack in 1985.

I am happy to remember him heading off into the sunset regularly ripping up opponents half his age in his final hurrah, leading from the front as ever, and pleased that he was able to step so seamlessly from leathers to blazer and embark upon a 30-year odyssey on the 'other' side of the fence.

*MARTIN ROGERS*

GENTLEMAN John, an accolade fully earned and deserved via sterling service upon both that side and this of the safety fence.

Actually, sterling's so wide of the mark. That's like saying politicians deserve to be paid more than nurses.

Because John Louis has more or less dedicated his life to all things sideways, and they're a rare breed indeed.

A confession. His first two years would more or less have passed an avid Wimbledon speedway supporter by. Thanks to buying *Speedway Star*, you couldn't escape the impact he and the Witches had on the British League Division Two scene.

But the Plough Lane Dons were a powerhouse of British League Division One then. Well, more a once mighty franchise in a slow decline actually, we just didn't realise it then.

South London patrons missed John's Division Two Riders' Championship victory by a whisker, as his victory was at Hackney, a year before the event was switched across town to SW17.

So, Thursday, April 6, 1972 certainly appears to be the first time my path would have crossed with JL's. It was a Spring Gold Cup encounter and gave us Wimbledonians an early opportunity to see what these Suffolk upstarts were all about.

No pretence here about owning a razor-sharp memory but, according to *Speedway Star,* John's first outing, against John Dews, Pete Murray and team-mate Alan Bellham, resulted in a fall. Next up, a 3-3 behind Sandor Levai, with Ronnie Moore the winner and Neil Cameron last.

But look at this. Heat 8, a paid win behind Olle Nygren and in front of Graeme Stapleton and Jim Tebby.

Heat 10, a win ahead of Trevor Hedge, Tebby and Bellham.

Heat 12, another win from Hedge, Nygren and Murray.

So, the first time we met, John went home with nine paid 11 from five outings, Ipswich losing 47-30.

A return visit, for league points, wasn't too far away. And, on that occasion, June 1, John dropped just one point in four rides, to 'necessary evil' (sorry, guest), Bob Kilby.

Match reporter Philip Rising was moved to write at the time: "Ipswich and John Louis in particular have made considerable progress since the Witches visited Plough Lane a few weeks ago. Louis really looked the part and looked like winning the second half final until he fell on the last lap."

Wimbledon 41 Ipswich 37. A clear indication of which direction both teams, as it happened, were starting to go in.

And the man with the trademark 'Tiger' leathers had left a calling card that spelt 'special' all over it.

Personal dealings with John were much more leaning towards the days long after those Tiger colours had been hung up to dry one last time.

In his first steps into management with Hackney in 1987, in fact. And he was always approachable, happy to chat and, not surprisingly, brought a depth of knowledge to the job that a fair few of his contemporaries could only dream about.

When the east London club found life in the top division a wee bit stressful, the drop into the lower level actually proved a master-stroke. John was THE ideal man to marshal a precocious bunch of kids, among them his own son Chris. And the Kestrels, as they were known, were a terrific team to follow, let along report on.

But try and get John to admit just how special Chris was. Forget it. So adverse was he to any favouritism, poor Chris barely got a mention! But like father, the son prove to be exceptional.

And it's fantastic to see both of them so heavily involved today. Also, a quote from John just a mere week or so ago from penning this, summed up what I admire about both of the Louis clan so much.

"Chris makes all the Ipswich decisions these days," John told Elvin King. "I have done my bit. I am basically a pair of hands.

"I am part of the gang that puts the fence up on Mondays after weekend stock car meetings, and I sweep out the pits and generally get things shipshape on Thursdays before we stage our home meetings."

That really is dedication to the Ipswich cause.

**RICHARD CLARK**
*Editor, Speedway Star*

**THERE have been many memorable on-track moments in the history of Ipswich Speedway but few stand the test of time as well as the 'Eric the Rake' incident.**

On August 27, 1970 those present saw one of the most dramatic finishes to a match that has ever been witnessed at Foxhall.

Rochdale were in town for a KO Cup semi-final and riding at No.1 for them was one of the top riders in the second division, Eric Broadbelt. As the riders came to the tapes for the final race, Hornets were four points down and needed a 5-1 to earn a draw. The programmed riders for Rochdale were the unbeaten Broadbelt and Alan Wilkinson, while Ipswich had John and reserve Ron Bagley, both of whom had dropped just one point to an opponent.

Team tactics were clear as Eric gated alongside John, then rode him to the fence between the first and second bend. John struggled in the deep dirt and could only watch as the other three riders were racing away from him down the back straight. Eric passed Ron to join his partner at the front.

John was now fired up and quickly caught up and passed his team-mate, then set about beating at least one of the Hornets.

But after he passed Wilkinson and put himself in a match-winning position, he made a determined effort to pass 'Broady' as well. It could have gone very wrong as he dived inside the leading rider on the third bend of the last lap. Eric moved out and fell.

It was now slow-motion time as John took the check flag. Would the red exclusion light come on? It didn't – and the crowd went wild, as Ipswich had progressed to the KO Cup Final.

Eric also went wild. He ran to the centre-green, picked up a grading rake and with the rake aloft, headed towards the back straight where John was on his slowing down lap.

At this point everyone in the stadium could see what was happening except John.

John Berry was mimicking a greyhound as he raced to stop a potentially dangerous situation. Eric dropped the rake before he got to JL but that didn't stop Berry from making a rugby tackle on him.

Eric received a two-week ban for his actions that day but has stubbornly remained tight-lipped about the incident – until now.

After constant badgering from me, he has finally spoken and this is his recollection of events: "Yes, I took John out but I was quite within my rights to. When you're in front you can ride where you like. But I must admit, I didn't expect to see him again.

"When he dived inside me, he did brush me with his back wheel. It wasn't hard but that's what I thought took me down.

"I was so incensed when John's exclusion light didn't come on that I ran to the centre-green and picked up a discarded rake. I lifted it above my head and began to run to the back straight, with John the only thing in my sight.

"But after a few steps I began to realise just how heavy those rakes are and I had to put it down – and then I was tackled by somebody.

"When I got back to the pits I was told by my mechanic that I had picked up a puncture in the rear tyre and that was obviously what took me down . . . but don't tell John that!"
**PETER THORPE**

**I WAS a 12 year old thrilled to be at Wembley for the 1972 World Final. John Louis was one of the English riders I was cheering for, along with the Boocock brothers.**

Although I was a Romford Bombers fan, I always took an interest in John's career and, thanks to him, I've been a Witches supporter for the last 10 years.
**NICK DOWELL**

**HOW ironic that we have the honour of publishing's John's story, as it was he who dominated the first meeting I recall attending.**

It was Sunday, October 18, 1970 at Rye House, an individual meeting for the Mike Letch Trophy in honour of the Australian junior who had been left paralysed in a track crash at the Hoddesdon venue just a couple of months earlier.

The line-up was made up of mainly south-eastern based riders but one stood out above all as the main attraction.

With only one thin rope separating the pits (located on the back straight) from the fans, you couldn't help but notice the biggest star in the distinctive stripy Tiger leathers who romped to an effortless 15-point maximum. I was only 10 but could see he was a bit special.

In my youth I watched as John earned lots of points at the expense of my local teams, Hackney, Rayleigh and Romford. As a Hawks' fan, he seemed to ruin every Good Friday with home and away maximums while most of us from the Essex end of the A12 privately envied our rival Witches' fans whose emerging team was led by an invincible colossus.

Funny how life pans out. Fast-forward 35 years from that Sunday afternoon at Rye House and I had the pleasure of interviewing John at his home for *Backtrack* magazine.

Another decade on and here we are, having now read what it took for a young kid from an ordinary background to go on and achieve extraordinary things through sheer professionalism, talent and dedication.

I can't think of another person in British speedway, rider or promoter, who has dedicated himself more and achieved so much for one club over such a long period than John Louis. It's a scandal that the people who govern his hometown haven't yet honoured his legacy by naming a local landmark after him (why not re-name it Louis Foxhall Road?), or preserved him in bronze in the town centre.

As you now know, he has appeared in front of The Queen twice already but it's about time he got the call to return to Buckingham Palace and collected the honours award his services to speedway so richly deserve.

*TONY McDONALD*
*Publisher, Retro Speedway*

------------------------------------------------------------

**Online comments posted on the British Speedway Forum**

**WembleyLion:** John Louis is my favourite rider of all time. A truly great rider and fantastic servant to speedway

**cityrebel:** What really stood out for me as a child were his 'Tiger' leathers, a real flash of colour when most riders were still racing in black.

**25yearfan:** John was one of England's finest and is Ipswich speedway's greatest rider. His brilliance in 1971 meant Witches had to move up into the first division, or go very stale in the second division without him.

I've seen no rider move up the ranks as quickly as John did. It seemed he went from unknown second-halver to star rider in a matter of weeks.

I remember going to the 1972 World Final only three years after he'd taken his first second half rides, John came fourth and half the crowd seemed to be from Ipswich. Indeed, at quite a few away meetings, at near rivals King's Lynn and Hackney, there seemed to be more Ipswich fans than home fans.

I remember going to a pub in Suffolk, just of the A140 {Norwich/Ipswich road), where they had a local singer who was singing a song about John Louis. That shows how popular John was in Suffolk in the heady years of the 70's.

I became a regular at King's Lynn on Saturdays in the summers of 1983-84, when the by now 40-plus John Louis was Lynn's best rider when the top flight of British speedway still had virtually all of the world's top riders in it.

**ColinMills:** john Louis was plastered over every inch of my wall as a child. I saw him win the Division Two 2 Riders' Championship and other highlights of his riding days were his team-riding with Ron Bagley and Mike Lanham.

I still have the cutting from the paper when he returned to Foxhall with Halifax. The report headline read: 'Tiger back at Foxhall and trouble'. Tim Hunt put him through the home straight fence. I loved the way he beat John Cook in Heat 4 – Tiger was the first visiting rider I shouted for!

John's leathers were probably the best in speedway. A legend at Foxhall.

**dontfortgetthefueltapsbruv (Richard Brabbin):** Mr Ipswich Speedway. Full stop.

John Berry rightly gets credited for the success story that was Ipswich Speedway upon its resurrection but every master craftsmen needs the best tools to work with. In John Louis he had just that – he was the perfect local hero to build around.

Goodness knows what he could've achieved had he started 10 years earlier.

Then, of course, not content with such a worthy riding career, he embarks on taking on the mantle of 'the boss'. While never as successful as Berry, trophy-wise (1998 aside – who could forget that year!), it could easily be argued John was more important than Berry in that without him there may no longer be an Ipswich Speedway. He has kept going through the tough times while, comparatively, Berry was there when you just had to open the gates.

In terms of a personal memory, I still have hanging in my wardrobe a racejacket I won as a prize towards the end of 1979. John raffled a few off in the last weeks of the season. My dad won but I got it.

Somewhere in the archives will be a picture of a skinny eight-year-old with a beaming smile on the centre-green at Foxhall, with John presenting it. That's me!

In summary, thanks John for all of that. And, of course, the dynasty continues with Chris . . .

**macca56:** I doubt if there is any other rider whose promoter would have taken his club up a division to keep a particular rider at that club.

I can't believe it is nearly 45 years since I first saw JL ride – as a guest for Eastbourne at Romford in October, 1970. John won his four heats by at least half a lap and set the fastest time of the night (I think JL then scored a paid max the following evening guesting for Hackney against West Ham).

I saw John in both the 1975 and 1976 World Finals but still consider that 1973 may have been his best chance of winning the title – but for his disqualification after the British-Nordic round.

Mention John Louis and team-riding always comes to mind. I can't forget John Earrey making the comment over the PA that JL had been warned by the referee for looking behind him more than forwards after one particular heat of selfless team-riding.

After the unveiling of the Prince Obolensky statue in Ipswich in 2009, BBC Radio Suffolk asked what other person should be honoured similarly. For his services to his sport and to his town, JL deserves that accolade.

### Comments posted on the John Louis Facebook Page

**Carl Squirrell:** John was always a great supporter of the Norfolk & Suffolk Junior Motorcycle Club who brought on many good riders

for the Ipswich speedway team. He often attended our race meetings and presented trophies and awards at the end of season dos. John presented an award (left) to my younger brother Adrian 'Fred' Squirrell, who sadly passed away earlier this year (2015).

**John Middleditch:** A legend! Have spent many nights in the past sinking pints with 'The Tiger' at The Farmhouse pub. He still calls me 'Centretrench' due to my surname! What a rider he was.

Remember my first meeting at Foxhall in 1971, England v Sweden, when I was only seven. He got an 18-point maximum and it cost just 2/6 to get in!

**Geoffrey Tomlinson:** After my first full season of going to Ipswich Speedway I met JL at Clacton, Essex in the close season, when JB bought the Witches to a sports exhibition in the Town Hall. What a great advert for speedway, he spent ages talking to me about his career, the bikes and racing techniques. Probably why I still love the sport to this day.

He was not only a great rider, but loved promoting the sport. Not many folk hadn't heard of the name Tiger John Louis in Suffolk and surrounding areas.

**David Nod Needham:** A great rider. If he wasn't leading he was always a 'Tiger' on the tail. A fantastic representative of what was arguably speedway's best era.

**Adrian Trevaskis:** When growing up in Suffolk in the late 60s and 70s, John was, and still is, a legend. He is Mr Ipswich Speedway. The team of 1998 was John's team and without doubt the best team that there has been in this country.

How he has not been honoured for his service to speedway, god only knows.

**Chris Gosling:** Being from Kings Lynn, and you ask me to comment on John Louis who had the audacity to come to Saddlebow Road on a regular basis and often ride better than our guys! John was a great servant to East Anglian speedway who gave of his best at all times. Those last two years when he rode for Lynn, while supposedly well past his best, only showed how good he really was. Even then he was more than capable of beating anyone anywhere. Nothing but respect for the man.

**Mike Hunter:** I can well remember the excitement of the early days of the rise of John Louis. He suddenly started appearing from nowhere in the scorers in Speedway Star and it was obvious he was a star in the making.

I first saw him in a Test match at Berwick, then the Division Two KO Cup Final, and what an exciting sight he was in his Tiger leathers.

I remember being at the British Final in 1972 when he qualified for the World Final. The Ipswich fans dominated the back straight.

I used to keep a book in his early days and noted down all his scores. His style, appearance and the instant rise to stardom just appealed to me and I loved following his progress. I've still got a model John Louis at home.

He was just a fantastic speedway phenomenon.

**Darren Fitch:** Let's get John the MBE he sooooo deserves . . .

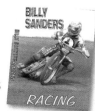